MEDIEVAL AND RENAISSANCE DRAMA IN ENGLAND

Editorial Board

Leeds Barroll
University of Maryland (Baltimore)

Catherine Belsey
*University of Wales
College of Cardiff*

David M. Bevington
University of Chicago

Barry Gaines
University of New Mexico

Jean E. Howard
Columbia University

Arthur F. Kinney
University of Massachusetts

Anne C. Lancashire
University of Toronto

William B. Long
Independent Scholar

Barbara Mowat
Folger Shakespeare Library

Lee Patterson
Yale University

John Pitcher
St. John's College, Oxford

E. Paul Werstine
*University of Western
Ontario*

MEDIEVAL AND RENAISSANCE DRAMA IN ENGLAND

Volume 23

Edited by
S. P. Cerasano

Associate Editor
Mary Bly

Book Review Editor
Heather Anne Hirschfeld

Madison • Teaneck
Fairleigh Dickinson University Press

© 2010 by Rosemont Publishing & Printing Corp.

All rights reserved. Authorization to photocopy items for internal or personal use, or the internal or personal use of specific clients, is granted by the copyright owner, provided that a base fee of $10.00, plus eight cents per page, per copy is paid directly to the Copyright Clearance Center, 222 Rosewood Drive, Danvers, Massachusetts 01923. [$10.00 + 8¢ pp. pc.] 978-0-8386-4269-6/10

Associated University Presses
2010 Eastpark Boulevard
Cranbury, NJ 08512

The paper used in this publication meets the requirements of the American National Standard for Permanence of Paper for Printed Library Materials Z39.48-1984.

International Standard Book Number 978-0-8386-4269-6 (vol. 23)
International Standard Serial Number 0731-3403

All editorial correspondence concerning *Medieval and Renaissance Drama in England* should be addressed to Prof. S. P. Cerasano, Department of English, Colgate University, Hamilton, N.Y., 13346. Orders and subscriptions should be directed to Associated University Presses, 2010 Eastpark Boulevard, Cranbury, New Jersey 08512.

Medieval and Renaissance Drama in England disclaims responsibility for statements, either of face or opinion, made by contributors.

PRINTED IN THE UNITED STATES OF AMERICA

Contents

Foreword	7
Contributors	9

Articles

Parallels and Poetry: Shakespeare, Kyd, and *Arden of Faversham* MACDONALD P. JACKSON	17
The "To be, or not to be" Speech: Evidence, Conventional Wisdom, and the Editing of *Hamlet* JAMES HIRSH	34
"Deep Prescience": Succession and the Politics of Prophecy in *Friar Bacon and Friar Bungay* BRIAN WALSH	63
Declamation and Character in the Fletcher-Massinger Plays JOHN E. CURRAN JR.	86
Reading Orlando Historically: Vagrancy, Forest, and Vestry Values in Shakespeare's *As You Like It* CHRIS FITTER	114
Rereading the Side Panels in *The View of London from the North* JUNE SCHLUETER	142

Reviews

Lloyd Edward Kermode, *Aliens and Englishness in Elizabethan Drama* CHARLES R. FORKER	161
Valerie Forman, *Tragicomic Redemptions: Global Economics and the Early Modern English Stage* INEKE MURAKAMI	164
Peter F. Grav, *Shakespeare and the Economic Imperative: "What's aught but as 'tis valued?"* ERIC V. SPENCER	167
Tom Rutter, *Work and Play on the Shakespearean Stage* C. BRYAN LOVE	170

D. K. Smith, *The Cartographic Imagination in Early Modern England: Re-writing the World in Marlowe, Spenser, Raleigh and Marvell* 173
 ELIZABETH JANE BELLAMY

Ian Munro, *The Figure of the Crowd in Early Modern London: The City and Its Double* 175
 MEG F. PEARSON

Tom MacFaul, *Male Friendship in Shakespeare and His Contemporaries* 178
 BEN LABRECHE

Amanda Bailey, *Flaunting: Style and the Subversive Male Body in Renaissance England* 180
 MARGARET ROSE JASTER

Todd H. J. Pettigrew, *Shakespeare and the Practice of Physic: Medical Narratives and the Early Modern English Stage* 183
 SAMANTHA MURPHY

Joan Fitzpatrick, *Food in Shakespeare: Early Modern Dietaries and the Plays* 185
 AMY L. TIGNER

Bradin Cormack, *A Power to Do Justice: Jurisdiction, English Literature, and the Rise of Common Law* 188
 ANDREW MAJESKE

Margreta de Grazia, *"Hamlet" without Hamlet* 190
 SAYRE GREENFIELD

Charlotte Scott, *Shakespeare and the Idea of the Book* 192
 JAMES J. MARINO

Index 196

Foreword

Medieval and Renaissance Drama in England, now over twenty years in publication, is an international journal committed to the publication of essays and reviews relevant to drama and theater history to 1642. *MaRDiE* 23 features essays by MacDonald P. Jackson on authorship as related to Shakespeare, Kyd, and *Arden of Faversham.* James Hirsch considers the editing of Hamlet's "To be, or not to be" in light of both conventional and emerging editorial theory. Politics and prophecy, as they influence *Friar Bacon and Friar Bungay,* is at the center of Brian Walsh's contribution, while John Curran uses declamation as a rhetorical strategy in order to focus on character in the Fletcher-Massinger plays. Chris Fitter considers vagrancy and "vestry values" in Shakespeare's *As You Like It* and June Schlueter reconsiders the matter of theatrical cartography and *The View of London from the North.* Not least of all, our collection of reviews range from books on early modern dietaries and Shakespeare's plays to those on male friendship and theater economics.

As ever, the publication of *MaRDiE* would not be possible without its many contributors and supporters. On this occasion I am pleased to welcome Mary Bly of Fordham University who, joining *MarDiE* as Associate Editor, will doubtless add her unique blend of wisdom and talent to future volume of this journal.

S. P. CERASANO
Editor

Contributors

ELIZABETH JANE BELLAMY is Professor and John C. Hodges Chair of Excellence in the English Department at the University of Tennessee, Knoxville. She is currently working on representations of the coastline in early modern English literature.

JOHN E. CURRAN JR. is associate professor of English at Marquette University. His recent book is *Hamlet, Protestantism, and the Mourning of Contingency: Not To Be* (Ashgate).

CHRIS FITTER is Associate Professor of English at Rutgers University at Camden. His first book, *Poetry, Space, Landscape,* has been reissued in paper, and he is currently completing *Radical Shakespeare: Politics and Stagecraft in the Elizabethan Plays.* His essays have appeared in *Shakespeare Studies, Milton Studies, ELR, ELH, Essays in Criticism,* and elsewhere.

CHARLES R. FORKER is Professor of English Emeritus at Indiana University, Bloomington. He is the editor of *Richard II* (2002) in the Arden 3 Shakespeare series. More recently, he has edited George Peele's *Troublesome Reign of King John* for the Revels plays (forthcoming 2010) and written a related article, "*The Troublesome Reign, Richard II,* and the Date of *King John:* A Study in Intertextuality" (forthcoming in *Shakespeare Survey,* 2010).

SAYRE GREENFIELD is a Professor of English at the University of Pittsburgh at Greensburg. His recent publications include "Quoting *Hamlet* Outside Britain in the Eighteenth Century," in *Shakespeare's World / World Shakespeare: The Selected Proceedings of the International Shakespeare Association World Congress, Brisbane* 2006, ed. Richard Fotheringham, Christa Jansohn, and R. S. White (Newark: University of Delaware Press, 2009), 237–46, and "Quoting *Hamlet* in the Early Seventeenth Century," *Modern Philology* 105.3 (2008): 510–34.

JAMES HIRSH is a Professor of English at Georgia State University. His recent publications include *Shakespeare and the History of Soliloquies* (FDUP) which won the 2004 South Atlantic Modern Language Association Book

Award, and articles on *Hamlet, Antony and Cleopatra, Henry V,* the commodification of Shakespeare, and covert appropriations of Shakespearean material by later writers.

MACDONALD P. JACKSON is Emeritus Professor of English at the University of Auckland. He edited *The Revenger's Tragedy* and served as an associate general editor for the Oxford *Thomas Middleton: The Collected Works* (2007), also contributing an essay titled "Early Modern Authorship: Canons and Chronologies" to the companion volume.

MARGARET ROSE JASTER is an Associate Professor at Penn State's Capital College in Harrisburg where she teaches courses in early modern English culture, drama, and Irish-American literature. She has published essays on clothing in early modern English culture, Shakespeare, early modern English-Irish relations, and twentieth-century treatments of *Macbeth* and Shane O'Neill.

BEN LABRECHE is an Assistant Professor at the University of Mary Washington. His current research concerns the development of political liberty in seventeenth-century England.

C. BRYAN LOVE is an Assistant Professor of English at the University of South Carolina Salkehatchie. His main area of interest is the London theatrical marketplace at the end of the sixteenth and beginning of the seventeenth centuries, with special focus on the children's theaters. His essays have appeared recently in the *Journal of the Georgia Philological Association* and *Renaissance Papers 2008.*

ANDREW MAJESKE teaches at John Jay College of Criminal Justice (CUNY). In 2006 he published *Equity in English Renaissance Literature,* and in 2009 he edited *Justice Women and Power in English Renaissance Drama* (FDUP).

JAMES J. MARINO is Assistant Professor of English at Cleveland State University. He has published articles and book chapters in *Shakespeare Quarterly, Renaissance Drama,* and *The Oxford Handbook of Early Modern Theatre.* His book, *Owning William Shakespeare: The King's Men and Their Intellectual Property,* is forthcoming.

INEKE MURAKAMI is an Assistant Professor at the University at Albany, SUNY. Her recent publications include "Wager's Drama of Convention, Class and State Constitution," *SEL* 47.2 (Spring 2007): 305–29, and "The 'bond and privilege of nature' in *Coriolanus,*" *Religion & Literature* 38.3 (March 2007): 121–36.

SAMANTHA MURPHY teaches in the English Department at the University of Tennessee, Knoxville. Her article, "Writing Britain: James VI & I and the National Body," was published in *Enculteration*, 6.1 (Spring 2008). It analyzes the relationship between authorship, nationality, and King James's hybrid body.

MEG PEARSON teaches early modern literature at the University of West Georgia as an assistant professor. Her recent publications have considered the function of spectacular figures such as Dog in *The Witch of Edmonton* and reframed the relationship between Titus and Aaron as pedagogical in *Titus Andronicus*. Presently she is at work on a larger piece comparing the dynamics of spectatorship in early modern paintings and plays.

JUNE SCHLUETER, Charles A. Dana Professor of English at Lafayette College, is co-author of *Reading Shakespeare in Performance: King Lear* and co-editor of *Acts of Criticism: Performance Matters in Shakespeare and His Contemporaries* (FDUP).

ERIC V. SPENCER is Associate Professor at the College of Idaho. He has written on Shakespeare's *Merchant of Venice* and *1 Henry IV*.

AMY L. TIGNER is an Assistant Professor in English at the University of Texas, Arlington. Dr. Tigner has published articles in *Modern Drama, English Literary Renaissance, Drama Criticism,* and *Global Traffic: Discourses and Practices of Trade in English Literature and Culture from 1550 to 1700,* and she is the founding editor of the new online journal, *Early English Studies,* at www.uta.edu/english/ees/index.html.

BRIAN WALSH is an assistant professor in the English Department at Yale University. His book *Shakespeare, the Queen's Men, and The Elizabethan Performance of History* is forthcoming.

MEDIEVAL AND RENAISSANCE DRAMA IN ENGLAND

Articles

Parallels and Poetry:
Shakespeare, Kyd, and *Arden of Faversham*

MacDonald P. Jackson

IN *Attributing Authorship: An Introduction,* Harold Love asserts that "literary quality is a genuine attribute of writing and one that can be recognised. As such it will be one of the criteria drawn on in conferring or denying attribution."[1] This seems to me sensible. In reaction to the excesses of eighteenth- and nineteenth-century scholars eager to foist onto some lesser dramatist anything of which they disapproved within the plays of the Shakespeare First Folio, there arose a distrust of any attempts at "disintegration" based on subjective assessment of merit. Shakespeare, it was insisted, could write poorly and other playwrights could write well. This is undoubtedly true. But Shakespeare, even at the beginning of his career as dramatist, was a better poet than Thomas Kyd, for example. The author of *The Spanish Tragedy* was a brilliant pioneer of stagecraft and dramatic plot construction, with a flair for the creation of striking theatrical moments and a sense of how to shape action to a climax. The verbal medium he devised—an elaborately patterned rhetoric, in which dialogue can become almost operatic—is an effective enough instrument for his purposes. But it lacks the linguistic subtlety, the lively play of imagery, and the rich metaphorical content that characterize Shakespeare's dramatic verse. Even without making a value judgement, we could nevertheless say that as poetic dramatists Kyd and Shakespeare exhibit different kinds of imagination and habits of mind.

This article aims to show how this crucial difference between Kyd and Shakespeare helps answer an old question: who wrote the anonymous domestic tragedy *Arden of Faversham?* That play was published in a quarto of 1592, probably having been first performed sometime within the period 1588–91.[2] Shakespeare's earliest plays are plausibly dated 1590–91.[3] Recent scholarship assigns Kyd's *The Spanish Tragedy* to 1587–88.[4] Kyd was also the undoubted author of a translation from Richard Garnier's French, *Cornelia,* composed not long before Kyd's death in August 1594.[5] A strong case has been made, on internal evidence, for thinking that *Soliman and Perseda* is also his. Entered in the Stationers' Register on November 20, 1592, and published shortly afterward in an undated octavo, it was almost certainly written after *The Spanish Tragedy,* but whether as early as 1588 or as late as 1591 remains in dispute.[6]

Recently Brian Vickers has argued that *Arden of Faversham, The True Chronicle History of King Leir, Fair Em the Miller's Daughter of Manchester,* and "parts of Acts 2 and 4, and the whole of Acts 3 and 5" of *1 Henry VI* should be added to Kyd's canon.[7] Using plagiarism software, he searched pairs of plays for shared three-word phrases (or "triples") and then, again with electronic aid, checked the substantial lists against a corpus of seventy-five non-Kyd plays "produced before 1596." He found that *Arden, Fair Em, King Leir,* and *1 Henry VI* each shared a fair number of triples or more extensive parallels with Kyd's plays alone among those of the period 1580–96. He concluded that the quantity of uniquely shared triples and the quality of the extended parallels clearly indicate Kyd's authorship of the nominated texts.

Elsewhere I have sought to demonstrate that these conclusions are unwarranted.[8] When the same electronic searches are carried out for three-word sequences shared by *Arden of Faversham* and Shakespeare's *2 Henry VI* and *The Taming of the Shrew, Arden,* a domestic tragedy, yields about as many unique matches with each of the Shakespeare plays, one a history and the other a comedy, as with all three of the canonical Kyd plays combined. Edward Archer clearly intended to ascribe *Arden of Faversham* to Shakespeare in his playlist appended to an edition of *The Old Law* in 1656, and although Archer made many gross blunders, Shakespeare's authorship of the play was considered likely by several nineteenth-century scholars, notable among them being the poet Swinburne.[9] However, early in the twentieth century several commentators argued for Kyd's authorship of *Arden of Faversham*. Charles Crawford, H. Dugdale Sykes, Félix Carrère, and others made out a case that convinced many, but was summarily dismissed by Kyd's editor Frederick S. Boas and pronounced "thoroughly unconvincing" by Kyd specialist Arthur Freeman.[10]

Let us, then, consider some passages in *Arden of Faversham* in relation to the contrasting styles of dramatic poetry of Shakespeare and Kyd. The most persistent feature of Shakespeare's language is its concreteness—its tendency to tie abstractions to physical phenomena, to express thoughts and feelings through images of objects and actions. Shakespeare is so alert to multiple meanings that imagery is often generated by a kind of wordplay. So in *King John,* Austria avers to Arthur that he will not return home

> Till Angers and the right thou hast in France,
> Together with that pale, that white-faced shore,
> Whose foot spurns back the ocean's roaring tides
> And coops from other lands her islanders,
> Even till that England hedged in with the main,
> That water-wallèd bulwark, still secure

> And confident from foreign purposes,
> Even till that utmost corner of the west
> Salute thee for her king.
>
> (2.1.22–30)[11]

Here "pale," as a fence or enclosure, leads into "coops" (meaning "encloses for protection"), "hedged in," and "water-wallèd bulwark," but also, as denoting pallor, leads into "that white-faced shore." The chalk cliff-face of the southeastern coast of England (or "Albion") is thus personified, and so the moribund metaphor in "the foot of a cliff" can be revived and drawn into the personification as a human foot "spurning back" the tides.[12]

Even in Shakespeare's very earliest plays this mode of operation, in which punning and imagery merge, is in evidence. For instance, in *2 Henry VI*, Suffolk, trying to convince King Henry of the Duke of Gloucester's hypocrisy, says:

> Smooth runs the water where the brook is deep,
> And in his simple show he harbours treason.
> The fox barks not when he would steal the lamb:
> *(To King Henry)*
> No, no, my sovereign; Gloucester is a man
> Unsounded yet, and full of deep deceit.
>
> (3.1.53–57)

The water metaphor in the semi-proverbial first line leads to the verb "harbours" in the next and gives concreteness and life to the otherwise almost dead metaphors of the words "unsounded" and "deep" in the last line. Most writers would refer to depths of deceit without evoking any image, but Shakespeare makes the depths real by juxtaposing "unsounded"—literally not measured with a plummet, as well as figuratively untried or unexamined. Even "The fox barks not when he would steal the lamb," which seems unrelated to the nautical imagery, is connected to it by an associational link in "bark": when Shakespeare uses the word "bark" in any sense, other senses are apt to be just below consciousness—the bark of a tree, for instance, and, as here, a sailing vessel (alternatively spelt "barque").

Arden of Faversham displays the same linguistic awareness. For example, Black Will, thinking of Alice Arden's promise of payment for acting as her husband's assassin, says:

> Why, this would steel soft-mettled cowardice,
> With which Black Will was never tainted with.
>
> (3.98–99)

"Mettle" is an abstract noun, deriving its meaning "courage" or "spirit" by metaphor from "metal," of which it is a variant. Here the verb "steel" draws attention to the original sense: even soft metal would be turned into hard steel, as the financial reward will harden Will's resolve. In her valuable book *Shakespeare's Wordplay,* M. M. Mahood noted that "although Shakespeare frequently puns on *metal* and *mettle,* there are many places in the plays where the two words coalesce into one significance."[13] They do so in the following passage from *2 Henry IV,* which affords a line remarkably similar to Black Will's. Morton says that report of Hotspur's death:

> took fire and heat away
> From the best-tempered courage in his troops;
> For from his metal was his party steeled;
> Which once in him abated, all the rest
> Turned on themselves, like dull and heavy lead.
>
> (1.1.112–18)

The fusion of abstract and concrete is complete and either spelling of the keyword would serve. From many other instances of such wordplay may be singled out Romeo's complaint that Juliet has made him effeminate, "And in my temper softened valour's steel" (3.1.115), where "temper" is doubly meaningful, as of course is "tempered" in the *2 Henry IV* passage. A search of the "Literature Online" (*LION*) electronic database reveals no play of 1580–96 that provides parallels as close to Will's "steel soft-mettled cowardice" as do *2 Henry IV* and *Romeo and Juliet,* while the only other instance of "never tainted with" falls within a scene of *1 Henry VI* that has been generally accepted as Shakespeare's (4.5.46), where it again refers to cowardice.[14]

Very common in early modern drama and poetry are allusions to the "closet" of the breast or heart. A closet is a small room, cupboard, or cabinet. As Marlowe employs the analogy in *Edward II,* it is stock poetic diction:

> My daily diet is heart-breaking sobs,
> That almost rents the closet of my heart.
>
> (5.3.21–22)[15]

Taken as genuinely figurative language, this is a muddle. Sobs that are consumed ("diet") almost tear or split ("rents") a closet. Words are being used loosely, without interacting to create any sensory stimulus to the imagination. In *Arden of Faversham* cliché is transformed. Will tells Michael:

> I am the very man,
> Marked in my birth-hour by the Destinies,
> To give an end to Arden's life on earth;
> Thou but a member but to whet the knife
> Whose edge must search the closet of his breast.
>
> (3.159–63)

The verb "search" here shows that the author is not using the word "closet" in any automatic and unimaginative way. His line is genuinely metaphorical. The searching of a closet blends with the kind of probing that Cassius commands from Pindarus: "with this good sword . . . search this bosom" (*Julius Caesar*, 5.3.40–41). Shakespeare twice uses the variant "the closure of my breast" so as to bring out the full force of the metaphor.[16]

Analysis of a few representative parallels that Vickers cites between *Arden of Faversham* and *Soliman and Perseda* reveals crucial differences in the way the shared three-word sequences or "triples" are used—differences that point to dissimilar kinds of poetic imagination and hence to separate authors. Among the triples that *Arden of Faversham* shares with *Soliman and Perseda* is "to everlasting night," preceded in both plays by the verb "to send." *Soliman and Perseda* has "to send them down to everlasting night" (5.2.110) and has earlier used "down to everlasting night" without the verb (1.1.26).[17] *Arden* has "And Arden sent to everlasting night" (5.9).

But if we consult the contexts in which the phrase occurs, the verbal parallel between the two plays appears less significant than the disparity in poetic quality. In *Arden,* the hired assassin Shakebag, after a brief and evocative tribute to the "sheeting darkness" that facilitates such villainy as he and his accomplice Black Will delight in, concludes that the "night" to which he is about to consign Arden will be an "everlasting one" (5.1–9). Not only is it to be under cover of literal night that Arden is dispatched to figurative night, but woven into the fabric of Shakebag's speech is an opposition between time and eternity. As Shakebag waits for night ("In which sweet silence such as we triumph," line 5) to drape the earth in "the black fold of her cloudy robe" (line 3), he says:

> The lazy minutes linger on their time,
> Loath to give due audit to the hour,
> Till in the watch our purpose be complete
> And Arden sent to everlasting night.
>
> (5.6–9)

The imagery and thought here are echoed in *The Rape of Lucrece.* Rapist Tarquin, experiencing minor delays as he approaches the sleeping Lucrece's bedchamber, takes them

> . . . as those bars which stop the hourly dial,
> Who with a ling'ring stay his course doth let
> Till every minute pays the hour his debt.
>
> (327–29)

The "bars" are the lines on the clock face that mark off the minutes, but they are also thought of as obstacles. They both punctuate the dial and appear to halt the movement of the hand, since early modern clocks "moved with regular jolts rather than a smooth movement."[18] "Let" means hinder. In both *Arden* and *Lucrece,* time is felt to slow down so as to postpone the moment at which the crime (anticipated as fulfillment) is committed. With "minutes," "linger," and "hour" compare "ling'ring," "minute," and "hour." In each case there is also a commercial metaphor. In *Arden* the minutes are "Loath to give due audit to the hour"—they are reluctant to render payment so as to square the final account that is owed ("due"). Similarly Tarquin is thwarted "Till every minute pays the hour his debt." "Audit" is a word of which Shakespeare is fond. In Sonnet 126 it is used in connection with time. Although Nature seems to have power to "kill" "wretched minutes" and so prevent the Fair Youth from aging, yet Time's "audit, though delayed, answered must be, / And her quietus is to render thee" (lines 11–12).

In Shakebag's speech "the watch" is a period of vigilance or "a time division of the night," but the word also evokes a timepiece or even "the marks of the minutes on a dial-plate." The word adds to the images of time set against "everlasting night." The idea of the minutes accumulating to make up the hour at which the assassins' "purpose be complete" is akin to King Henry's desire to sit and "carve out dials quaintly, point by point":

> Thereby to see the minutes how they run:
> How many makes the hour full complete.
>
> (*3 Henry VI*, 2.5.24–26)

Arden of Faversham is full of anticipations of *Macbeth,* and Shakebag's "sheeting darkness" is well on the way to Lady Macbeth's "blanket of the dark" (1.5.52). There are, as Fluellen might have said, bedclothes in both, with their connotations of nighttime. But "sheeting darkness" also carries suggestions of winding-sheets. This is *OED*'s only example of the present participial adjective, meaning "swathing, enfolding." Its earliest example of the past participial adjective "sheeted" is in *Hamlet*'s "the sheeted dead" (Additional passage A.8), where the sheets are shrouds, and its earliest example of "sheet" as a verb is from *Antony and Cleopatra,* where "snow the pasture sheets" (1.4.65). So Shakebag's speech displays a typically Shakespearean verbal inventiveness.

In Shakebag's speech "Black night hath hid the pleasures of the day" and with its "sheeting darkness" conceals the would-be assassins "with the black fold of her cloudy robe," so that they may send Arden to "everlasting night." Likewise, in *Richard III* (1.3.264–67), Queen Margaret harangues Gloucester as butcher of her sun-like son ("now in the shade of death"), whose beams "thy cloudy wrath / Hath in eternal darkness folded up." Gloucester "turns the sun to shade." Neither Kyd nor Marlowe uses "fold" as noun or verb in connection with darkness. Shakespeare does so not only in *Richard III* but also in *Venus and Adonis,* where "the merciless and pitchy night" did "Fold in" Adonis, obscuring him from Venus's sight (821–82), and in *The Rape of Lucrece,* where Tarquin's crime is "folded up in blind concealing night" (675).

Finally, with regard to the context of the triple "to everlasting night," when *LION* is set to search all authors living in the years from 1000 to 1700 for juxtapositions of "minute(s)," "hour," and inflections of the verb "to linger," it finds only two instances besides those in *Arden of Faversham* and *The Rape of Lucrece*—in the anonymous play *Mucedorus* and in a poem called "The Hour-glass" by Rowland Watkins in *Flamma Sine Fuma* (1662). In *Mucedorus* (Q 1598, B1ʳ) the lingering is of a person and is quite distinct from "each minute of an hour." Watkins has:

> The sand within the transitory glass
> Doth haste, and so our silent minutes pass.
> Consider how the ling'ring hour-glass sends
> Sand after sand, until the stock it spends.
> (*Flamma Sine Fuma,* 1662, E5ᵛ)

Here the sand in the glass "Doth haste" and the hourglass lingers. The ideas are different from those in the *Arden* and *Lucrece* passages, and in any case the poem was written about seventy years later.[19]

As poetry, the passage in which "to everlasting night" occurs within *Soliman and Perseda* lacks the interest of the *Arden* lines. Soliman, apostrophizing the dead Erastus, vows that he himself will kill the two janissaries who strangled him; Soliman's hand

> shall help
> To send them down to everlasting night,
> To wait upon thee through eternal shade.
> Thy soul shall not go mourning hence alone.
> (5.2.109–12)

There is no complex interplay of images here, just a straightforward reference to the classical descent into Hades. This is true also of Kyd's first use of the phrase. In the chorus involving Love, Fortune, and Death that opens the play, Death asserts: "I will not down to everlasting night / Till I have moralized this tragedy" (1.1.26–27).

Another triple common to *Arden of Faversham* and *Soliman and Perseda* is "with eager mood." The dying Soliman entreats Perseda:

> And, sweet Perseda, fly not Soliman
> Whenas my gliding ghost shall follow thee
> With eager mood thorough eternal night.

> And now pale death sits on my panting soul
> And with revenging ire doth tyrannize.
>
> (5.4.149–53)

Here "eager mood" takes its place in an assembly of nouns preceded by the most obvious epithets: "sweet Perseda," "gliding ghost," "eternal night," "pale death," "panting soul," "revenging ire." The excerpt is a tissue of inert expressions and other men's inventions.

There could hardly be a greater contrast than with the rich particularity of the lines in which "with eager mood" appears in *Arden*. Greene advises Black Will and Shakebag as they prepare to attack their victim:

> Well, take your fittest standings, and once more
> Lime your twigs to catch this weary bird.
> I'll leave you, and at your dag's discharge
> Make towards, like the longing water-dog
> That coucheth till the fowling-piece be off,
> Then seizeth on the prey with eager mood.
> Ah, might I see him stretching forth his limbs
> As I have seen them beat their wings ere now.
>
> (9.38–45)

The metaphorical hunting scene has been clearly visualized by the poet and vividly presented. A "water-dog" is "a dog trained to retrieve waterfowl." Shakespeare refers to a "water-spaniel" ("a variety of spaniel, much used for retrieving waterfowl") in *The Two Gentlemen of Verona* (3.1.269) and to "water-rugs" (belonging to "a shaggy breed of water-dog") in *Macbeth* (3.1.95). The retriever crouches, belly to the ground, longing for the moment when the bird is shot, and then dashes to seize the prey "with eager mood"—the phrase assumes a certain concreteness in the context. The eagerness is in the dog's very nature.

The opening image of "smearing . . . twigs with a sticky substance known as bird-lime to catch birds"[20] is one to which Shakespeare frequently returns. There are three such bird-snaring images in *2 Henry VI*: "Madam, myself have limed a bush for her, / And placed a choir of such enticing birds / That she will light to listen to their lays, / And never mount to trouble you again" (1.3.91–94); "And York and impious Beauford that false priest, / Have all limed bushes to betray thy wings, / And fly thou how thou canst, they'll tangle thee" (2.4.54–56); "Like lime twigs set to catch my wingèd soul" (3.3.16). There are many other cases: "lay lime to tangle her desires" in *The Two Gentlemen of Verona* (3.2.68); "Birds never limed no secret bushes fear" (*The Rape of Lucrece*, 88), whereas "The bird that hath been limèd in a bush / With trembling wings misdoubteth every bush" (*3 Henry VI*, 5.6.13–14); "they are limed with the twigs" (*All's Well That Ends Well*, 3.5.23–24);

and so on. But Kyd also uses the image in *The Spanish Tragedy:* "I set the trap, he breaks the worthless twigs, / And sees not that wherewith the bird was limed" (3.4.41–42).

It is the detailed picture of the water-dog—which reads like the work of a country man who has experienced hunting for waterfowl at first hand—that most suggests Shakespeare. For anything comparable in the drama of the late 1580s and early 1590s we would have to turn to Shakespeare, as in *1 Henry VI,* 4.2.45–52:

> How are we parked and bounded in a pale!—
> A little herd of England's timorous deer
> Mazed with a yelping kennel of French curs.
> If we be English deer, be then in blood,
> Not rascal-like, to fall down with a pinch,
> But rather, moody-mad and desperate stags,
> Turn on the bloody hounds with heads of steel
> And make the cowards stand aloof at bay.

The imagery in that speech, of hunting for deer, governs Arden's narrative of his dream at 6.6–31.

That Shakespeare had handled a "fowling-piece" is suggested by Robin Goodfellow's (Puck's) account, in *A Midsummer Night's Dream,* of the "rude mechanicals'" reaction to Bottom's metamorphosis into an ass. When they catch sight of him:

> As wild geese that the creeping fowler eye,
> Or russet-pated choughs, many in sort,
> Rising and cawing at the gun's report,
> Sever themselves and madly sweep the sky—
> So, at his sight, away his fellows fly. . . .
>
> (3.2.20–24)

Again we have the fowl, the stalker's stealthiness (water-dog "couching," fowler "creeping"), the firing of the gun, the beating of wings. In *The Merry Wives of Windsor,* Page, Ford, Caius, and Evans are said to have gone "a-birding" (3.3.221, 3.5.43, 3.5.119, 4.2.7) and "fowling-pieces" in the Quarto (1602) become "birding-pieces" in the First Folio (1623) (4.2.50).

Both *Arden of Faversham* and *Soliman and Perseda* contain references to "a sudden qualm." In Kyd's play, Lucina asks "What ails you, madam, that your colour changes?" and Perseda replies "A sudden qualm" (2.1.49–50). In *Arden,* Franklin asks "What ails you, woman, to cry so suddenly?" and Alice replies "Ah, neighbours, a sudden qualm came over my heart" (14.301–2). Both question and answer share a three-word sequence. But in this case it is worth consulting every instance of the word "qualm" in plays of 1580–96. Some plays use "qualm" without offering anything much by way of parallelism with *Arden* or *Soliman and Perseda*. Greene's *Friar Bacon and Friar Bungay* has "a qualm did cross his stomach then" (1.18)[21] Greene and Lodge's *A Looking Glass for London and England* has "to ease a woman when a qualm of kindness come too near her stomach" (1100–1102). Lyly's *Sapho and Phao* has "or else a woman's qualm" (3.1, p. 86).

Other plays offer more. Alice's "qualm came over my heart" is paralleled in "a qualm that often cometh over my heart" of Lyly's *Endimion* (3.4, p. 170) and in an exchange in Shakespeare's *Love's Labour's Lost:* Katherine remarks, "Lord Longaville said I came o'er his heart. / And trow you what he called me?," which elicits the Princess's quip "'Qualm', perhaps" (5.2.278–79). Evidently qualms are apt to come over the heart. In *2 Henry VI,* Gloucester says "Some sudden qualm hath struck me at the heart" (1.1.52). In the bad quarto (1594) of the same play this becomes "Pardon, my lord, a sudden qualm came over my heart" (A3r).[22] It is possible that a reporter corrupted the text preserved in the Folio through recollection of Alice's "a sudden qualm came over my heart." Whatever the reason, the quarto *Contention* shares with *Arden of Faversham* this uninterrupted seven-word sequence.

But it is Gloucester's use of the verb "struck" that points to the most significant link with a "qualm" in *Arden*. Gloucester is reading out an agreement that Suffolk has engineered between King Henry and the French King Charles in which lands held by the English are to be released to the French. He breaks off, dropping the paper: "Pardon me, gracious lord. / Some sudden qualm hath struck me at the heart / And dimmed mine eyes that I can read no further" (1.1.51–53). In *Arden of Faversham,* Franklin is urged by Arden to continue his a tale of an adulterous wife. Franklin attempts to excuse himself:

> I assure you, sir, you task me much.
> A heavy blood is gathered at my heart,
> And on a sudden is my wind cut short
> As hindereth the passage of my speech.
> So fierce a qualm yet ne'er assailèd me.
>
> (9.63–67)

In both passages the qualm strikes or assails, is sudden, and affects the heart. The attack stops Gloucester from continuing to read aloud and Franklin from continuing to narrate. In one further mention of a qualm in the drama of 1580–96, Greene writes "A sudden qualm / Assails my heart" in *James IV* (5.1.65-2). Here is the same verb that Franklin employs in *Arden*. I doubt that we can possibly establish relationships of influence or agency between all these early modern qualms, though the parallel between Franklin's qualm in *Arden of Faversham* and Gloucester's in *2 Henry VI* strikes me as the most evidential of authorship. But the crucial matter to which I want to draw attention is the Shakespearean way in which "fierce" and "assailèd" interact in Franklin's "So fierce a qualm yet ne'er assailèd me." *2 Henry VI* has "struck" and *James IV* even has "Assails." But the addition of the simple adjective "fierce" brings out the latent metaphor in "assailèd": the two words act upon each other to create a line with real metaphorical life.

To examine one further parallel, Crawford and Sykes, arguing for Kyd's authorship of *Arden of Faversham,* compared "forge distressful looks" in *Arden* (8.56) with "forge alluring looks" in *Soliman and Perseda* (2.1.117). Since *LION* yields no further instances of the forging of looks in English drama of the period 1576–1642, from the opening of the Theatre to the closing of the theatres, there is almost certainly a connection between these two. But studying them in context leads to the conclusion that identity of authorship is most improbable.

In *Arden of Faversham,* Mosby, with characteristic egotism, accuses the sighing Alice of feigning misery only to make him feel miserable too:

> Ungentle Alice, thy sorrow is my sore;
> Thou know'st it well, and 'tis thy policy
> To forge distressful looks to wound a breast
> Where lies a heart that dies when thou art sad.
>
> (8.54–57)

The author of *Arden* is alive to the language he is using. The implications of the latent metaphor in "forge" (one forges weapons) are fully appreciated, and carried on in "wounds" and "dies." This strand of imagery begins in the earlier lines of Mosby's speech when he compares Alice's sighs to "a cannon's burst / Discharged against a ruinated wall"—sighs that break his "relenting heart in thousand pieces" (51–53); and the word "policy" contributes to the thread with a hint of military strategy. Shakespeare similarly exploits the underlying, primary sense of the verb "forge" in 137:

> Why of eyes' falsehood hast thou forgèd hooks,
> Whereto the judgement of my heart is tied?
>
> (lines 7–8)

The fashioning of hooks from metal (probably with the aid of beams flashing from the eyes) is implicit in this intricate image of false beguiling.

In *Soliman and Perseda,* Perseda exclaims:

> Ah, how thine eyes can forge alluring looks
> And feign deep oaths to wound poor silly maids.
>
> (2.1.117–18)

Kyd (if it be he) uses "forge" prosaically to mean "contrive" with no interest in its derivation. The word "wound" is present but fails to connect with any other word to generate a metaphorical charge in the lines. How, one may ask, can eyes feign oaths, let alone deep ones? The playwright responsible for *Soliman and Perseda* did not trouble himself with such questions. The author of *Arden of Faversham* awakes the dormant metaphors in words; the author of *Soliman and Perseda* bundles together his "alluring looks," "deep oaths," and "silly maids," and lets the metaphors sleep.

In illustration of the Shakespearean vitality of much of the language of *Arden of Faversham,* I cited the way that the verb "steel" brings out the "metal" in "soft-mettled" in Black Will's avowal of his resolve to kill Arden. His speech continues

> I tell thee, Greene, the forlorn traveller
> Whose lips are glued with summer's parching heat
> Ne'er longed so much to see a running brook
> As I to finish Arden's tragedy.
>
> (3.100–103)

Not only does the language have a vividness and concreteness never on display in Kyd's plays, but it contains three significant links to early Shakespeare. The phrase "summer's parching heat" is found in *2 Henry VI,* which has "In winter's cold and summer's parching heat" (1.1.78). It appears in no other play of 1576–1642, and the whole of *LION* English drama contains only one eighteenth- and one nineteenth-century echo of the phrase.[23] In the very next line "a running brook" is shared with *The Taming of the Shrew* (Ind.2.49) and with no other play of 1576–1642. Indeed, the phrase appears in only one other *LION* work—whether poetry, drama, or prose—before the nineteenth century, and that is John Studley's translation of Seneca's *Medea,* a closet drama of 1566. Thirdly, "Whose lips are glued" has its counterpart in "That glues my lips" in *3 Henry VI* (5.2.38). This image of glued lips constitutes a third Shakespearean link that is unique in early modern drama. And the three links—within two consecutive lines—are to three of Shakespeare's first four plays, according to the Oxford *Textual Companion,* which dates them 1590–91.

Moreover, the *Arden* lines have close parallels in *Venus and Adonis,* written in 1592–93 and published in 1593. Venus eagerly anticipates a kiss from Adonis: her "lips were ready" but he "turns his lips another way" (89–90). Then "Never did passenger in summer's heat / More thirst for drink than she for this good turn" (91–92). In both *Arden* and Shakespeare's poem the "lips" of the traveler (or "passenger," which means traveler) thirst for drink in "summer's . . . heat." The other element in the *Arden* image is present in a later stanza of *Venus and Adonis,* where Venus presses her "thirsty lips"

(543) on Adonis's mouth, until the pair, "Their lips together glued, fall to the earth" (545).[24]

The Shakespearean linguistic alertness typified by the juxtaposition of "fierce" and "assailed" in relation to a "qualm" thus appears within a speech that not only has a Shakespearean poetic vigor but displays striking parallels with Shakespeare's earliest works.

One more example of Shakespearean wordplay-cum-image-making in *Arden of Faversham* seems worth noting, since it includes a submerged pun found also in *Macbeth*, which, as mentioned above, *Arden* often anticipates.[25] Quarreling with Alice, her lover Mosby protests that, in carrying on an affair with her:

> I left the marriage of an honest maid
> Whose dowry would have weighed down all thy wealth,
> Whose beauty and demeanour far exceeded thee.
> This certain good I lost for changing bad,
> And wrapped my credit in thy company.
> I was bewitched—that is no theme of thine!—
> And thou unhallowed hast enchanted me.
> But I will break thy spells and exorcisms
> And put another sight upon these eyes
> That showed my heart a raven for a dove.
> Thou art not fair—I viewed thee not till now;
> Thou art not kind—till now I knew thee not.
> And now the rain hath beaten off thy gilt
> Thy worthless copper shows thee counterfeit.
>
> (8.88–94)

Mosby's character is here reflected in the imagery he uses. His concern with the "dowry" and the "wealth" that he has lost reappears in puns on "changing," "credit," and "company," and in the final image in which he compares Alice to a counterfeit gold coin. "Credit" is good reputation in general but also has specific application to financial credit-worthiness or solvency; "company" is both society and a business concern. Later in the play the commercial sense of "company" draws out the metaphorical content of "purchase": "Your company hath purchased me ill friends" (14.209).[26] Shakespeare several times quibbles on "company."[27] *The Two Gentlemen of Verona* affords a good illustration. Valentine says: "Sir Thurio borrows his wit from your ladyship's looks, and spends what he borrows kindly in your company" (2.4.36–40), and the commercial references are continued in "bankrupt," "exchequer," and "treasure" (40–42). Shakespeare brings *Arden*'s "credit" and "company" together in *The Merchant of Venice*, where Tubal tells Shylock: "There came divers of Antonio's creditors in my company to Venice" (3.1.105–6).

The opposing of dove and raven to contrast value and worthlessness or to emphasize the deceptive nature of appearances is Shakespearean, as is the image of the gilding of copper to symbolize falseness in love.[28] But it is the word "wrapt" to which I want to draw attention. In *Shakespeare's Wordplay,* Mahood notes Banquo's remarks about Macbeth's strange behavior when he learns that he has been made Thane of Cawdor: "Look how our partner's rapt" (1.3.141). As she says, "the secondary meaning of 'wrapped' is shown to be in the air by his next words":

> New honours come upon him.
> Like our strange garments, cleave not to their mould
> But with the aid of use.
>
> (1.3.143–45)[29]

Mosby's unconscious wordplay on "wrapped" (meaning involved, implicated, invested)[30] works in the other direction, the homophone "rapt" connecting with the subsequent "bewitched," "enchanted," "spells," and "exorcisms."

Mahood quotes Coleridge's appreciation of Shakespeare's "never broken chain of imagery, always vivid, and because unbroken, often minute." As she explains, illustrating the point by analysis of a passage in *Romeo and Juliet,* "it remains unbroken because its images are linked by unconscious wordplay."[31] In an earlier article I showed how four threads of imagery—relating to horticulture, spoken and written language, conflict and violence, and parts of the body—run through Arden's twenty-line speech in scene 4 (1–20), being inherent in words that often carry multiple meanings and interweave the threads.[32] Complex sensory content animates the emotional, ethical, and theological abstractions. The rhetorical structure of the speech, at least in its opening lines, is scarcely less elaborate than that of certain set pieces in Kyd's *The Spanish Tragedy,* but the interplay of words and images fleshes out the skeleton of rhetoric in ways typical of Shakespeare but not of Kyd. And the sources of imagery in *Arden of Faversham* are those upon which, early in his career, Shakespeare repeatedly draws.

In the present article I have examined a handful of phrases shared between *Arden of Faversham* and *Soliman and Perseda* or other early modern plays. Their treatment in *Arden,* as opposed to their treatment by Kyd and others, exemplifies, in a small compass, the essence of the Shakespearean process described by Coleridge and analyzed by Mahood. There can be no doubt of the immense value of numerical approaches to questions of authorship. Objective counts of particular features can discriminate between one playwright and another. But traditional literary critical methods also have their place. Vickers's pioneering employment of plagiarism software to identify sequences of words that anonymous plays share with Kyd has considerable potential. But when his results for numbers of three-word sequences that *Arden of Faversham* shares with Kyd but not with other plays of 1580–96 are set against the results of a search of three-word sequences similarly unique to *Arden of Faversham* and *2 Henry VI* or *The Taming of the Shrew*, it turns out that each of the two early Shakespeare plays yields many more unique triples than does any play by Kyd. And analysis of the literary qualities of the contexts in which shared triples occur within *Arden of Faversham* and *Soliman and Perseda* reinforces the verdict that Kyd is much less likely than Shakespeare to have written the pertinent passages in *Arden*. Swinburne had no head for statistics, but, as a poet himself, he recognized that the play contained dramatic verse of Shakespearean distinction. Shakespeare remains a strong candidate for the authorship of at least a substantial part of *Arden of Faversham*.

Notes

1. Harold Love, *Attributing Authorship: An Introduction* (Cambridge: Cambridge University Press, 2002), 94.

2. Matters of text and dating are ably discussed by M. L. Wine in his Revels edition, *The Tragedy of Master Arden of Faversham* (London: Methuen, 1973), from which my quotations from the play are taken and to which my scene and line references refer: Wine divides the play into scenes only.

3. I have relied on the Oxford chronology, in Stanley Wells and Gary Taylor with John Jowett and William Montgomery, *William Shakespeare: A Textual Companion* (Oxford: Clarendon Press, 1987), 69–133.

4. Lukas Erne, *Beyond* The Spanish Tragedy: *A Study of the Works of Thomas Kyd* (Manchester: Manchester University Press, 2001), 58–59.

5. ibid., 203–16.

6. For authorship and date of *Soliman and Perseda*, see Erne, *Beyond the Spanish Tragedy*, 157–67. Arthur Freeman, *Thomas Kyd: Facts and Problems* (Oxford: Clarendon Press, 1967) inclined toward 1591–92. In *The Tragedye of Solyman and Perseda Edited from the Original Texts* (New York: Garland, 1991), John J. Murray thinks it "not unreasonable to conclude . . . that Kyd reworked his play in its present surviving form around the year 1591" (xii). It is listed under 1590 in Alfred Harbage rev. S. Schoenbaum, *Annals of English Drama 975–1700* (London: Methuen, 1964). Scholarship on the play was surveyed by Jill Levenson, "Anonymous Plays: *Soliman and Perseda*," in *The Predecessors of Shakespeare: A Survey and Bibliography of Recent Studies in English Renaissance Drama*, ed. Terence P. Logan and Denzell S. Smith (Lincoln: University of Nebraska Press, 1978), 230–39

7. Brian Vickers, "Thomas Kyd, secret sharer," *Times Literary Supplement*, April 18, 2008, 13–15. The data on which this article draws are posted on the website of the London Forum for Authorship Studies: http://ies.sas.ac.uk/events/seminars/LFAS/index.htm.

8. MacD. P. Jackson, "New Research on the Dramatic Canon of Thomas Kyd," *Research Opportunities in Medieval and Renaissance Drama* 47 (2007): 107–27.

9. That Archer intended to ascribe *Arden of Faversham* to Shakespeare, but that columns were accidentally misaligned was demonstrated by W. W. Greg, "Shakespeare and *Arden of Feversham*," *Review of English Studies* 21 (1945): 134–36. Greg assessed the reliability of attributions in Archer's and other seventeenth-century playlists in "Author Attributions in the Early Play-Lists, 1656–1671," *Edinburgh Bibliographical Society Transactions* 2 (1938–45): 305–29. For Swinburne, see Algernon Charles Swinburne, *A Study of Shakespeare* (London: Chatto and Windus, 1880), 129–41. For other supporters of the Shakespeare theory, see the account of scholarship on the authorship question by M. P. Jackson, "Material for an Edition of *Arden of Feversham*" (BLitt thesis, University of Oxford, 1963), 129–264, and Levenson, "Anonymous Plays: *Arden of Feversham*," in *Predecessors*, 240–52; also Wine, *tragedy of Master Arden*, lxxxi–xcii.

10. Frederick S. Boas, ed., *The Works of Thomas Kyd* (Oxford: Clarendon Press, 1901), lxxxix; Arthur Freeman, *Thomas Kyd: Facts and Problems* (Oxford: Clarendon Press, 1967), 179–80. The case for Kyd is assessed by Jackson, "Materials," 91–115, and fully documented by Levenson, *Predecessors*, 240–52.

11. I quote from *William Shakespeare: The Complete Works: Compact Edition*, ed. Stanley Wells and Gary Taylor (Oxford: Clarendon Press, 1988). But throughout this article I have used the familiar titles *2 Henry VI* and *3 Henry VI*, rather than Oxford's *The First Part of the Contention* and *Richard Duke of York*.

12. This passage was discussed by W. H. Clemen, *The Development of Shakespeare's Imagery* (London: Methuen, 1951), 75. Throughout the present article my definitions of words are taken from *OED*.

13. M. M. Mahood, *Shakespeare's Wordplay* (London: Methuen, 1957), 16.

14. At http://lion.chadwyck.co.uk. In quoting from *LION* I modernize spelling and punctuation. For the authenticity of *1 Henry VI*, 4.5, see Brian Vickers, "Incomplete Shakespeare: Or, Denying Coauthorship in *1 Henry VI*," *Shakespeare Quarterly* 58 (2007): 311–52, especially 339, where the ascription of 4.5 to Shakespeare is pronounced "uncontroversial."

15. *Christopher Marlowe: The Complete Plays*, ed. J. B. Steane (Harmondsworth, Middlesex: Penguin, 1969, repr. 1975).

16. *Venus and Adonis*, 782; Sonnet 48.

17. I quote *Soliman and Perseda* from *Works*, ed. Boas, but modernize his old spelling and punctuation.

18. William Shakespeare, *The Complete Sonnets and Poems* (Oxford: Oxford University Press, 2002), ed. Colin Burrow, commentary on *Lucrece*, 327.

19. Shakespeare seems to have unconsciously recalled the *Arden* passage in *Cymbeline*, 5.6.51–53, where the words "minute," "ling'ring," "time," "purposed," and "watching" echo the vocabulary of Shakebag's speech, and the construction "in which" (plus noun) recurs.

20. Wine, commentary on *Arden*, 9.39.

21. This excerpt and those that follow are modernized from *LION* and may be found by keying words into the search boxes, but references are to the following editions: Robert Greene, *Friar Bacon and Friar Bungay*, ed. Daniel Seltzer (Lincoln:

University of Nebraska Press, 1963), Regents Renaissance Drama; Thomas Lodge and Robert Greene, *A Looking-Glass for London and England,* ed. W. W. Greg (Oxford: Oxford University Press, 1932), Malone Society Reprint; *Sapho and Phao* and *Endimion,* in *The Plays of John Lyly,* ed. Carter A. Daniel (Lewisburg: Bucknell University Press; London: Associated University Presses, 1988); Robert Greene, *The Scottish History of James the Fourth,* ed. Norman Sanders (London: Methuen, 1970). Daniel's edition lacks line numbers, so page references are given.

22. Wine, commentary on *Arden,* 14.301–2.

23. Shakespeare's poem *The Rape of Lucrece* has the line "That knows not parching heat nor freezing cold" (1145). George Lillo echoes Shakespeare in *The London Merchant* (1731), with "the summer's parching heat and winter's cold" (2.11.68–69) and Alfred Austin borrows "Summer's parching heat" in his *Savonarola* (1881), 1.1. p. 15. References are to George Lillo, *The London Merchant,* ed. William H. McBurney (Lincoln: University of Nebraska Press, 1965) and to *Savonarola* (London: Macmillan, 2nd ed. 1891).

24. Furthermore, the word "parch" (in any form) is found near "lips" in no other play *LION* of 1576–42 except *King John:* "parchèd lips" (5.7.40).

25. Likenesses were discussed by Percy Allen in a chapter on "*Arden of Feversham* and *Macbeth*" in his *Shakespeare, Jonson, and Wilkins as Borrowers* (Oxford: Cecil Palmer, 1928), 19–20, and, more fully, by Robert F. Fleissner, "'The Secret'st Man of Blood': Foreshadowings of *Macbeth* in *Arden of Faversham,*" *University of Dayton Review* 14 (1979–80): 7–13. See also MacDonald P. Jackson, "Shakespearean Features of the Poetic Style of *Arden of Faversham,*" *Archiv für das Sudium der neueren Sprachen und Literaturen* 230 (1993): 279–304, at 288 n. 17.

26. The process, as regards "purchase," is similar to that in *Julius Caesar,* when Metellus recommends that the conspirators plotting Caesar's assassination enlist the support of Cicero, because "his silver hairs / Will purchase us a good opinion, / And buy men's voices to commend our deeds" (2.1.144–46). "Silver," primarily an adjective of color indicating the venerable Cicero's age, also suggests the precious metal and so revives the moribund metaphor in "purchase" (obtain) and "buy" (secure). Shakespeare uses Alice's expression "purchase friends" in *2 Henry VI,* 1.1.223 (following "cheap pennyworths"), *Titus Andronicus,* 2.3.275, and *The Rape of Lucrece,* 963 (where it is followed by the line "lending him wit that to bad debtors lends").

27. For example, in *1 Henry IV,* 2.2.11; *Love's Labour's Lost,* 5.2.224; *Much Ado About Nothing,* 3.3.57.

28. For raven and dove, see *A Midsummer Night's Dream,* 2.2.120; *Twelfth Night,* 5.1.129; *2 Henry VI,* 3.1.75–76; *Romeo and Juliet,* 3.2.76; *Pericles,* sc.15.32. For gilding copper, see *Troilus and Cressida,* where Troilus vows fidelity to Cressida: "Whilst some with cunning gild their copper crowns, / With truth and plainness I do wear mine bare" (4.4.105–6).

29. Mahood, *Shakespeare's Wordplay,* 165.

30. Had Shakespeare used any one of these words, it would have been with full consciousness of its Latin derivation (the rolling up of cloth, folding, clothing). He chooses "wrapped," rather than a synonym from which the original physical sense has been lost.

31. Mahood, *Shakespeare's Wordplay,* 13.

32. Jackson, "Shakespearean Features" (as in n. 25 above), 283–86.

The "To be, or not to be" Speech: Evidence, Conventional Wisdom, and the Editing of *Hamlet*

James Hirsh

SUBSTANTIAL, conspicuous, and varied pieces of evidence demonstrate that Shakespeare designed the "To be, or not to be" speech to be perceived by experienced playgoers of his time as a feigned soliloquy. Plentiful evidence within the play implies that Hamlet pretends to speak to himself but actually intends the speech itself or an account of it to reach the ears of Claudius in order to mislead his enemy about his state of mind. External evidence demonstrates that experienced playgoers of the period did indeed make the inference intended by Shakespeare. I pointed out much of this evidence in a 1981 article and further evidence in subsequent articles and in a 2003 book.[1] The present essay will add numerous important confirming pieces of evidence. This accumulation of evidence refutes the post-Renaissance conventional assumption that the speech is meant to represent a sincere expression of Hamlet's thoughts. Post-Renaissance editors and commentators have ignored or dismissed this evidence and have projected post-Renaissance attitudes onto Shakespeare. The orthodox assumption leads to misunderstandings about the "To be" speech, about the character of Hamlet, about other features of the play, about Shakespeare's artistic goals and techniques, about Renaissance dramatic practices, and about the history of subjectivity.

Evidence that the "To be" speech was designed as a feigned soliloquy

(1) The content and form of the "To be" speech are radically different from the content and form of every one of Hamlet's extended soliloquies elsewhere in the play. In each of those speeches Hamlet exhibits a passionate, obsessive focus on his personal situation—on his mother's marriage to his hated uncle, on the Ghost's accusation, on his desire for revenge, and on his own machinations. In each speech Hamlet uses first-person-singular pro-

nouns at a rate of at least one per four lines. In the soliloquy that ends the scene (2.2) before the one in which the "To be" speech occurs (3.1), Hamlet uses first-person-singular pronouns thirty-six times in fifty-nine lines. In sharp contrast, the "To be" speech is conspicuously impersonal. In a speech containing a long catalogue of grievances that might lead someone to contemplate suicide, Hamlet fails to mention any of the particular grievances that occupy his full attention during every one of his extended soliloquies elsewhere in the play. The omission of any reference to his personal situation is coupled with another kind of omission that makes the speech a tour de force of impersonality. In the entire thirty-four lines of the speech until he overtly addresses Ophelia, Hamlet never once uses a first-person-singular pronoun.

(2) Near the end of the scene (1.5) in which the Ghost tells Hamlet that he was murdered by Hamlet's uncle, Hamlet tells Horatio and Marcellus that in future he will "put an antic disposition on"[2] (1.5.171). The obvious reason that Hamlet will put on an act is to mislead Claudius or agents of Claudius about his state of mind. An alert playgoer realizes that, from this moment on, whenever Hamlet knows or suspects that Claudius or anyone Hamlet regards as an agent of Claudius is present, anything Hamlet says or does may be put on.

What is an "antic disposition"? Or, more precisely, what is an "Anticke disposition" (Q2 and F)? The post-Renaissance association of this word with playfulness seriously misleads playgoers and readers about its meaning in Shakespeare's works. In Shakespeare's works its connotations included "grotesque," "macabre," and "morbid." Shakespeare repeatedly associated the word with death in general and suicide in particular. According to Richard II, "within the hollow crown" of a king "Keeps Death his court, and there the antic sits" (3.2.160, 162). In *Hamlet* itself, Shakespeare associated the word specifically with suicide. The words now distinguished in both spelling and pronunciation as "antic" and "antique" were differentiated in Shakespeare's age neither in spelling (each was variously spelled "anticke," "antick," "antik," or "antike") nor in pronunciation (each was pronounced with the stress on the first syllable).[3] When Horatio declares his intention to commit suicide he repeats the word he heard Hamlet use in 1.5 as if its association with suicide literally went without saying: "I am more an antique Roman than a Dane" (5.2.341, Q2: "antike," F: "Antike"). "An antique Roman" means "a person intent on committing suicide" since many famous ancient Romans committed suicide. The antic/antique disposition Hamlet repeatedly puts on for agents of his enemy is a general disgust with life so sweeping that it makes him suicidal, oblivious to the contingencies of his particular situation, and incapable of action. Like a method actor, Hamlet uses emotions he has actually felt in his fabrication of this fictional disposition. In his soliloquy in 1.2, Hamlet expressed disgust with life and a longing for death. But the contrast between that soliloquy and the antic/antique disposition he puts on for agents of his enemy is striking and profound. In 1.2 his disgust and longing for death were provoked by an intensely personal grievance—his mother's marriage to his hated uncle. By omitting all references to his personal grievances when in the presence of agents of his enemy, Hamlet tries to convey the impression that his disgust with life is merely the result of a generic melancholy temperament, an antic/antique disposition, not any personal grievance.

(3) As a sincere expression of wholly impersonal attitudes unconnected with Hamlet's particular situation, "To be" the speech could have been located at any of numerous other points in the play, but Shakespeare chose to locate it in the midst of an eavesdropping episode. Claudius and Polonius plan to eavesdrop on an encounter between Hamlet and Ophelia and take their hiding place when they hear Hamlet approach.

(4) Hamlet has been summoned to this particular location by his deadly enemy. Shortly before Hamlet arrives, Claudius explains to Gertrude, "We have closely sent for Hamlet hither" (29). Arriving at a location to which his enemy has summoned him, Hamlet would expect that agents of that enemy are present, that the walls have ears. This is precisely the kind of situation in which Hamlet will put on his antic/antique disposition.

(5) Shortly before Hamlet enters, Polonius instructs his daughter, "walk you here" (42). The obvious purpose of this instruction is to make Ophelia as conspicuous as possible (in motion as well as in plain sight) so that Hamlet will notice her as soon as he arrives. Polonius and the King of Denmark will be waiting behind the arras for the commencement of the conversation between Ophelia and Hamlet, so Polonius wants it to commence without delay. It is not credible that Ophelia flagrantly disobeys her father by hiding at the approach of Hamlet. It is not credible that, upon arriving at the place to which he has been summoned by a man whom he suspects of having already murdered one Hamlet, Hamlet would fail to look around for the presence of agents of that enemy. It is thus not credible that Hamlet would fail to notice the conspicuous presence of his former girlfriend.

(6) As Hamlet well knows, Ophelia is the obedient daughter of the chief henchman of Hamlet's enemy. She would report to her father anything Hamlet might tell her, so Hamlet cannot and does not confide in her. Hamlet would not regard her presence at the location to which he has been summoned by his enemy as a coincidence.

(7) This situation contributes to a pattern established in earlier scenes. Hamlet regards his mother's marriage to his hated uncle as a betrayal. In the immediately preceding scene, Hamlet insistently pestered Rosencrantz and Guildenstern about whether they were "sent for" (2.2.274, 278, 281, 288). They hesitated to answer presumably because it would have been embarrassing to tell their friend to his face that they were sent for to ascertain the cause of his insanity. But this hesitation is enough for Hamlet to regard them as

agents of his enemy. In an apostrophe in a soliloquy guarded in an aside from their hearing, Hamlet says, "Nay then I have an eye of you" (290). A man who regards former friends as enemy agents because of a momentary hesitation would feel even more deeply betrayed by a former girlfriend he encounters at the location to which he has been summoned by his enemy. In Hamlet's eyes Claudius has corrupted his mother, his school friends, and now his former girlfriend.

(8) Elsewhere in the play Hamlet resents and repeatedly mocks Polonius's meddlesomeness. When Hamlet encounters the daughter of the meddlesome henchman of his enemy in the location to which Hamlet has been summoned by his enemy, he would not assume that Polonius would trust his naive daughter's ex post facto account of her meeting with Hamlet. Hamlet's expressed attitude toward Polonius elsewhere implies that he would suspect as a matter of course that the meddlesome Polonius is eavesdropping in the present circumstance. That Hamlet does indeed make this assumption is confirmed by evidence item 29.

(9) Throughout the play Hamlet exhibits both aptitude and zeal in devising and carrying out clever stratagems. He puts on an antic/antique disposition, attempts to catch the conscience of the King, and foils Claudius's plan to have him executed in England. Hamlet shows particular enthusiasm for devising counter-plots, for turning against his enemies the plots they have initiated against him.[4] He gleefully describes to Horatio how he turned Claudius's plot to have him executed into a plot to have Rosencrantz and Guildenstern executed. Hamlet's behavior in 3.1 is a key link in the chain of this pattern. Arriving at the location to which he has been summoned by his enemy and finding the daughter of his enemy's henchman walking in circles and trying to act naturally, he devises a scheme to turn against his enemies the stratagem that they have initiated against him. He pretends to be so melancholy, to be in the grip of such an antic/antique disposition, that he is oblivious of Ophelia's presence, and he launches into a feigned soliloquy to convey (ultimately) to his enemy that his mental state has rendered him incapable of taking any action. Hamlet can be sure that an account of his melancholy speech will reach Claudius. Even if the King himself is not eavesdropping in the location to which he has summoned Hamlet, the meddlesome Polonius almost certainly is. At the very least, Ophelia will dutifully report on the speech to her father, who will dutifully report it to the King.

(10) Hamlet's feigned soliloquy is only one of a number of episodes that exhibit Hamlet's strong histrionic impulse. After the Mousetrap episode, he asks Horatio, "Would not this . . . get me a fellowship in a cry of players?" (3.2.275–78).

(11) In the long preceding scene (2.2), Hamlet repeatedly puts on his antic/antique disposition to mislead agents of his enemy.

> *Polonius.* Will you walk out of the air, my lord
> *Hamlet.* Into my grave. . . .
> *Polonius.* My lord, I will take my leave of you.
> *Hamlet.* You cannot take from me any thing that I will not more willingly part withal—except my life, except my life, except my life.
>
> (206–7, 213–17)

Immediately after identifying Rosencrantz and Guildenstern as agents of Claudius in a soliloquy guarded in an aside—"Nay then I have an eye of you"—Hamlet tells them that he is overwhelmed by disgust with every aspect of the world. Hamlet's purpose in making this speech to agents of his enemy is to convince that enemy that he poses no threat. To help playgoers make the connection between Hamlet's speech in 1.5 about the "disposition" he will put on and the description of his mental state that Hamlet feeds Rosencrantz and Guildenstern in 2.2, Shakespeare even plants that particular word in the later speech: "indeed, it goes so heavily with my *disposition,* that this goodly frame, the earth, seems to me a sterile promontory" (297–99, italics added).

(12) There are numerous conspicuous similarities between the "sterile promontory" speech and the "To be" speech. Like the "sterile promontory" speech, the "To be" speech expresses a philosophical melancholy that would render the speaker incapable of engaging in any kind of vigorous action. Like the "sterile promontory" speech, the "To be" speech conveys a disgust with life by means of a catalogue of examples. As in the "sterile promontory" speech, the examples in the "To be" speech are generalized and unconnected with the speaker's actual and particular circumstances. Like the "sterile promontory" speech, the "To be" speech is eloquent. Like the "sterile promontory" speech, the "To be" speech is spoken while at least one person whom Hamlet has reason to regard as an agent of his enemy is present and visible to Hamlet.

(13) In the "To be" speech, Hamlet describes "death" unequivocally as "the undiscovered country from whose bourn / No traveller returns" (78–79). Hamlet cannot have forgotten the most memorable experience of his life, his encounter with what appeared to be the ghost of his own father.[5] The passage makes sense only as a ploy to deceive the agent of his enemy in full view and ultimately his enemy. In 1.5, Hamlet repeatedly and passionately demanded that his companions swear that they will never tell anyone else about the Ghost. If news that the Ghost of the man Claudius murdered is haunting the castle did reach Claudius, Claudius would assume as a matter of course that the motive of the Ghost's visitation was to demand that his son revenge the murder. In case someone has informed Claudius about the Ghost, Hamlet expresses, in his supposedly self-addressed speech, an utter disbelief in ghosts. This passing remark in a supposedly self-addressed speech is de-

signed to convey the impression that he has not encountered the Ghost of his father and is therefore ignorant of Claudius's murder of old Hamlet.[6]

(14) At the very end of the preceding scene, Hamlet exuberantly declared, "the play's the thing / Wherein I'll catch the conscience of the King" (2.2.604–5). In his next speech, the "To be, or not to be" passage, Hamlet declares that "we" are incapable of action without expressing regret that this incapacity in his own case will prevent him from carrying out his plan for verifying that his father was murdered by his uncle. In the scene following the "To be" scene Hamlet exuberantly pursues his plan to catch the conscience of the King without expressing relief that he has overcome "our" incapacity for action.

(15) Renaissance drama contains a vast number of eavesdropping episodes, which occur in plays of all genres and in a wide variety of circumstances. In no other period of Western drama do eavesdropping episodes occur so often in serious plays. Playgoers evidently relished eavesdropping episodes, and dramatists exercised great ingenuity in devising novel variations.

(16) Eavesdropping episodes occur in almost all of Shakespeare's plays and in a wide variety of dramatic circumstances, and many of these episodes are intricate. In more than one play, for example, Shakespeare created episodes involving concentric circles of eavesdroppers. One character (or group) eavesdrops upon a second character (or group) while a third character (or group) eavesdrops upon all the other characters.[7] Some of Shakespeare's most subtle, ingenious, and daring eavesdropping episodes occur in his tragedies.

(17) In one eavesdropping variation that Shakespeare used in more than one play, a character or group has reason to suspect that an eavesdropper is present and uses the opportunity to mislead the eavesdropper. Two examples of this variation occur in *Much Ado about Nothing* (in 2.3 and 3.1), written about two years before *Hamlet*.

(18) Although there are three other characters within earshot when Hamlet arrives on stage in 3.1, none of the three can see what he does as he enters. The eavesdroppers stationed behind the arras can hear him, but they cannot see him. On her father's orders, Ophelia has her eyes glued to a book. Shakespeare constructed the situation in such a way that the actor playing Hamlet could provide visual clues—the direction of his gaze, facial expressions, gestures, body language, and movements—indicating that Hamlet is alert and aware of the presence of Ophelia when he arrives at the location to which he has been summoned by his enemy. As he enters, the actor playing Hamlet could halt and look directly at Ophelia for a moment before beginning to speak. These visual clues could have been calibrated to any degree of subtlety or obviousness desired by Shakespeare in consultation with Richard Burbage.[8]

(19) Many of the eavesdropping episodes in Renaissance drama involve

soliloquies and asides. A remarkably precise and complex set of conventions governed soliloquies, asides, and eavesdropping in the period. (a) As a matter of course, all words spoken by an actor represented words spoken by the character. (b) Even soliloquies, words that a character did not intend to be heard by any other character, represented speeches (rather than interior monologues), as demonstrated, for example, by the startling number of soliloquies in Renaissance plays that are overheard by eavesdroppers. (c) A character could direct a speech to the hearing of one or more characters but guard it in an aside from the hearing of one or more other characters of whose presence the speaker was aware. (d) A character could also guard a self-addressed speech in an aside from the hearing of all the other characters of whose presence he was aware. Such a speech is a soliloquy guarded in an aside. (e) A character could not guard a speech from the hearing of another character if the speaker did not know for certain that the other character was within earshot. A mere suspicion that another character was present did not enable a character to guard a speech. (f) Like any other skill, guarding an aside could be performed well or badly. An aside had to be actively and continuously guarded. If a speaker became so preoccupied by what he was saying to himself that he lowered his guard, the other characters on stage would begin to hear what he was saying to himself. Such a complex set of conventions that now seem patently unrealistic could be maintained in Renaissance drama because they came into operation in the vast majority of plays of the period, and experienced playgoers were quite familiar with them. Dramatists rigorously followed these conventions because they created opportunities for complex eavesdropping episodes that evidently delighted playgoers of the period.[9]

(20) Shakespeare showed great ingenuity in employing these complex conventions governing soliloquies, asides, and eavesdropping throughout his career and in plays of all genres. Many of these episodes violate post-Renaissance canons of verisimilitude. About half of Shakespeare's plays, for example, contain episodes in which a character's self-addressed speech is overheard.[10] Shakespeare constructed numerous episodes on the assumption that experienced playgoers would grasp intricate and subtle operations of these conventions. In *Julius Caesar* (1599) 2.4, for example, within six lines (39–44), Portia (1) speaks overtly to her servant Lucius ("I must go in"); (2) then speaks in a soliloquy fully guarded in an aside ("Ay, me! how weak a thing / The heart of woman is!"); (3) then, while continuing to speak to herself in a soliloquy, becomes so fixated on the hypothetical audience of her apostrophe that (as her subsequent fully guarded aside indicates) she ceases to guard her soliloquy adequately from Lucius ("O Brutus, / The heavens speed thee in thine enterprise!"); (4) then realizes that she had ceased to guard her soliloquy adequately in an aside and speaks to herself now in an adequately guarded soliloquy-aside ("Sure the boy heard me"); (5) then overtly addresses Lucius to try to explain away her insufficiently guarded

soliloquy ("Brutus hath a suit / That Caesar will not grant"); (6) then adequately guards a soliloquy in an aside ("O, I grow faint"); (7) then overtly addresses Lucius ("Run, Lucius, and commend me to my lord"). Shakespeare followed the conventions governing soliloquies, asides, and eavesdropping not because he was conventional in the pejorative sense, but rather because those conventions allowed him to create daringly original dramatic episodes.

(21) In several plays, Shakespeare created situations in which a character pretends to be talking only to himself but actually allows his speech to be heard by another character who the speaker knows or suspects is within earshot in order to mislead that character about his state of mind. One example of a feigned soliloquy occurs in 1.2 of *Lear*. Noticing the approach of his brother, Edmund pretends to speak to himself. In his feigned soliloquy he expresses a "melancholy" (135) disposition in order to give Edgar the false impression that he is incapable of action when, in fact, he has already set in motion a plot against his brother.

(22) There are striking similarities between what Edmund is doing in 1.2 of *Lear* and what so much other evidence implies that Hamlet is doing in 3.1 of *Hamlet*. Like Edmund, Hamlet pretends to be speaking only to himself but actually allows another character who is in full view to hear his speech. Like Edmund, Hamlet gives voice in his feigned soliloquy to a melancholy disposition in order to deceive someone into believing he is incapable of action when, in fact, he has already set in motion a plan of action. The situation in *Lear* is a greatly condensed version of the situation in the earlier play.

(23) Shakespeare often employed the technique of implication. Many of these implications are quite subtle and challenge the ability of playgoers to make inferences. Shakespeare was willing to take the risk that some playgoers would fail to make the appropriate inference. The first fifty-six lines of *The Merchant of Venice* (1596–97) focus on the mystery of Antonio's sadness. Neither Antonio nor his friends arrive at a satisfactory explanation. Later in the scene, playgoers learn that Antonio already knows that Bassanio wants to woo an heiress who lives at Belmont. Antonio loves Bassanio and will provide him with money to travel to Belmont. But if Bassanio marries the heiress and moves to her residence, Antonio will no longer see his dear friend on a daily basis. Shakespeare easily could have provided an explicit solution to the initial puzzle of the play but instead chose to allow playgoers themselves to put two and two together.

In *Lear* 4.6, when Oswald threatens the life of Gloucester, Edgar begins to speak in a peasant dialect: "Chill not let go, zir, without vurther cagion" (235, "I will not let go, sir, without further occasion"). The reason for this odd behavior does not become apparent until after the fact and then only by implication. After Edgar kills Oswald, he apostrophizes the corpse: "I know thee well; a serviceable villain" (252). Edgar has not yet revealed his identity to his father but has dropped his verbal impersonation of Poor Tom. This suggests that Edgar wants the blind Gloucester to recognize who his companion is on his own. If Edgar knows Oswald well, then Oswald knows him well. If Edgar—who is no longer visibly disguised as Poor Tom—spoke in his usual manner, Oswald might recognize him and address him by name. Gloucester would learn the identity of his companion from a serviceable villain rather than on his own. So Edgar disguises his speech. Shakespeare could have given Edgar a self-addressed aside explaining his ploy but chose not to do so. The number of elements in *Hamlet* implying that the "To be" speech is a deceptive ploy far exceed the number of elements in *Lear* implying that Edgar's use of a peasant dialect is a deceptive ploy.

Shakespeare often devised implications that depended on playgoers' familiarity with the conventions governing soliloquies and eavesdropping. An example occurs in *King Lear* 2.2. After Kent is placed in the stocks and is left alone, he falls asleep. Edgar enters and begins a soliloquy without noticing the presence of Kent. Experienced Renaissance playgoers knew that soliloquies represented speeches by characters and that they would be overheard as a matter of course by other characters of whose presence the speaker was unaware unless there was some clearly dramatized impediment. Kent's sleeping state is such an impediment. But why would the dramatist bring Edgar on the stage already occupied by a sleeping Kent? Shakespeare encouraged experienced Renaissance playgoers to hope and expect that Kent would awaken while Edgar was speaking and hear the remainder of Edgar's self-addressed speech. Kent would quickly realize that Edgar is innocent of the charges against him and would presumably make his presence known to Edgar, and these two sympathetic and victimized characters, who have much in common, would join forces. When Edgar leaves without interacting with Kent, Renaissance playgoers would have suffered disappointment in response to this lost opportunity. During the course of the play, characters often have their hopes raised only to have those hopes ultimately dashed. In this episode Shakespeare created a situation in which playgoers undergo a similar experience themselves. This profound artistic effect depended on the *implicit* operation of the Renaissance conventions governing soliloquies and eavesdropping.[11]

A dramatist who intends to write thought-provoking plays will often use implication rather than explication. You cannot provoke people into thought if you do all their thinking for them. Ben Jonson, who was less daring in his use of implication than Shakespeare, wrote that "a writer should always trust somewhat to the capacity of the spectator."[12]

(24) Shakespeare created a number of situations in which he expected playgoers to realize without any overt explanation in the dialogue that a character is feigning or has feigned a self-addressed speech. Shakespeare devised just such an episode in *Othello*, which was probably the next tragedy he wrote

after *Hamlet*. At a crucial moment in *Othello* a character (a) pretends to speak only to himself, but (b) actually speaks to be heard by another character in order to mislead that character about his state of mind, and (c) does not explain his ploy in a genuine self-addressed speech. Entering with Othello as Cassio takes leave of Desdemona, Iago pretends to speak only to himself but actually allows Othello to hear his words: "Hah? I like not that" (3.3.34). This is a lie. Iago himself has engineered the meeting of Desdemona and Cassio to arouse Othello's jealousy. But Iago does not speak these words openly and directly to Othello. Othello asks him to repeat what he said. Presuming that Othello actually did hear what he said, Iago is evasive in order to convey the false impression that he does not want Othello to know what Iago said in order to convince Othello of the sincerity of Iago's expression of unease at seeing Cassio and Desdemona together. Later in the episode it becomes evident that Iago did allow Othello to hear what he said and that it has been preying on Othello's mind. Othello brings it up: "I heard thee say even now, thou lik'st not that, / When Cassio left my wife. What didst not like?" (109–10). Iago's deceptive ploy is obvious to playgoers because they know in advance that Iago plans to deceive Othello.

This situation has striking similarities to the situation in 3.1 of *Hamlet*. Iago has stated his intention to deceive Othello. Hamlet has stated his intention to put on a false disposition, presumably whenever Claudius or anyone he regards as an agent of Claudius is present. When Iago says, "Hah? I like not that," he is in the presence of Othello, the person he intends to deceive. When Hamlet speaks the "To be" speech, he is in a location to which he has been summoned by his enemy, a place where walls can be expected to have ears and where the person who is in full view can be counted on to report what Hamlet says to her father, the henchman of his enemy. Playgoers know that what Iago says in the presence of Othello is a misrepresentation of what he is actually thinking. Playgoers know that what Hamlet says in the presence of the obedient daughter of the henchman of his enemy is a misrepresentation of what is actually on Hamlet's mind. Playgoers know that Hamlet is obsessed by his personal grievances and know that he has encountered what appeared to be the ghost of his father, whereas in the "To be" speech he omits all mention of his personal grievances and declares unequivocally that death is "the undiscovered country from whose bourn / No traveller returns." A playgoer capable of putting two and two together in the one case is capable of putting two and two together in the other. Indeed, Hamlet's implicitly feigned soliloquy would have posed far less of a challenge to Renaissance playgoers' powers of inference than Iago's would have posed. (a) The number of elements in *Hamlet* implying that the "To be" passage is a feigned self-address far exceed the number of elements in *Othello* implying that Iago's "Hah? I like not that" is a feigned self-address. (b) Iago's feigned self-address is only five syllables long whereas Hamlet's occupies thirty-four lines, so playgoers at *Othello* had much less time to make the inference. Shakespeare was apparently so satisfied with the implicitly feigned self-addressed speech in *Hamlet* that he used the very same device in his next tragedy in a greatly abbreviated form.

(25) Shakespeare included an episode involving an implicitly feigned soliloquy in *All's Well That Ends Well,* also written shortly after *Hamlet.* In 1.3 the Steward reports to the Countess that he overheard an offstage self-addressed speech by Helena:

> I was very late more near her than I think she wish'd me. Alone she was, and did communicate to herself her own words to her own ears; she thought, I dare vow for her, they touch'd not any stranger sense. Her matter was, she lov'd your son. Fortune, she said was no goddess, that had put such differences betwixt their two estates. (106–12)

Many details in the play imply that this account of a supposed self-addressed speech is bogus. (a) Rather than inconveniencing Helena, the purported invasion of Helena's privacy by the Steward leads directly to the precise outcome Helena desires. The Steward's report arouses the sympathy of the Countess, who gives her servant Helena approval and the necessary means to travel to Paris and thereby to cure the King, who in gratitude forces Bertram to marry Helena. If it were a pure accident that the Steward overheard Helena, it was an extremely lucky accident for Helena. (b) In a genuine soliloquy only a short time earlier in the play Helena explicitly and passionately expressed her intention to achieve her goal by taking matters into her own hands and not to rely on lucky accidents:

> Our remedies oft in ourselves do lie,
> Which we ascribe to heaven. The fated sky
> Gives us free scope, only doth backward pull
> Our slow designs when we ourselves are dull.
>
> (1.1.216–19)

This is glaringly at odds with Helena's passive sorrow at the operations of "Fortune" in her supposed self-addressed speech. (c) Elsewhere in the play Helena exhibits an extraordinary determination to take matters in her own hands rather than to rely on Fortune. (d) Elsewhere in the play Helena exhibits an extraordinary facility in devising and carrying out elaborate deceptions to get what she wants. (e) Elsewhere in the play Helena enlists other characters by persuasion or bribery to help her carry out her deceptions. (f) Later in the play, the Countess chastises the Steward for his delay in giving her the letter in which Helena declares that she is going to Spain. If he had given the Countess the letter earlier, Helena could have been prevented from leaving, as the Countess remarks and as the Steward acknowledges (3.4.19–24). Like his earlier prompt reporting of Helena's supposedly self-addressed speech, the Steward's delay in delivering Helen's letter to the Countess is an accident too good to be true for Helena. As a direct result of the Steward's delay, Helena can pursue her current project without interference from the Countess. Just as the letter delivered to the Countess by the Steward misleads the Countess about Helena's intentions (Helena is actually headed to Florence, not Spain), the supposedly self-addressed speech supposedly overheard by the Steward misleads the Countess about Helena's state of mind at that point in the play. (g) In his report to the Countess about Helen's supposed self-addressed speech, the Steward (an amateurish liar) explicitly denies the possibility that Helena was perpetrating a deception: "she thought, I dare vow for her, they touch'd not any stranger sense." If Shakespeare did not intend to imply that Helena persuaded or bribed the Steward to give the Countess a false report that he overheard a self-addressed speech in which Helena pathetically bewails her fate, Shakespeare botched the job by including so many elements before, during, and after the episode that individually and collectively point to that as the only reasonable inference.

Helena's feigned soliloquy has a very specific similarity with the feigned soliloquies of Hamlet and Edmund. In each case, the speaker, who has set in motion a plan of action, wishes to convince the target of the deception that the speaker is passive.

(26) Shakespeare was not the only dramatist of the period to construct episodes involving implicitly feigned soliloquies. An example occurs in John Fletcher's *A Woman's Prize* (1611).[13] In 4.2, Petruchio notices the approach of his second wife Maria and decides to eavesdrop. In a series of speeches, Maria complains that she has been prevented from tending to her sick husband by officious nurses and that Petruchio has treated her unkindly by ordering the removal of furnishings from the house. These complaints make no sense as sincere self-addressed speeches. They contradict what playgoers witnessed earlier in the play: Maria herself fabricated the rumor that Petruchio has the plague, hired the nurses who keep him confined, and ordered the removal of the furnishings. Maria's complaints in 4.2 make sense only if Maria spotted Petruchio as he took up his hiding place and decided to take advantage of the situation by misleading him about her state of mind by pretending to talk to herself. Maria never explains her ploy in a genuine soliloquy guarded from Petruchio's hearing. Fletcher expected playgoers to realize that Maria's speeches are feigned soliloquies simply on the basis of incongruities between the content of those speeches and what playgoers witness in other episodes, perhaps supplemented by visual clues conveyed by the boy actor portraying Maria. This particular example is particularly relevant to the present argument for several reasons: (a) it occurs in a play written for the King's Men during the time that Shakespeare was a leading member of the company; (b) Fletcher's play is a sequel to one of Shakespeare's own plays (*The Taming*

of the Shrew); (c) Fletcher would shortly become Shakespeare's replacement as the leading playwright of the King's Men and probably was already being vetted or groomed for the job; (d) Fletcher would shortly collaborate with Shakespeare on as many as three plays (*Henry VIII, Cardenio,* and *The Two Noble Kinsmen*). The implicitly feigned soliloquy in *A Woman's Prize* was obviously created with the approval of Shakespeare and his company. That approval was a forgone conclusion since Shakespeare himself had created similar situations in his own plays.

(27) After feigning a speech in order to convey the impression that he suffers from an incapacitating generic melancholy, Hamlet then pretends that he has just noticed the presence of Ophelia: "Soft you, now, / The fair Ophelia" (87–88). He pretends that he is still speaking only to himself and pretends to guard these words from her hearing but actually allows her and any eavesdroppers who may be present to hear them. Like Iago's "Hah? I like not that," Hamlet's "Soft you, now? The fair Ophelia" is a feigned soliloquy in a feigned aside.

(28) During his encounter with Ophelia, Hamlet berates her and implies that she is dishonest. The obvious cause of this outburst is Hamlet's anger at Ophelia for participating at this very moment in a plot to find out what is on his mind.

(29) In the course of this tongue-lashing, Hamlet asks a superficially incongruous question: "Where's your father?" (129). Hamlet (a) assumes that her meddlesome father is eavesdropping and that Ophelia is a knowing participant in the eavesdropping plot and (b) wants to humiliate the woman whom he now regards as an agent of his enemy by forcing her to tell an outright lie ("At home, my lord" [130]).

(30) Hamlet's deception becomes an element of a profound dramatic irony. After executing a magnificent thirty-four-line feigned soliloquy to mislead agents of his enemy into believing that he has no personal grievance and that he is utterly incapable of action, Hamlet becomes so enraged at Ophelia's pose of innocence while she is at this very moment participating in what Hamlet regards as a plot against him that he abandons his pretense of passivity. In the process of berating and humiliating a woman whom he regards as a betrayer, he reveals that he is angry, bitter, "revengeful" (124), and "ambitious" (124). Ironically, the situation that he momentarily turned against his enemy has ultimately revealed to his enemy that he does indeed pose a threat.

(31) At three points during his encounter with Ophelia, Hamlet says "Farewell" (132, 137, 140) but does not actually leave. The obvious explanation for this is that he hopes Polonius, who Hamlet suspects is eavesdropping and who can hear but not see Hamlet, will assume Hamlet has left and emerge from his hiding place. The Lord Chamberlain would thus be embarrassingly exposed as an eavesdropper. Hamlet elsewhere shows a zest not merely for deceiving but also for making fools of those he regards as his enemies, espe-

cially Polonius. The exposure of Polonius as an eavesdropper will also humiliate Ophelia. Her declaration only two lines before Hamlet's first "farewell" that her father is "At home" will be promptly and emphatically exposed as a lie. But the eavesdroppers cautiously stay in hiding until Hamlet has gone for good.

(32) Shakespeare often dramatizes the sad fact that eloquence is no guarantee of sincerity. Many eloquent characters in Shakespeare's plays are deceptive. In 3.1 of *Hamlet* Shakespeare pushes this theme to its limit. That the supremely eloquent "To be, or not to be" speech is a deceptive ploy drives home the point that there is no level of eloquence that guarantees sincerity.

(33) Another disturbing notion illustrated by Hamlet's deception in this episode is that in the process of combating an enemy one regards as evil, one may begin to resemble one's adversary. In the process of combating a deceptive schemer, Hamlet has become a deceptive schemer. Ironically and disturbingly, Hamlet becomes a mirror image of his enemy. Hamlet's ploy in the "To be" episode is a major element in this pattern.

(34) Yet another major theme developed in the episode also concerns Hamlet's growing resemblance to his enemy. Claudius treats other people as objects to be used or disposed of merely to serve his purposes, and so does Hamlet. Claudius has deceived Polonius and Ophelia into believing he cares about his nephew's welfare and makes use of those unwitting agents in a plot to uncover the intentions of a potential rival for his throne. In the same episode Hamlet makes use of Claudius's agents—who are no more witting of Hamlet's actual purposes than they are of Claudius's—in an attempt to mislead his enemy about his state of mind.

(35) *The Conspiracy of Charles, Duke of Byron* (c. 1607), a play by George Chapman, contains a speech (a) that is located in an eavesdropping episode, (b) that is a feigned soliloquy, and (c) that is obviously modeled on the "To be, or not to be" speech. Aware of the presence of Byron, La Fin decides to deceive him by pretending to talk to himself but actually allowing Byron to hear his speech. He describes his plan in a genuine soliloquy guarded in an aside from Byron's hearing: "A feigned passion in his hearing now, / Which he thinks I perceive not."[14] A dramatist's decision whether or not to have a character explain such a ploy depended on the particular circumstances. Shakespeare chose to make Edmund's deception of Edgar explicit (just barely), but he expected playgoers to infer entirely on their own that when Iago says "Hah? I like not that" the speech is a feigned self-addressed speech.

La Fin's eighteen-line feigned soliloquy has manifest and manifold resemblances to Hamlet's "To be" speech. Like Hamlet, La Fin pretends to be suffering from melancholy. Like Hamlet, La Fin expresses a longing for death. Like Hamlet, La Fin never refers to his personal situation. Hamlet's speech consists largely of a catalogue of generic miseries of life. La Fin's speech consists largely of a corresponding catalogue of generic joys of life that have been "eclipsed" (20) from his perspective as a result of his melancholy. Like Hamlet, La Fin never once uses a first-person-singular pronoun. Hamlet refers to "that sleep of death" (65), La Fin to "the death of sleep" (17). Like the "To be" speech, La Fin's speech is spoken while another character is in full view on stage. Chapman clearly made the correct inference that Hamlet's "To be" speech was a feigned soliloquy.

(36) *The Broken Heart* (c. 1630) by John Ford contains a speech (a) that occurs in an eavesdropping episode; (b) that is feigned soliloquy, (c) that is not accompanied by an explanation of the ploy by the perpetrator, and (d) that conspicuously alludes to the "To be, or not to be" speech. Aware of the presence of other characters, Orgilus pretends to talk to himself but actually speaks to be heard by them in order to mislead them about his state of mind. Orgilus does not explain his ploy. Ford expected playgoers to make the inference that the speech is feigned. He provided contextual clues, including incongruities between what Orgilus says here and what playgoers otherwise know about him. An additional technique by which Ford implied that the speech is a feigned soliloquy is the inclusion of clear reminders of Hamlet's feigned soliloquy. Orgilus pretends to engage in a philosophical debate with himself about the futility of action. Near the beginning of the speech occurs the infinitive phrase "to appease the raging sea,"[15] which echoes the infinitive phrase "to take arms against a sea of troubles," which occurs near the beginning of the "To be" passage. Like Chapman, Ford realized that the "To be" speech was a feigned soliloquy.

Evidence that Renaissance playgoers perceived the "To be" speech as a feigned soliloquy

The foregoing catalogue includes evidence not only that the "To be" passage was designed by Shakespeare to be perceived by playgoers as a feigned soliloquy but that it was indeed perceived as such. This evidence is of two kinds. (1) Shakespeare himself included feigned self-addressed speeches, including implicitly feigned self-addressed speeches, in no fewer than three plays (including two tragedies) in the years immediately following the first performance of *Hamlet,* and each of those speeches (Helena's, Iago's, and Edmund's) has one or more specific additional similarities to the "To be" speech, as indicated above. In the cases of the implicitly feigned soliloquies perpetrated by Iago and Helena, Shakespeare included far fewer clues than in the case of Hamlet's implicitly feigned soliloquy. Shakespeare would not have repeated this plot device if the experiment in *Hamlet* had been a failure, if he had judged that most playgoers failed to catch any of the numerous clues that Hamlet was feigning a self-addressed speech. (2) At least two particular playgoers, the dramatists George Chapman and John Ford, recognized that the "To be" speech was a feigned soliloquy. Each designed a speech (a) that occurs in an eavesdropping episode, (b) that is a feigned soliloquy, and (c) that specifically alludes to the "To be" speech, which also occurs in an eavesdropping episode.

A comparison with the conventional post-Renaissance assumption

Shakespeare included a large number of clues in the play that all point in the same direction. An individual playgoer would have to notice only one or two in order to infer that the "To be" speech is a feigned soliloquy. Shakespeare was evidently attempting to lead as many playgoers as possible to make the inference to which all these pieces of evidence point. If Shakespeare did not intend to imply that the "To be, or not to be" speech is a deceptive ploy, he bungled the job by inadvertently including so many elements before, during, and after the episode that individually and collectively point to that implication. Indeed, it is hard to imagine that a play could contain a greater number of independent clues that all point to a single implication. In addition to the many other important functions of this episode, Shakespeare was clearly using it to explore an element of his craft, to experiment with the artistic technique of implication. One should not confuse the technique of implication with the technique of leaving something open to multiple interpretations. The explanation presented here is the only one that makes sense of the relevant evidence.

Someone who adheres to the conventional assumption that the "To be" speech is a genuine soliloquy has to try to explain away *on the basis of an independent rationale* each of the pieces of evidence catalogued above. The resulting argument would be a ramshackle collection of makeshift rationalizations, such as the following. (1) When Hamlet arrives at the location to which he has been summoned by his enemy, he does not notice the presence of Ophelia because he is lost in his sublime meditation on life and death. (2) When Hamlet arrives at the location to which he has been summoned by his enemy, it does not occur to him that his enemy or an agent of that enemy might be in hiding. (3) Although Hamlet tells his companions in 1.5 that he will put on an act, it does not occur to him to do so in the location to which he has been summoned by his enemy. (4) Although Shakespeare's plays contain other episodes in which characters who have reason to believe eavesdroppers are present mislead the eavesdroppers and in 3.1 Hamlet has reason to believe eavesdroppers are present, Hamlet does not take this golden opportunity to mislead his enemy because it would be unseemly for a princely hero to stoop to such a low tactic. (5) Although in every one of his extended soliloquies elsewhere in the play, Hamlet is obsessed with his personal grievances, he fails to mention any of them in the "To be" speech because his sublime meditation has momentarily abstracted him from his personal situation. (6) When Hamlet describes "death" as "the undiscovered country from whose bourn / No traveller returns," he means that no traveler returns from death to take up permanent residence among the living. (7) Similarities between the "To be" speech and the "sterile promontory" speech, which Hamlet feeds to agents of his enemy to convince them that he suffers from a general debilitating malaise rather than any particular personal grievance, are purely coincidental. (8) When Hamlet does finally notice Ophelia, he regards the presence of the daughter of his enemy's henchman at the location to which he has been summoned by that enemy as purely coincidental. (9) When Hamlet asks Ophelia "Where's your father?" he does so because a moment earlier Polonius stuck his head out of the arras and Hamlet spotted him. (10) Although Shakespeare's plays contain many subtle implications that test playgoers' powers of inference, he would not have attempted to lead playgoers to realize on the basis of multiple conspicuous clues that Hamlet was feigning a soliloquy because Shakespeare was afraid that some playgoers might miss all the clues. (11) Although there are striking similarities between this episode and episodes involving feigned soliloquies in Shakespeare's other plays, no situation elsewhere in his plays is identical to this one in every single respect. Iago's implicitly feigned self-addressed speech ("Hah? I like not that"), for example, is much shorter than the "To be" speech. The length of the "To be" speech is a guarantee of its sincerity. (12) Although Shakespeare frequently dramatized the fact that eloquence is not a guarantee of sincerity, the "To be" speech is so eloquent that it must be sincere. (13) It is purely accidental that so many pieces of evidence conflict with the notion that the "To be" speech is sincere and so many pieces of evidence imply that the speech is a feigned soliloquy. (14) At no point did Shakespeare or members of his company notice that, by sheer accident, many elements in the play conflict with the notion that the "To be" speech is sincere and that many elements suggest that it is a feigned soliloquy, and so Shakespeare never altered the play to correct the misimpression inadvertently fostered by these elements. (15) Modern audiences would not be able to infer that the "To be" speech is a feigned soliloquy, so neither would Renaissance audiences. (16) It is purely coincidental that two other Renaissance dramatists designed episodes in plays written after *Hamlet* in which characters mislead eavesdroppers by means of feigned soliloquies that have conspicuous similarities to the "To be" speech, which also occurs in an eavesdropping episode.

Someone who concurs with the conventional post-Renaissance assumption that the "To be" speech is sincere unavoidably commits himself to this entire collection of makeshift propositions or to a similarly large collection of similarly makeshift propositions in order to explain away the numerous pieces of evidence that conflict with the conventional assumption. Someone with a respect for evidence would not be satisfied with such a hodgepodge of feeble rationalizations. Nor would someone with a respect for evidence be satisfied with a defense of the conventional assumption that dealt with only a few of the many pieces of inconvenient evidence catalogued here and that simply ignored the numerous remaining pieces. If ever a situation called for Occam's razor, this is it. If a single explanation accounts for many pieces of evidence, that explanation is more likely to be correct than a series of separate, ad hoc explanations, one for each piece of evidence, even if the alternative explanations for each individual piece of evidence are equally credible.[16] As the number of pieces of evidence increases, the probability that the single explanation is the correct one increases exponentially. In the present case, the probability that each of the thirty-six pieces of evidence catalogued above actually has another explanation and that it is *purely coincidental* that *all* of them point to the single inference that the "To be" passage was designed as a feigned soliloquy would be infinitesimal even if the two explanations for each individual piece of evidence were equally credible.

Furthermore, in the present case the alternative explanations for many individual pieces of evidence are *not* equally credible. The *only* credible explanation for many pieces of evidence is that the "To be" speech was designed as a feigned soliloquy. For example, a strenuous act of prestidigitation is required to make the assertion that no traveler returns from the bourn of death mean anything other than what it seems to mean. It is not credible that Hamlet would find his way to the location to which he has been summoned by his deadly enemy and then forget what brought him there. It is not credible that Chapman and Ford would both model feigned soliloquies in eavesdropping episodes on a speech in *Hamlet* that also occurs in an eavesdropping episode if the passage in *Hamlet* were not also a feigned soliloquy. And so on. Any one of these pieces of evidence alone invalidates the conventional assumption about the speech. This case involves a fusillade of smoking guns. Some features of *Hamlet* are ambiguous or mysterious. This is not one of them.

The notion that the "To be" speech is a sincere expression of Hamlet's thoughts resembles the notion that someone else wrote the works generally attributed to Shakespeare. In that case, the anti-Stratfordians have to explain away many substantial, conspicuous, and varied pieces of evidence from Shakespeare's age that indicate that Shakespeare was the author of those works. Someone who adheres to the conventional post-Renaissance assumption that the "To be" speech is a genuine soliloquy has to explain away the many substantial, conspicuous, and varied pieces of evidence *from Shakespeare's age* catalogued here that contradict that assumption. The assumption that the "To be" was designed as a genuine soliloquy is based entirely on *post-Renaissance* theatrical, critical, and editorial traditions that arose in the late seventeenth century.

The fact that in countless successful post-Renaissance productions of *Hamlet* the "To be" passage has been staged as a sincere expression of Hamlet's innermost thoughts has no bearing on the case. There have also been countless successful post-Renaissance productions of *Hamlet* in which the role of Ophelia has been performed by an actress, but that does not change the fact that in Shakespeare's theater the part was played by a boy actor. If historicist scholarship has taught us anything, it is that we should not project our own assumptions, perspectives, aesthetic tastes, or other attitudes onto earlier cultures. We should acknowledge that people of an earlier age may have had different tastes than we do. One cannot base conclusions about the attitudes of people living in an earlier given age on evidence drawn from later ages. In order to ascertain the attitudes of people in an earlier age, cultural historians must locate and analyze evidence from the age itself. Renaissance drama contains countless self-addressed speeches by characters and countless eavesdropping episodes, and a startling number of episodes that combine these elements in various ways. Renaissance audiences apparently enjoyed such episodes, and Renaissance dramatists competed with one another in creating novel variations. The fact that these episodes have seemed patently unrealistic to commentators of later ages does not change the fact that Renaissance dramatists and playgoers delighted in them.

That Shakespeare designed the "To be" episode as a feigned soliloquy does not mean that a modern acting company is obliged to stage it as a feigned soliloquy. Most of Shakespeare's own works are themselves adaptations of earlier works, and we do not condemn him for departing from his sources, so we should not condemn modern performers for altering a feature of a play by Shakespeare. Each production should be judged on its own merits as a work of art. But we should not confuse the artistic freedom to adapt a prior work of art in the creation of a new work of art with the freedom to make false statements about the prior work. A modern company that casts an actress as Ophelia would not claim that Ophelia was originally played by a woman. That claim would conflict with plentiful evidence from Shakespeare's age. Similarly, a modern company that stages the "To be" speech as a genuine soliloquy should not claim that Shakespeare must have designed the episode to be perceived by playgoers of his time as a genuine soliloquy. That claim would conflict with plentiful evidence from Shakespeare's age that the speech was designed as a feigned soliloquy.

This is not an inconsequential matter. The argument presented here provides insights not only into the most famous passage in world literature, but also into numerous other important matters: the character of Hamlet, themes of the play, Shakespeare's dramatic purposes and techniques, and Renaissance dramatic conventions. Its ramifications extend deeply into cultural history, as noted by Jeffrey Kipnis:

In a striking parallel to Hirsh's critique, Ernst van de Wetering and other art historians have raised doubts over the assumption about Rembrandt's self-portraits that prevails among scholar and layperson alike. Hirsh and van de Wetering argue that our modern sense of self is unwittingly retrojected onto premodern representations of self-address, as if the self were natural and remained constant in history.[17]

The cliché that the "To be" passage represents Hamlet's "innermost thoughts" distorts the history of subjectivity.

Concealment in plain sight

How did the erroneous notion that Shakespeare designed the "To be" passage to be dramatized as a sincere expression of Hamlet's thoughts arise? And how is it possible that the evidence—the substantial, plentiful, conspicuous, and varied evidence from Shakespeare's own age indicating that the speech was designed to be perceived as a feigned soliloquy—could have been ignored for over three hundred years? (1) The only texts of the play with any authority lack explanatory stage directions. (2) Professional theatrical activity was banned in England for eighteen years (1642–60). By the time theatrical activity resumed, stage conditions had profoundly changed. (3) Applying new principles of verisimilitude, neoclassical critics ridiculed self-addressed speeches by dramatic characters as unrealistic, and this attitude has prevailed ever since. Instead of occurring in all or nearly all plays and in an enormous range of dramatic situations, as they did during the Renaissance, they have occurred only infrequently in post-Renaissance drama. (4) Eavesdropping episodes occur with astonishing frequency in Renaissance drama, and dramatists competed with one another in creating subtle, intricate, and novel variations, but such episodes lost their appeal after the Renaissance and occur infrequently in drama of later ages. (5) As a result of the two preceding changes, the complicated conventions that governed soliloquies, asides, and eavesdropping in Shakespeare's age ceased to operate. Because these conventions were complex and violate post-Renaissance canons of verisimilitude, they have never been revived. The operations of these conventions in Renaissance drama have created difficulties for post-Renaissance performers and have confused commentators. (6) According to Colley Cibber, what did thrill playgoers of the Restoration period were the "charms of harmonious Elocution."[18] (7) William Davenant was given the exclusive right to stage a group of plays by Shakespeare, including *Hamlet*. Davenant relentlessly adapted Shakespeare's plays (a) to make them simpler and easier to understand and (b) to bring them into line with the dramatic conventions and aesthetic tastes of the new age, which were profoundly different from the conventions and tastes of the previous age. (8) The leading man in Davenant's company was Thomas Betterton, whom Cibber singled out as the greatest practitioner of elocution: "When these flowing Numbers came from the Mouth of a *Betterton* the Multitude no more desired Sense to them than our musical *Connoisseurs* think it essential in . . . an *Italian* Opera" (1:106, italics in the original). (9) By staging the eloquent "To be" speech as a sincere expression of Hamlet's thoughts, Davenant and Betterton (a) turned it into a great opportunity for Betterton to show off his elocution and (b) eliminated a deceptive ploy that, as a result of the changes in conventions and tastes, would have aroused the puzzlement, laughter, or contempt of their audiences. (10) Betterton was by far the most famous and influential performer of the part of Hamlet from 1661 to 1709. (11) Betterton's performance of the "To be" speech as a sincere expression of Hamlet's thoughts was so impressive that at least one playgoer, Samuel Pepys, committed the passage to memory and paid a composer to set it to music.[19] (12) From Betterton's age to the present, the passage has been staged innumerable times as a sincere expression of Hamlet's thoughts. (13) From Betterton's age to the present, a vast amount of commentary has reinforced the notion that the speech is a sincere expression of Hamlet's thoughts. (14) No editor of the play has ever provided readers with correct information about the conventions governing soliloquies, asides, and eavesdropping in English Renaissance drama. Without such information, post-Renaissance readers cannot make the inference that the "To be" speech is a feigned soliloquy, an inference that would have been obvious to Renaissance playgoers. (15) Countless teachers have instructed countless students that the "To be" speech is a sincere expression of Hamlet's innermost thoughts. (16) Countless allusions to the passage in popular culture convey the impression that the speech is a sincere expression of Hamlet's thoughts. (17) As a result of this indoctrination, long before people ever see or read *Hamlet,* they accept as a certainty that the "To be" speech is a sincere expression of Hamlet's thoughts, so when they eventually do see or read the play, they ignore evidence that the speech is a deceptive ploy. (18) The fame of the speech as a sincere expression of Hamlet's thoughts grew until it became the most famous passage in world literature. Like Poe's purloined letter, the "To or not to be" speech has been concealed in plain sight. (19) Hamlet has been sentimentalized in countless post-Renaissance performances and commentaries as a sensitive, brooding hero. The chief prop for this view is the supposedly sincere "To be" speech. (20) Hamlet has been sentimentalized in countless post-Renaissance performances and commentaries as a romantically mysterious character. If Hamlet is mysterious, one need not bother trying to figure out why his "To be" speech does not make sense as a sincere expression of his thoughts in its dramatic context. (21) Sentimental attitudes toward Hamlet encouraged a yearning for direct access to his so-called innermost thoughts, a yearning supposedly satisfied by the supposedly sincere "To be" speech. (22) The relationship between Hamlet and Ophelia has been sentimentalized in countless post-Renaissance performances and commentaries. This attitude would be threatened by the recognition that in 3.1 Hamlet regards Ophelia as an agent of his enemy when he finds her in the location to which he has been summoned by that enemy. (23) Eloquence is often sentimentalized, especially by people who love literature. Someone who sentimentalizes eloquence is not inclined to notice the plentiful evidence that the supremely eloquent "To be" speech is a deceptive ploy. (24) As a result of all these other factors, the assumption that the "To be" speech is a genuine soliloquy became such a deeply entrenched orthodox dogma that it can be maintained despite being at odds with the relevant evidence from Shakespeare's time. (25) The principle that any proposition, no matter how long-held, deeply entrenched, or passionately cherished, must be abandoned if it is shown to be at odds with the relevant evidence is not adhered to as rigorously in the humanities as in some other disciplines.[20] (26) It would not serve the practical self-interest of individual Shakespeare scholars to acknowledge that the Emperor has no clothes, to acknowledge that an assumption propped up by post-Renaissance performance history, post-Renaissance scholarly tradition, and post-Renaissance popular culture is false.

The Scholarly Tradition

A scholar might reasonably suppose that the conventional post-Renaissance assumption about the "To be" speech would not have become so widely and so deeply held for so long if someone somewhere in the vast commentary on *Hamlet* had not made a cogent and comprehensive argument that would refute the argument presented here—even if the scholar himself has no idea who that someone was. In fact, no scholar who has adhered to the conventional assumption that the "To be" speech is sincere has ever attempted to account for more than a small selection of the evidence presented here. Adherents of the conventional assumption have never needed to present an argument. Betterton's performances in the late seventeenth century so firmly established the speech as a genuine soliloquy that from that point onward people ignored the Renaissance evidence that it was designed as a feigned soliloquy.[21] Most commentators on *Hamlet* have not confronted any of the evidence described above and have simply assumed as a matter of course that the "To be" speech is a genuine soliloquy. A few commentators have tried to explain away a few isolated pieces of evidence with makeshift rationalizations.[22] Samuel Taylor Coleridge, for example, explained away the "No traveller" passage as follows:

> If it be necessary to remove the apparent contradiction—if it be not rather a great beauty—surely it were easy to say that no traveller returns to this world, as to his home, or *abiding-place*."[23]

In order explain away a passage that does not make sense if the speech is sincere, Coleridge simply added words to what Hamlet says in order to make him mean what Coleridge required him to mean. A traveler can return to a locale other than his home, as indicated by the passage in which Laertes asks Claudius for "leave and favor to return to France" (1.2.51). Evidently not satisfied with Coleridge's "easy" rationalization, Harold Jenkins (editor of the 1982 Arden edition of the play) fabricated his own:

> The truth surely is that we must not, and we do not (as Hamlet himself does not) connect the Ghost at all with this general reflection. Shakespeare allows Hamlet to utter it because it is what would occur to any well-read Renaissance man meditating upon death.[24]

This explains away the incongruity of the passage by turning Shakespeare into an inferior dramatist, one who gives a character a speech that makes no sense in the context of the experience of that character in order to insert into the play an irrelevant commonplace.

The Editorial Tradition

No edition of *Hamlet* has ever alerted readers to the plentiful evidence that indicates that the "To be" speech was designed to be perceived by Renaissance playgoers as a feigned soliloquy. Ann Thompson and Neil Taylor, the editors of the 2006 Arden edition, dismiss in a footnote the possibility that the "To be" passage might be a feigned soliloquy:

> Q2's placing of Hamlet's entry before 54 rather than after it has allowed editors to argue that he sees the King and Polonius 'withdrawing' and that this motivates his suspicion at 129 ["Where's your father?"]. It would be very unusual for Shakespeare, or any dramatist of this period, not to clarify the situation if Hamlet is consciously directing his soliloquy or his subsequent speeches at listeners; compare, for example, the moment in George Chapman's *The Conspiracy of Charles Duke of Byron* (1608) where La Fin signals his 'fake soliloquy' by beginning with the words 'A fained passion . . .' and later pretends shock: 'what! Did your highness hear?' (2.1.1–5, 24).[25]

This dismissal gives the erroneous impression that the only evidence suggesting that the "To be" passage is a feigned soliloquy is the location of a stage direction in Q2. The editors ignored the dozens of other pieces of evidence described earlier in the present essay, some of which are very conspicuous. For example, they suggest that the only reason Hamlet might be suspicious when he enters this scene would be if he spots the King and Polonius as they withdraw. But Hamlet has grounds more relative than this for being suspicious. He was summoned to this location by his enemy, and playgoers are informed of that summons only twenty-six lines before Hamlet's entrance.

The assertion that "It would be very unusual for Shakespeare, or any dramatist of this period, not to clarify the situation if Hamlet is consciously directing his soliloquy or his subsequent speeches at listeners" does not survive scrutiny. (1) A dramatist can "clarify" a situation that is "very unusual" or even unique by clearly implying what playgoers need to know. It is very unusual for an aristocratic character in a Renaissance play to adopt a peasant dialect at the moment his father's life is threatened, but Edgar does this without any explicit rationale. What he was up to becomes clear, but only in retrospect and only by implication. (2) A great many elements clearly imply that the "To be" speech is a feigned soliloquy, and numerous elements clearly contradict the notion that the speech is sincere. (3) Perhaps Thompson and Taylor actually meant to assert that it would be unlikely for Shakespeare not to make Hamlet's ploy *explicit* in the dialogue. But, as demonstrated above, Shakespeare and other Renaissance dramatists did, in fact, create other situations in which a character executes a ploy similar to Hamlet's without providing an explanation of the ploy in the dialogue. Shakespeare and his fellow dramatists could confidently rely on implication rather than resorting to explication in these situations because experienced playgoers were quite familiar with intricate eavesdropping episodes and must have enjoyed novel variations, or else dramatists of the time would not have created so many variations. Indeed, that dramatists would design implicitly feigned soliloquies was an almost inevitable result of the competition among dramatists of the period to design clever and novel eavesdropping episodes. When a particular type of dramatic situation becomes popular, dramatists eventually design more complex variations, and detailed explication begins to seem superfluous and clumsy. Skillful dramatists reduce explication to a minimum and sometimes rely solely on implication.

The Arden editors cite one case in which the perpetrator (La Fin) of a feigned soliloquy explicitly describes his ploy, as if this were evidence that Shakespeare would not have constructed a situation in which he expected playgoers to infer on the basis of obvious clues that a character is feigning a soliloquy. This argument is faulty in at least four respects. (1) The fact that one kind of event occurs once does not prove or in any way suggest that a different kind of event is unlikely. (2) The feigned soliloquy in Chapman's play that occurs in an eavesdropping episode is manifestly based on the "To be" speech, which also occurs in an eavesdropping episode. Evidence the Arden editors present to dismiss the notion that the "To be" speech was feigned actually indicates that another dramatist of the period understood that the speech was feigned. (3) The Arden editors mention one case in which a character who feigns a soliloquy explains his tactic, but they fail to mention that in other Renaissance plays (by Shakespeare, Fletcher, and Ford) a character who feigns a self-addressed speech to mislead another character does not explain his or her tactic. (4) The number of contextual clues Shakespeare provided to imply that Hamlet feigns the "To be" speech far exceeds the number of contextual clues provided in any of those examples.

The Arden editors address only a small number of the many pieces of inconvenient evidence and attempt to sweep them away with makeshift rationalizations.

> **No traveller returns** The Ghost has made a rather notable return, but Hamlet presumably means that under normal circumstances death is irreversible. (286)

The Hamlet imagined by the Arden editors asserts without qualification that no traveler returns from death because he has encountered only one traveler who has returned from death and that encounter does not count because it was not an everyday occurrence.

> **closely sent** . . . When [Hamlet] appears he does not make any mention of the fact that he is responding to a message from the King, though some performers make a show of looking carefully around them. . . . This slight awkwardness may refer to the larger problem of the placing of "To be or not to be." (281)

The Arden editors suggest that the absence of an explicit confirmation by Hamlet that he has been summoned to this location by the King somehow conflicts with ("though") the notion that he would be wary when he arrives at the location. But there are two obvious reasons why Shakespeare did not have Hamlet explicitly mention that he has arrived at the location to which he has been summoned by his enemy. (1) To do so would have been superfluous and redundant. In line 29 Claudius asserts that he has "sent for" Hamlet "hither." When Hamlet arrives hither at line 55, a playgoer should remember what has brought Hamlet hither. (2) Hamlet has reason to suspect that Polonius is eavesdropping in this location (see evidence items 8 and 29) but does not know this for certain. According to Renaissance conventions governing soliloquies, asides, and eavesdropping (see evidence item 19), Hamlet could not have guarded a genuine soliloquy in a genuine aside from an eavesdropper in hiding on the mere suspicion that the eavesdropper was present. The Arden editors have invented a "slight awkwardness" where none exists. There is no reason to believe either (a) that Hamlet has forgotten that he has been summoned to this spot by his enemy or (b) that the placing of the "To be" speech is a "problem."

The "problem" of the "placing" of the "To be" speech is also discussed briefly in the Introduction:

> the entire speech appears in a different place in Q1, during the equivalent of 2.2, much earlier than in the other texts . . . and several modern stagings of Q2/F

Hamlet have adopted the Q1 placing as being, for their purposes, more logical than the Q2/F placing in 3.1. While Hamlet's soliloquies are among the best-known and indeed best-loved features of the play, they seem, on the basis of the earliest texts, to be movable or even detachable: there is no sign in Q1 or F of Hamlet's last soliloquy. (18)

This version of the "problem" is as flawed as the one on page 281. (1) The assertion that "the entire speech appears in a different place in Q1, during the equivalent to 2.2" conveys the erroneous impression that *only* the speech occurs in a different location in Q1 and therefore that the "To be" speech does not take place in an eavesdropping episode in Q1 as it does in Q2 and F. In fact, in Q1 the entire eavesdropping episode occurs in the earlier scene. In all three texts the "To be" speech is located in an eavesdropping episode. (2) The placement of the speech in post-Renaissance productions has no bearing on the issue of its placement in Shakespeare's design of the play. (3) The fact that one soliloquy is not included in two texts of the play does not in any way suggest that Shakespeare designed all soliloquies "to be moveable or even detachable." The Arden edition gives readers the impression that Shakespeare wrote soliloquies as lyric poems, which he then inserted into plays at random. On the contrary, a hallmark of Shakespeare's artistry is that each speech, including each soliloquy, reflects the particular personality and particular situation of the speaker. And the present essay has demonstrated that, as a feigned soliloquy, the "To be" speech is deeply embedded in its particular dramatic context. Indeed, it is hard to imagine a dramatic speech more deeply embedded in its particular dramatic context.

In order to preserve the orthodox post-Renaissance assumption that the "To be" speech is a genuine soliloquy, the Arden editors inadvertently mislead readers about aspects of the character of Hamlet, about other features of this play, about Shakespeare's artistry, and about Renaissance dramatic practices. The Arden edition does not represent an aberration from the editorial tradition. That tradition has inadvertently taken Davenant and Betterton's simple and sentimental adaptation as if it were Shakespeare's conception and have thereby eliminated Shakespeare's subtle, complex, and disturbing implication. Some editors dispose of the inconvenient evidence even more efficiently than do the Arden editors. In the Yale edition of the play, Burton Raffel altered a stage direction to prevent readers from even considering the possibility that the speech might be insincere.

Enter Hamlet (thinking himself alone)[26]

Raffel does not explain why someone who has arrived at the location to which he has been summoned by his enemy and in which his former girlfriend is conspicuously present could possibly think himself alone.

In light of the plentiful, varied, and substantial evidence presented here, what should future editors of *Hamlet* do? Although Shakespeare used implication rather than explication in his design of the "To be" episode and expected playgoers of his time to infer that the "To be" passage is a deceptive ploy by Hamlet, post-Renaissance editors cannot follow Shakespeare's lead. The implication that would have been obvious to Renaissance playgoers has been and will continue to be very far from obvious to post-Renaissance readers because of the numerous factors described above ("Concealment in Plain Sight"). Hamlet's ploy has to be explained to modern readers. Because the orthodox dogma that the speech is a sincere expression of Hamlet's innermost thoughts is reinforced by manifold and pervasive forms of cultural indoctrination, a full and fair account of the evidence that conflicts with this dogma should be supplied so that the notion that the speech is a feigned soliloquy is not dismissed peremptorily by readers. An editor who remains fully committed to the conventional assumption can then present his or her counterargument and allow readers to make up their own minds. By taking these steps, editors will show their respect for the principle that scholarship should be based on evidence.

I dedicate this essay to the memory of Thomas Moisan, a distinguished scholar and an extraordinary friend who showed remarkable personal and professional courage.

Notes

1. James Hirsh, "The 'To be or not to be' Scene and the Conventions of Shakespearean Drama," *Modern Language Quarterly* 42 (1981): 115–36; "Shakespeare and the History of Soliloquies," *Modern Language Quarterly* 58 (1997): 1–26; "To Take Arms against a Sea of Anomalies: Laurence Olivier's Film Adaptation of Act Three, Scene One of *Hamlet*," *EnterText* 1 (2001): 192–203; *Shakespeare and the History of Soliloquies* (Madison, NJ: Fairleigh Dickinson University Press, 2003).

2. William Shakespeare, *The Riverside Shakespeare,* ed. G. Blakemore Evans, 2nd ed. (Boston: Houghton Mifflin, 1997). *Hamlet* was probably first performed in 1600 or 1601. Dates in parentheses after the titles of Shakespeare's other plays are probable dates of first performances.

3. According to the headnote to the entry on "antique" (1:94) in *The Compact Edition of the Oxford English Dictionary* (1971), the words now distinguished as "antic" and "antique"

> both were spelled *antik(e, antick(e* in 16th. c. . . . the identity of pronunciation remained longer; Dr. Johnson says *antique* 'was formerly pronounced according to English analogy, with the accent on the first syllable; but now after the French with the accent on the last, at least in prose; the poets use it variously.

4. In Q2 Hamlet enthusiastically describes the thrill he derives from counter-plots: " 'tis the sport to have the engineer / Hoist with his own petard, an't shall go hard / But I will delve one yard below their mines, / And blow them to the moon" (3.4.206–9).

5. Even though Hamlet wants to confirm the authenticity of the Ghost, he would not assert unequivocally and matter-of-factly that ghosts do not exist.

6. In addition to the two characters who have sworn not to reveal that they have seen the Ghost, Hamlet knows of at least one other character (Barnardo) who has seen it. As far as Hamlet knows, other inhabitants of the castle may have seen it as well and may have reported its visitation to the King.

7. In *Troilus and Cressida* (1601–2) 5.2, for example, Troilus and Ulysses eavesdrop upon Cressida and Diomedes while Thersites eavesdrops upon all four of those characters.

8. Shakespeare designed the episode so that, in addition, Hamlet could enter in time to spot Claudius and Polonius as they take their hiding place, allowing Burbage to add an additional visual clue by directing his gaze at the backs of the actors playing Claudius and Polonius, but this would have been merely an optional confirmation of the implication that is well-established by many other factors.

9. For plentiful evidence supporting all of these points, see Hirsh, *History,* chaps. 4–6.

10. For a catalogue of such episodes, see Hirsh, *History,* 125–46.

11. This effect has been destroyed by those editors, beginning with Alexander Pope, who have designated Edgar's soliloquy as a separate scene. Readers are thus prevented from hoping that Edgar and Kent might interact and from feeling disappointment when the two maltreated characters do not join forces.

12. Ben Jonson, *The Masque of Queens* (1609), in *Selected Masques,* ed. Stephen Orgel (New Haven: Yale University Press, 1970), lines 95–96.

13. John Fletcher, *A Woman's Prize,* in *English Renaissance Drama: A Norton Anthology,* ed. David Bevington et al. (New York: Norton, 2002).

14. George Chapman, *The Conspiracy and Tragedy of Charles, Duke of Byron,* ed. John Margeson (Manchester: Manchester University Press, 1988), 3.1.1–2.

15. John Ford, *The Broken Heart,* ed. T. J. B. Spencer (Manchester: Manchester University Press, 1980), 1.3.105.

16. A similar principle in the sciences is known as parsimony. Neither Occam's razor nor parsimony means that the most *obvious* solution is best. On the contrary, according to these principles, a single explanation that accounts for a large number of pieces of evidence is preferable to a series of separate, ad hoc explanations, one for each piece, even if the ad hoc explanations are orthodox, familiar, and soothing and the single explanation is unorthodox, counterintuitive, and disturbing.

17. Jeffrey Kipnis, "Introduction: Act Two," *Written into the Void: Selected Writings, 1990–2004,* by Peter Eisenman (New Haven: Yale University Press, 2007), xxv.

18. Colley Cibber, *An Apology for the Life of Mr. Colley Cibber Written by Himself* (1740), ed. Robert W. Lowe, 2 vols., 1889 (rpt. New York: AMS Press, 1966), 1:105.

19. Samuel Pepys, *The Diary of Samuel Pepys,* ed. Robert Latham and William Matthews (Berkeley: University of California Press, 1970), 5:320.

20. For detailed accounts of many of these factors, see Hirsh, *History,* chap. 10.

21. No purpose would be served by supplying a list of the countless books and

articles on the play that fail to present a coherent and comprehensive counterargument to the argument presented here.

22. A genealogy/taxonomy/refutation of these rationalizations is provided in Hirsh, *History,* 325–434.

23. Samuel Taylor Coleridge, *Coleridge's Writings on Shakespeare,* ed. Terence Hawkes (New York: Capricorn/Putnam, 1959), 105. The italics occur in the original.

24. Harold Jenkins, ed., *Hamlet,* Arden Shakespeare, 2nd series (London: Methuen, 1982), 491.

25. Ann Thompson and Neil Taylor, eds., *Hamlet,* Arden Shakespeare, 3rd series (London: Thomson, 2006), 284.

26. Burton Raffel, ed., *Hamlet* (New Haven: Yale University Press, 2003), 96. The entire stage direction is in italics.

"Deep Prescience": Succession and the Politics of Prophecy in *Friar Bacon and Friar Bungay*

Brian Walsh

In a well-known episode from the *Faerie Queene* (1590), the seer Merlin delivers a political prophecy to Britomart which predicts the ascension of a "royall virgin" to the throne of England. It is an instance of what Marjorie Garber calls "hindsight masquerading as foresight," as Spenser ascribes to a figure of the deep past the ability to foresee the reign of Queen Elizabeth, perhaps associating her rule with providential design.[1] The prophecy takes a strange turn almost immediately, though. This vision of the Elizabethan era that begins gloriously stops abruptly, as the future becomes ominously oblique. Spenser ends the prophecy with a startling phrase to describe what Merlin sees, but will not name, beyond Elizabeth: a "ghastly spectacle" by which he is "dismayd."[2] Merlin's refusal to continue is represented as his unwillingness to report what he sees. But in fact it is an acknowledgment of authorial limits. Spenser had appropriated a fabled, potent wizard to use in this scene, but he could not endow him with the power to see any more of the future than the poet himself could apprehend while writing in the late sixteenth century. Although by the end of the 1580s James VI of Scotland had emerged as Elizabeth's most likely heir, this was by no means certain, nor was the smooth accomplishing of such a theoretical transition something that could be confidently expected.[3] Critics of the poem have long recognized that when readers of the *Faerie Queene* are shut out of a vision of life beyond Elizabeth with such alarming language, Spenser's homage to his monarch is tinctured with disquietude over her failure to produce an heir. The moment, albeit indirectly, highlights fear of a succession crisis as a topic of literary speculation in the last decades of the sixteenth century, even among those ostensibly dedicated to praising the Queen.

A similar moment occurs in a near-contemporaneous work, Robert Greene's *Friar Bacon and Friar Bungay* (ca. 1589), performed by the Queen's Men. At the close of this play, set in thirteenth-century England, Friar Bacon delivers a vision of the future to King Henry III and his court that culminates in the ascension of "Diana's rose" and the peace and plenty her reign will bring.[4] While this speech does not contain the foreboding tone of Merlin's in the *Faerie Queene,* it likewise cannot purport to see any hint of stability beyond the last Tudor monarch. As in Spenser's case, Greene's attempt to ascribe a sense of the future to the past is perforce limited by the state of his own knowledge in the present in which he lives. While critics have written at length about the political implications of Merlin's prophecy in the *Faerie Queene,* and the ways it complicates our sense of Spenser's political and theological commitments, the parallel moment in *Friar Bacon and Friar Bungay* has not been closely studied in these terms.[5] It is largely taken for granted that *Friar Bacon and Friar Bungay* is a patriotic celebration of England and Elizabeth, and that this speech is the ecstatic climax of its praise.[6] Closer examination of Bacon's prophetic speech and the play as a whole expands this narrow picture. The speech notes the nation's dependence on Elizabeth for peace and prosperity, but also implicitly suggests that England has no future beyond her, a backhanded compliment to the Queen that recognizes her impressive tenure and points out her inability to secure long-term stability for her people.

I will demonstrate the validity of this premise in the first section of this essay. Yet, I do not want here simply to reverse the critical orthodoxy and claim that *Friar Bacon and Friar Bungay* undermines rather than lauds Elizabeth. In the second section, then, I will explore how we can acknowledge that reading and still arrive at a more nuanced assessment of how the play reflects on monarchical authority in the past and present, and on its prospects for the future. The dramatic context of this work is crucial to understanding its potential effect on audience perception of Elizabeth, especially the effect of Bacon's resounding prophecy. As part of a live performance, a prophetic speech works differently on playgoers than such speeches might in written prose or poetry. It brings the time-scheme of the stage in dialogue with the complex temporal dimensions of "hindsight masquerading as foresight" in a way that makes the audience acutely aware of its own present moment. *Friar Bacon and Friar Bungay* uses prophecy ascribed to the past not merely to cast an ominous shadow over the nation and its aging ruler, but to cast this shadow *and* direct its audience to concentrate on the realities of the present as a means to prepare for and produce a desirable future.

"Time Was . . . Time is Past": Political Prophecies from Virgil to Greene

Friar Bacon, renowned for his facility with "magic's mystery," spends a good deal of the play anticipating the culmination of his greatest endeavor, the animation of a brazen head that will "unfold strange doubts and aphorisms" and "compass England with a wall of brass" (II.13, 25, 29). If the scholarly consensus that dates *Friar Bacon* to 1589 is correct, this would be a particularly potent fantasy just one year after the Armada.[7] The successful repulsion of the Spanish forces did not allay English anxiety about another such attempt. The desire to create a barrier around England, a literal realization of Gaunt's notion in *Richard II* that England is a "fortress," expresses a fantasy of English impenetrability. When Bacon first explains the project of raising the brass wall, he declares that it will prevent even "ten Caesars" with "all the legions" of Europe from touching "a grass of English ground," calling attention to the Roman conquest of Britain as a precedent for successful invasion that makes the magical defense system necessary (II.58–60).

Bacon's wall is never accomplished. His anticipation of it as a future guarantee of English security is a desire that is deferred indefinitely, as Elizabethan audiences would be all too aware. Before the brazen head that was to build the wall is mysteriously destroyed, its cryptic pronouncement shuts off consideration of the future at all, speaking only in the present and past tenses: "time is," "time was," and "time is past" (XI.53, 64, 73). The failure of Bacon to gain control of the head and harness its power marks a limit to his ability to control the future of the nation. The fact that the head stops speaking with the phrase "time is past" leaves audiences with a haunting intimation of stasis rather than the hope of future strength for England.[8] The threat of no future is a menace to all comic worlds. This menace is encapsulated in the phrase "time is past," and is dramatized in *Friar Bacon and Friar Bungay* in another scene involving Bacon's necromancy. This one involves his "glass prospective," a magic mirror through which far-flung simultaneous actions can be seen. In Bacon's cell at Oxford, two young students watch through the glass as their fathers in Fressingfield fight and kill each other. Each man in the duel assures the other that they will be outlived by a son who can avenge him. But as the fatal fight unfolds, the two students immediately attempt to take revenge and kill each other. The next generation is cut down, even as the previous one falls, shutting off the promise of continuity through children. Bacon, when showing his glass to Prince Edward in an earlier scene when the prince is scheming to bed the pastoral beauty Margaret, the "Fair Maid of Fressingfield," had said to him "Sit still, my lord, and mark the comedy" (VI.48). As the two scholars arrive to watch their fathers' encounter in Fressingfield, Bacon ominously says "I smell there will be a tragedy" (XIII.36). The play makes explicit the generic turn from the world of wooing country girls and the hope of sexual fulfillment and propagation that it implies to the world of murderous passion and revenge, and the hopelessness of death that it implies. When Margaret, an object of male desire throughout the play, threatens to enter a nunnery, she adds virginity as a different kind of threat to comic closure.

Friar Bacon and Friar Bungay, a generic mixed bag that combines elements of history, romance, and tragicomedy, does ultimately achieve a comic telos despite the dark turn in Bacon's cell and Margaret's tentative chastity.[9] The young scholars cannot be resurrected, but Margaret embraces her role as a wife and future mother, just as Prince Edward joins with Princess Eleanor to form a dynastic match. The various plot threads become untwisted, and the play begins to sort itself out as a more or less traditional comedy replete with a concluding gala feast for a double wedding between young lovers. The feeling of stasis conveyed in the "time is past" utterance would thus seem to be overturned by the play's ending. Just before the play concludes, Friar Bacon steps forth to deliver his prophecy, adding more emphasis to the event as a celebration of futurity:

> I find by deep prescience of mine art,
> Which once I tempered in my secret cell,
> That here where Brute did build his Troynovant,
> From forth the royal garden of a king
> Shall flourish out so rich and fair a bud
> Whose brightness shall deface proud Phoebus' flower,
> And over-shadow Albion with her leaves.
> Till then Mars shall be master of the field;
> But then the stormy threats of wars shall cease.
> The horse shall stamp as careless of the pike;
> Drums shall be turned to timbrels of delight;
> With wealthy favours plenty shall enrich
> The strond that gladded wandering Brute to see,
> And peace from heaven shall harbour in these leaves
> That gorgeous beautifies this matchless flower.
> Apollo's hellitropian then shall stoop,
> And Venus' hyacinth shall vail her top;
> Juno shall shut her gilliflowers up,
> And Pallas' bay shall bash her brightest green;
> Ceres' carnation, in consort with those,
> Shall stoop and wonder at Diana's rose.
>
> (XVI.42–62)

A look at what lies ahead, these lines at first glance are an appropriate theme for a wedding party. But by considering the implications of how the speech itself concludes, and some of its key literary antecedents and analogues, we can begin to put pressure on the full extent of its hopefulness.

The king's response to the remarkable speech is incomprehension: "This prophecy is mystical" (63). More properly, Bacon's prophecy is *Merlinic*. The tradition of such prophecies began with Geoffrey of Monmouth's stories about the Welsh figure of Merlin in his *History of the Kings of Britain*. The Merlinic prophecy is usually very dense, to the point of inscrutability, and it typically employs elaborate natural imagery. For instance, in Geoffrey's book Merlin produces a series of visions in a "prophetic trance," such as this one: "The Lion of Justice shall come next, and at its roar the towers of Gaul shall shake and the island Dragons tremble. In the days of this Lion gold shall be squeezed from the lily-flower and the nettle, and silver shall flow from the hoofs of lowing cattle."[10] Howard Dobin, in his study of vaticinal discourses in early modern English literature and politics, notes that ostensibly such visions can yield stable meanings, but that "prophecy in the Merlinic tradition of obscurantist symbolic rhetoric forecloses the chance of ever recovering . . . single truth." He goes on to argue that the "peculiarities of prophetic style cancel the possibility of locating definitive meaning" because of the "inexhaustibly polysemic nature of prophetic texts."[11]

Bacon's prophecy fulfills the requisite cryptic quality of the Merlin prophetic tradition for those on stage who hear it; the king's response that it is "mystical" shows that he has no interpretation, and no one else speaks in response to it. Henry quickly shifts his words to address all his guests with a speech that concludes the play and is most concerned with the wedding festivity to ensue. For the onstage auditors, the prophecy is baffling and could mean anything. But its meaning is clearer for those in the audience of a performance of *Friar Bacon and Friar Bungay.* The speech is delivered by a character based on the famed Oxford philosopher Roger Bacon, to the court of King Henry III of England, just as his son, Prince Edward, is about to marry Eleanor of Castile. From this purported thirteenth-century perspective, the speech foresees a period of internecine conflict for England—when "Mars shall be master of the field"—before a time of peace brought about by a "fair bud" who comes from the "royal garden of a king." The prophecy predicts the long and traumatic civil wars England will endure in the fifteenth century, as well as the rise of Elizabeth as the fair bud of a royal king—which could refer either to Henry VII or Henry VIII—to inaugurate a period of peace and plenty. The "future" predicted here culminates in a world that marvels at the majesty and benevolence of a ruler identified as "Diana's rose."

This name combines the "Tudor Rose" badge first adopted by Henry VII as the symbol of his house, with Diana, the mythical virgin huntress. It is an unmistakable reference to Elizabeth. It is here that the speech fails to conform to the central tenet of Merlinic prophecy according to Dobin. For while it is too abstruse for Henry and the rest of the characters Bacon addresses to comprehend, its meaning, in particular its closing reference to "Diana's rose," is intelligible to an Elizabethan audience. For playgoers at a performance of *Friar Bacon and Friar Bungay,* the prophecy sets forth the rhetoric of an idealized Tudor status quo, a rhetoric with which they would be familiar. The play relies here on the assumption that audiences will take for granted that this prophecy has already come true, and that they are, in their present-tense moment, enjoying its fruits. What Bacon describes as his "prescience" is more accurately, for playgoers, a kind of *reminiscence.*

Greene wrote this speech in the Galfridian tradition of Merlinic prophecy, but he had an even more ancient model for the thrust of it. The prophecy assigned to the past that ends in the present time of a work's audience is a Virgilian motif. It originates in Anchises' prophecy to Aeneas in book 6 of the *Aeneid.* There, when Aeneas meets his father in the underworld, Anchises delivers a vision of the Roman future. This vision predicts the growth of Rome as the pinnacle of earthly governments. It also foresees the emergence of a particular ruler, "the man you heard so often promised— / Augustus Caesar, son of a god, who will / renew a golden age in Latium."[12] Anchises can see far into the future, but no further than the time of the poet who gives him a voice during the reign of Augustus. This passage from the *Aeneid* foregrounds the issue of succession. As Aeneas approaches his father, we read that "Anchises, lost in thought, was studying / the souls of all his sons to come." Virgil includes reference here to one who might succeed Augustus, the young man Marcellus, "a victor / who towers over all!"[13] The historical Marcus Claudius Marcellus, Augustus's nephew and his son-in-law, was sometimes identified by Roman historians and later by Renaissance commentators as Augustus' heir. But we quickly learn from Anchises, in a series of wrenching lines, that this hope for the future has expired. Marcellus died at the age of twenty-three. For Virgil's original audience, the poem's announced heir was already being mourned. The series of visions that began as an outline of the Roman future ends in grief over the loss of a potential bridge forward.

Spenser, in his scene featuring the truncated prophecy of Merlin to Britomart, adopted this motif from the *Aeneid,* filtered through its prior use in canto 3 of Ariosto's *Orlando Furioso.* There, a prophecy that is given in a cave by Merlin to a female knight also becomes deliberately vague when it reaches the present of the poem's composition, albeit in a distinct way. As one critic points out, for Ariosto to complete the genealogy of the ruling house he has set forth, he would have to mention a pair of traitorous relatives who had been imprisoned for attempting a coup, thus tainting the family his poem seeks to praise.[14] He is content, therefore, to focus on the fecundity of his patron, Alfonse d'Este, and ignore Alfonse's unseemly brothers. While Ariosto is his more immediate precedent for the prophecy, Spenser adheres closely to the Virgilian original in that his poem becomes opaque not out of fear of naming inconvenient possible heirs, but because there is no certain heir to name. John Watkins puts the matter succinctly:

> By 1590, Elizabeth's commitment to virginity had cost her the opportunity ever to produce an heir. In imagining the Tudor future, Spenser yielded Ariosto's Estense confidence to the uncertainty and trepidation with which Virgil imagined the fate of Rome after Augustus' death.[15]

The prophetic genealogies of Spenser's Merlin and of Anchises are rhetorical statements, couched in the past, that indict the present. They construct interlocking links in a genealogical chain, but in each case, the last link is open-ended. This creates the potential for chaos: in 1601, two years before Elizabeth died, one Englishmen noted that "there are 12 competitors that gape for the death of that good old Princess the now Queen."[16] On a very practical level, of course, the omission in Spenser is due to the fact that it was illegal to openly discuss the succession. But by walking up to the very edge of such a discussion, Spenser calls attention to it and to the unsure status of the future. The "dismay" Spenser's Merlin feels when he perceives what lies, or what does not lie, beyond Elizabeth parallels Anchises' anguish over the death of Marcellus: both of these uncomfortable moments convey fears of an uncertain future, a fear that in Spenser's poem is amplified by the very subject being taboo.[17] Securing a peaceful succession is traditionally one of the cardinal responsibilities of any ruler so as to avoid the scramble for power the statement about "competitors" for the English crown predicts. Spenser, in homage to Virgil, illuminates Elizabeth's failure to do so.

Bacon's prophecy at the close of *Friar Bacon and Friar Bungay* can also be placed in this tradition. As we have seen, the play is conscious of the threat of stasis, of a world without a future, seen in the deaths of the young scholars, Margaret's temporary embrace of chastity, and the disturbing utterance of the brazen head, "time is," "time was," and "time is past," words that refuse to recognize a future tense. Such threats are allayed in part by the couplings with which the play ends. And yet the specific promise for the future that the key coupling of Edward I and Eleanor of Castile represents is *already the past* for the Elizabethan audience. They are not living in a time when an heir flourishes, or at a time of anticipation for the birth of another heir, as the characters within the play are. There is no option set forth for continued succession beyond the Elizabethan present in the ending, an impression that is made especially vivid through the structure of the play. Bacon's prophecy is positioned to force the audience to meditate on its own limited vision to a greater degree than its precedents. The moments I have considered in the *Aeneid* and the *Faerie Queene* are clearly meant to be important and memorable, but they occur in the middle of long poems. In both cases, and especially in the *Faerie Queene*, there is an immediate return to a world of action, where densely packed narrative episodes follow hard upon these prophecies. In *Friar Bacon*, the passage is the penultimate speech of the play, so that it might still be ringing in playgoers' ears when they leave the theater. The Elizabethan audience can feel a measure of satisfaction that they live in the promised time of Bacon's prophecy, but the play also leaves them with no sense of their own future; only a finite sense of the future as it has been projected onto the past.

Greene's play highlights succession as a fraught issue for Elizabethans in other ways that amount to a critique of their Queen. For instance, Edward's title underlines his status as a monarch-in-waiting. Edward is frequently referred to, by himself and others, as the "Prince of Wales," a title named at least ten times over the course of the play.[18] The title Prince of Wales as applied to Prince Edward here is anachronistic. This moniker was first given by Edward himself as a title for the heir apparent to his own son, the eventual Edward II (an act dramatized in George Peele's *Edward I,* probably first performed a few years after *Friar Bacon and Friar Bungay*). The play is careful in many other regards to cultivate a sense of historicity. Bacon is based on a historical figure, and Greene places him among the monarch with whom he was contemporary, Henry III. This is a shift from the prose source for the play, in which the English king is unnamed, which gives that work a more timeless feel.[19] Now, the premature use of "Prince of Wales" amid the play's other gestures toward crafting a sense of the past is minor enough as anachronisms in early modern plays about the past go.[20] But the appearance of this title, with its connotations of a living male heir, and the frequency of its use here, seem significant. The prince is represented as a lustful young man, a would-be Tarquin whose desire to rape a subject is curbed and whose erotic energy is redirected toward his eventual wife, Eleanor. In focusing on the trajectory of his sexual desire finding the proper object, the play presents a picture of the triumph of Edward's orderly reproductive energy as much as it presents a more general moral about tyranny and the maturation of a ruler who must first learn to rule himself. In other words, the play focuses audience attention on Edward becoming a lawful progenitor. *Friar Bacon and Friar Bungay* also repeatedly reminds its audience that Edward is the Prince of Wales, the heir to the throne, and through this they are repeatedly reminded of King Henry's potency and the promise of succession that it has provided. Edward's virility, too, is clearly on display. At first it is sinister, but by the end it is connected directly to the glorious future of Bacon's prophecy. His speech is prompted by Henry's pointed question to Bacon before the wedding of his son: "what shall grow from Edward and his queen?" (XVI.41).

When Margaret agrees to abandon her plans to enter a nunnery and marry Lacy, her true love, her capitulation is humorously pithy and free of elaborate justification: "The flesh is frail" (XIV.86). Importantly, her desire for sexual fulfillment with Lacy and the promise of children it implies comes within the context of marriage, the legal means by which reproduction can have binding, practical consequences for the future. Likewise, and more importantly for the nation, Edward's rejection of his frivolous lust for Margaret, and his subsequent embrace of licit sexual expression and reproduction with Eleanor, gives hope for the maintenance of England's ruling dynasty. As with the title Prince of Wales, the particular dynasty this marriage will perpetuate is named explicitly in the play many times, a move that is again unprecedented in the prose source. King Henry and Prince Edward refer to themselves, or are referred to by others, with the name "Plantagenet" six times over the course of *Friar Bacon and Friar Bungay*.[21] Just as invocation of Prince of Wales as a name for the designated male heir to the throne reminds audiences that in their moment, there is none, the repetition of the Plantagenet name serves to highlight the difference between that ruling family and the one that reigns in the present of the play's performance, the Tudors. The juxtaposition, at least in terms of reproductive success, is not flattering for Elizabeth's house. The relative fecundity of the Plantagenets is on display in *Friar Bacon and Friar Bungay*. Here, the play ends with a king who is still reigning and about to supervise the marriage of his son, an eventual king, to a woman with whom he will father another eventual king, who in turn fathers Edward III, famed source of numerous sons, the "seven vials of his sacred blood."[22]

The allusion to Diana and her virginity in Bacon's speech is an obvious reminder that Elizabeth's reign has not included the festive comic moment of marriage or the hope of reproduction and dynastic continuity that marriage promises. Greene reminds us of this fact subtly in the final scene of the play. Twice in this scene, once before the prophetic speech, and once within it, Bacon employs the phrase "matchless"; first to describe England, then Elizabeth (XVI.39, 56). The most obvious meaning of the term in both instances is "incomparable," or "peerless." But lurking behind the expression is another meaning, one that is especially poignant as a description of the Queen: unmarried, i.e., without a match. Elizabeth's matchless life stood in contrast to the generative matches of Henry III and Edward I on display. The play's final speech at first appears as an encomium in praise of Elizabeth and the halcyon order she inaugurates. But in fact, it is an *elegy* for the twilight of the Tudors, the ruling house whose extinction was well within sight for the English in the last decade of the sixteenth century.

King Henry's speech closes out the play with the reverberating final line "Thus glories England over all the west" (XVI.76). Some critics have been too quick to suture these final words of Henry's to Bacon's prophecy, as though the logical outcome of the prophecy is the proclamation of eternal English glory.[23] This is a deceptively triumphalist view of the final scene. Henry's words do not address the larger destiny of England, or even Bacon's speech, which he has simply characterized—perhaps even dismissed—as "mystical." They speak to the limited moment of the wedding feast, where, Henry claims, should the European monarchs present have "frolic hearts," England will have preeminent glory while it contains these joyful heads of state for the duration of their visit. Henry's heady sounding final phrase, in other words, is embedded only in the moment of comic celebration it depicts. Bacon's speech looks farther ahead, to the Elizabethan present, and it ends with Elizabeth herself. Like the brazen head's syntax, there is no future tense, no sense of what comes next. Audiences leave the playhouse with no reassuring fantasy of future glory; rather, they leave knowing only that the time of their present is fading into an uncertain future, and perhaps with a foreboding sense that the time of their sovereign and their nation is indeed about to be "past."

"Time is": Performance, Prophecy, and Possibility

Plays unfold under the pressure of real time. This fact has special significance for plays that depict the historical past as *Friar Bacon* seeks to do. The time-scheme of drama demonstrates the constructed nature of historical narratives, for audiences observe history being made before their eyes within the confines of a playhouse, out of the materials of theater, chief among them living human bodies. This present-past dialectic produces a heightened awareness of the absence of the past by showing the artificial means necessary to create some experience of it. *Friar Bacon and Friar Bungay* constructs an Elizabethan version of the medieval past, and posits within that past a vision of the future that dead ends in the present. Based on this, we might simply pronounce *Friar Bacon and Friar Bungay* to be one of the many cultural products of the late sixteenth century that reflect anxieties over a possible English succession crisis. Anxiety about the succession was real, and most probably did inflect this play and the blank sense of futurity it represents. But it need not be the whole story. I want, then, to consider some alternate ways to understand the effect of the play's meditation on succession questions, ones that don't necessarily eschew uneasiness about the future, but that connect that uneasiness to a sense of possibility.

We can begin such a consideration by pressing further on the temporality of live performance just mentioned. The liveness of drama always foregrounds a keen sense of the present. Greene exploits this and heightens the sensation of being present in the theater to an exceptional degree in *Friar Bacon and Friar Bungay*. In particular, the play repeatedly forces audiences to consider its own act of spectatorship in attending a play, that is, what it means to look and observe in the moment of performance. This is achieved in one place through Bacon's "glass prospective," the device that allows those who look into it to see events happening in distant locales. Two scenes of double staging are designed around the glass, which creates a radical sense of simultaneous action. In the second, as we have seen, two students watch from Oxford as their fathers kill each other in Fressingfield. In the first, Bacon allows the lovesick Edward to watch from Oxford as his friend Lacy, who had pledged to woo Margaret in Fressingfield on his behalf, in fact reveals his own love for Margaret, a love which she also feels for him. This scene emphasizes more overtly than the other the complicated dynamics of staging simultaneity. The precise blocking for this scene is not clear in the quarto text, but presumably Bacon and Edward are visible on one part of the stage, while Margaret, Lacy, and Friar Bungay are visible on another. They are separated by the glass which supposedly allows Edward to see across the distance that divides him from Lacy and Margaret. At one point, Bacon must restrain Edward from stabbing the mirror. The Prince becomes angry when he realizes that Lacy and Margaret are in love. When the Prince offers to "stab them," Bacon cries out "Oh, hold your hands, my lord, it is the glass!" calling attention to the glass as a lifeless thing, and, indeed, a mere *prop* (VI.127, 128). Edward's excuse that "Choler to see the traitors gree so well / Made me think the shadows substances" (129–30) brings to mind discourses of representation, and builds an analogy between looking through the glass and looking at a play, where spectators must always be mindful of taking the action on stage too seriously.[24] Bacon reminds the Prince that " 'Twere a long poniard, my lord, to reach between / Oxford and Fressingfield" (131–32), a clever line that undermines the work the glass supposedly does by alerting playgoers to the artifice of the split stage device: presumably, the actor playing Edward could in fact stab the actors playing Lacy and Margaret if he failed to respect their fictional distance, just as any playgoer could mar the play they are watching should they shout out that there is no real expanse of space between the actors on stage. Theatrical convention allows audiences to entertain the fiction that they are able to see actions occurring in two different locales at once, in Oxford and in Fressingfield. As Bacon's sly comment reminds us, though, the outrageous conceit of the scene calls attention to its own staginess, and makes the audience aware that the ability to see distinct locations in one moment is an aesthetic construct that depends for its success on their own complicity with the theatrical event taking place before them.

The benefit of complying in this way is theatrical pleasure itself. Such pleasure is on display in many forms in *Friar Bacon and Friar Bungay,* but nowhere more so than in the scene of the "conjuring contest" between the two eponymous friars and the German Vandermast. The contest is done for the benefit of King Henry and his fellow princes, thus providing an onstage audience with whom playgoers in the theater must watch the spectacle, an effect that helps remind those playgoers of their own act of looking. That this episode struck a memorable chord with audiences is clear from the fact that it, and its aftermath—Vandermast being carted off stage by a devil—is referenced a few times in the sequel to *Friar Bacon and Friar Bungay,* a now-obscure play called *John of Bordeaux.*[25] Bungay begins the contest by making appear "the tree leaved with refined gold / Whereon the fearful dragon held his seat / That watched the garden called Hesperides, / Subdued and won by conquering Hercules" (IX.79–82). A spectacular stage direction follows: "*Here* Bungay *conjures, and the tree appears with the dragon shooting fire*" (83 s.d.). Vandermast does him one better, promising to "raise him [Hercules] up as when he lived, / And cause him pull the dragon from his seat, / And tear the branches piecemeal from the root" (89–91). With Vandermast's cry of "Hercules, *prodi, prodi,* [come forth] Hercules," the stage direction tells us that "Hercules *appears in his lion's skin*" (92, 97.s.d.). He then follows Vandermast's instructions to begin tearing down the tree.

Bungay starts the contest by using his power to bring a fantastic prop onto the stage, complete with a potent stage effect "*The dragon shooting fire.*" When Vandermast calls on Hercules to appear, his language makes clear that has not really brought forth Hercules. He describes the figure he has brought forth as "The fiend *appearing like* great Hercules" (99, emphasis added). Like Faust, in Marlowe's contemporary necromancer play, who can only bring forth "such spirits as can lively *resemble* Alexander" the Great, Vandermast admits that he's in fact called on a devil to come forth and portray Hercules, rather than reincarnated some genuine article.[26] He and Bungay have, in effect, arranged a reenactment of a piece of ancient mytho-history that is fantastic to behold but that is also rooted in the dynamics of professional playing, making the conjuring contest another figure for theatrical performance. One magician has supplied the prop, the other has supplied the actor. Bacon then enters to provide the climax, exercising his supreme authorial power, as he thwarts Vandermast by overriding his ability to control the spirit playing Hercules. Bacon also delivers the comical dénouement of the episode, as he calls on another devil to kidnap Vandermast and take him back to Germany, in effect ending the playlet the magicians have put on for the court, and for the theater audience.[27]

In an earlier scene that also participates in this pattern of theatrical self-consciousness, the clown Rafe is dressed as Edward. When some skeptical Oxford dons challenge this, doubting the buffoonish man could be the Prince of Wales, Edward's friends admit the fraud, but ask for the scholars' indulgence: "I must desire you to imagine him [Rafe] all this forenoon the Prince of Wales" to which one, Mason, agrees: "I will" (VII.114—16). Greene dramatizes here the moment of audience acceptance of the conditions of performance; it is a miniature performance of the theatrical contract itself. *Friar Bacon and Friar Bungay* calls attention in these scenes to the dynamics of impersonation and audience collusion, and it presents in return for audience complicity the fantastic and amusing spectacles that props and theatrical bodies can provide. These fantastic moments are calculated to disallow audiences to forget they are looking at theatre in action; each moment contains some version of the "I will" concession from the scholar Mason, a moment when collective awareness of the artifice of the stage is acknowledged but not bemoaned as a bar to audience enjoyment. I believe that through the strategic moments in which the play goes out of its way to call attention to its own theatricality—as in the glass prospective scenes, the conjuring contest scene, and the concluding pact of the Rafe impersonation scene—*Friar Bacon and Friar Bungay* keeps audiences attentive to the sensation of being in the theater and enjoying acts of theatrical labor.[28] The play is ostensibly about the past, and, in Bacon's speech, about the future. But the various elements of performance I have been tracking here conspire with the content of the play as a whole and that speech especially to ensure that it continually alerts playgoers to the fact of the *present tense* they occupy and in which they are witnessing, and participating in, a real-time event of theater.

The play asks audiences to think about themselves as audiences at a play, and thus cultivates an interpretive space in which playgoers can engage with and stay mindful of the ideas the play communicates. This is especially possible because theater is, of course, not merely a visual medium. The meta-theatrical consciousness I am talking about comes in part through witty turns of phrase. Greene's powerful verse ensures that the play's *language* is compelling throughout. A great deal of the pleasure of *Friar Bacon and Friar Bungay* must surely come from the many gorgeous passages, rich with classical allusion and vivid imagery, that the characters speak. The play even shows the consequences of not paying close attention to language at some key moments. The brazen head is destroyed in part because the clown Miles cannot understand that its words have meaning and demand interpretation. Bacon's prophecy itself demonstrates that magic can be represented verbally as well as visually, helping to heighten audience interest in the "lush" poetry of the play and what it conveys.[29] Greene and the players offer a good deal of raw spectacle in this play. But they skillfully embroider it with expressive poetry and pointed meta-theatrical comments that create alert audiences who are continually challenged to exercise their minds in response to the play's visual and verbal stimuli rather than to accept it simply as wondrous display.

If we apply this notion that Greene uses theatrical action and dramatic language in *Friar Bacon* to engage audience perception about the issues the play broaches, and that in doing so he ensures that audiences are acutely sensitive to their own present-tense moment in the theater—and thus how the past and future the play proffers are constructs of the present—we can begin to imagine a more complex range of response to the rhetoric of succession in the play. Such rhetoric need not point only to nostalgia for a more fruitful past. The heightened sense of being present in the theater helps to create a "historical distance" effect for audiences, putting the events of the play at a temporal arm's length.[30] The frequent use of the name Plantagenet that I noted earlier can be understood in this context as a code for what is old and even obsolete rather than only a positive alternative to the issueless Elizabeth.[31] As noted earlier, Edward and Eleanor, the young couple entering marriage as the play ends, are vessels of futurity only in the fiction of the play's historical conceit. In fact, by the end of the sixteenth century, they had been resting around the shrine of Edward the Confessor in Westminster Abbey for almost three hundred years. They lay beneath elaborate tombs in an ancient burial site that, in sixteenth-century London, was already being frequented by visitors interested in history.[32] The tombs themselves were indices of an antiquated world of Catholic ritual and mourning practices, designed originally to be sites of intercessory prayers that were later outlawed by the Reformation.[33] Far from signifying only as bright and fertile signs of the future, Edward and Eleanor could also signify as relics from the distant past, enlivened on stage, but only for the transient time of a performance, and only by the most artificial acts of impersonation.

Elizabethan audiences may also have been aware of the product of the marriage with which the play ends: Edward II, son of Prince Edward and Eleanor of Castile. While his birth and eventual ascension, and his own fathering of a son, all speak well to the benefits of dynastic continuity, Edward's status as a defective king was established in the chronicles of the sixteenth century, a story compelling enough that it was soon to serve as the basis of its own play by Marlowe.[34] The instability of his reign could serve as evidence that governments based on royal primogeniture always run the risk that an unfit or controversial heir will come to power, a realization that might help to dampen some degree of enthusiasm for reproduction as the main criteria and hope of political succession. Even Edward II's famed son King Edward III presented a troubling object lesson to Elizabethans, one later to be exploited by Shakespeare in his history plays: the dangers of royal "overproduction." The existence of too many heirs can create succession crises as easily as the existence of no heirs can.

Bacon's prophecy asserts that Elizabeth "grows" from Edward and Eleanor, even though her lineal connection to the Plantagenet House is less direct than such language suggests. This attenuated descent makes evident that political continuity does not have to be strictly patrilineal in nature. In an even simpler sense, the very fact that audiences are continually made aware that the family depicted in *Friar Bacon* is not technically the same as the one currently in power reveals that ruling houses can peter out or be otherwise removed from power by various forces of rupture. This perhaps creates space to recognize precedent for other, even nonbiological, forms of succession such as Elizabeth's death will necessitate. Bacon's final speech invokes the "wandering Brute" as part of a conventional link between the Trojans who supposedly landed on Britain and the Tudors (XVI.54). But mentioning this figure, even as it does the political work of implying that the Tudors are a restoration of the island's first legitimate rulers, also reminds playgoers that restoration is made necessary because of the mutability of governments and ruling houses. From Brute, to Plantagenet, to civil wars, to Tudor, and after that, to the unknown: interruption and change are unavoidable aspects of having a government at all.[35]

Henry calls Bacon's prophecy mystical. What I am getting at here is some sense in which it might be, for Elizabethan audiences, something almost *practical.* In a pioneering study of political prophecy in medieval and Renaissance England, Rupert Taylor notes that prophecies commonly flourished in times of "crisis," and that they were "numerous at the time of the Armada."[36] The specter of Spanish invasion in the 1580s was seen by some as a possible sign of the Apocalypse. The confrontation from the English perspective was in many senses a battle between the true faith and Antichrist. English victory gave rise to providential self-assurances about God's favor.[37] But this did not quell the atmosphere of crisis that, as Taylor notes, spurred the production of many political prophecies. Reinhart Koselleck, in his penetrating study of prophecy and national temporalities, has argued that the pressure of unresolved Apocalyptic anxiety created a crucial transformation in the prophetic culture of early modern Europe. Koselleck argues that, on the Continent, when early modern wars of religion were brought to an end through negotiation and compromises such as the *Cuius regio, eius religio* ("whose realm, his religion") principle, rather than through final victory or defeat, a new perspective on the future began to emerge:

> The experience won in a century of bloody struggles was, above all, that the religious wars did not herald the Final Judgment, at least not in the direct manner hitherto envisaged . . . and this disclosed a new and unorthodox future.

The defeat of the Armada was a decisive victory for the English, but it did not foreclose the possibility of future Spanish, or indeed Catholic threats. In other words, it was not the "Final Battle," but one in a potentially limitless series of battles. Koselleck goes on to say that, once nations realized that wars oriented around religious conflict, however they concluded, did not in fact bring on the Apocalypse, the question arises of "the actual conceptions of futurity occupying the space of the waning future," and that one of these conceptions is "rational prognosis," which he calls the "counterconcept of contemporary prophecy." Koselleck argues that "while prophecy transgressed the bounds of calculable experience, prognosis remained within the dimensions of the political situation."[38]

This notion of a turn from reliance on prophecy to prognosis can be helpful in assessing Bacon's speech. Bacon calls on his "deep prescience," but as we have seen, its depth is backward rather than forward. The political prophecy offered by Bacon's speech is used up in its recitation; it has exhausted its value for Elizabethan audiences in being a set of beautiful verse lines that help close out an enjoyable play and in affirming the official discourse of their current monarch's glory. It cannot give them hope or clarity about the future, but only communicate to them their own past. And in so doing, it shows the need for something else to emerge to ensure a stable future, a different attitude toward what is to come than can be offered by hindsight that masquerades as foresight: perhaps the rational prognosis of Koselleck's analysis. The defeat of the Armada did not mean the defeat of Catholicism or of hostile foreign powers, much less the end of time. Likewise, the death of

Elizabeth need not mean the ruin of England. It means, rather, that something like rational prognosis is needed to create a desirable future beyond her life and reign. By stopping as it does with Elizabeth, Bacon's speech reminds audiences that they are living in a time of imminent rupture. They will experience the death of not only a monarch, but of a dynasty. They will see momentous change take place. What kind, of course, is left unknown. This suspense can be understood only as causing anxiety, but it can also be understood as salutary, as a kind of imperative for staying alert in the present to the reality of potential future pitfalls.

We noted above one of the obvious pitfalls of an uncertain succession in the statement from 1601 that "there are 12 competitors that gape for the death of that good old Princess the now Queen." In the scene when the two men of Fressingfield, Lambert and Serlsby, fight and kill one another, the play presents a microcosm of the perils of such competition: civil war, one of the chief threats of a succession crisis. This peril is exaggerated when their sons kill each other as well, showing how internecine conflict—here between two neighbors and then two fellow Oxford students—spawns a multigenerational cycle of destruction that is detrimental to the land as a whole. Moreover, Bacon's speech itself spells out the danger of civil war. Elizabeth's reign is the peaceful answer to the time when "Mars shall be master of the field" (49). Audiences may not know who will replace her, but her reign is held out as a time free of civil conflict and thus a model of national cohesion that should be emulated.

Likewise, in terms of international conflict, the play emphasizes friendship, concord, and openness. As many critics have pointed out, it is ultimately appropriate that the brass wall Bacon hopes to see built around England never materializes, for the nation cannot so thoroughly enclose itself and hope to survive in an increasingly interdependent world where opportunities for stabilizing alliances and economic expansion beyond Europe were mushrooming.[39] National rivalry is indeed played out as harmless academic dispute between the English friars and Vandermast—where even the vanquished and obnoxious German ends up safely back in his university study—not as costly battles on land or sea. *Friar Bacon and Friar Bungay* was performed at a moment when war with Spain was a constant threat, and yet Eleanor of Castile and her father are portrayed in a wholly sympathetic light.[40] The king's final words, "Thus glories England over all the west," celebrate a triumph of hospitality, not military prowess: it is Henry's hope that England will gain renown through the presence of friendly foreign powers together celebrating an international marriage. The play's ending conveys a message that diplomacy and dynastic matches are preferable to foreign wars as forms of international policy. The Wars of the Roses period was also a time of conflict with France and Scotland; civil war and foreign war were linked in the English historical consciousness. The halcyon period of Elizabeth's rule that Bacon's speech constructs implies a link between peace at home among the English, and peace between England and other nations: it is when "peace from heaven shall harbour in these leaves" that the world "shall stoop and wonder at Diana's rose."

When Miles ignores the initial utterance of the brazen head, "time is," he misses the call to action in the present he was supposed to heed. The bumbling clown is a figure for unreadiness. While *Friar Bacon and Friar Bungay* does not convey anything like specific directives, it does contain something like broad, pragmatic advice. It forces audiences to recognize they do not live in the time the play represents, a time when a living king could give his blessing to a son on his marriage day, and further that even if they did, all ruling families are eventually subject to extinction. Audiences must accept that they have to be prepared, unlike the cowardly, easily distracted Miles, for the decisive moment when their Queen will die and the nation as a whole will go through a transition. While Greene does not have the prescience to see deeper into the future than Bacon and indicate exactly what shape that future will take, he can offer a general message that will be relevant for such a moment of transition: he highlights the dangers of ruthless ambition for personal gain, seen in the early threat of the Edward-Margaret plot, as well as such dangers in Bacon's own pretenses to greatness and power; the play further promotes an ideal of unity at home, between gentry through the negative example of Lambert and Serlsby and their sons, and through the eventually positive example of the relationship between the scholars Bungay and Bacon, as well as the bonds that are sealed between monarchy and the nobility, as in the reconciliation of Lacy and Edward, and between the aristocracy and common citizens, seen in the marriage of Lacy and Margaret.[41] The play further promotes a policy of nonbelligerence abroad in the community of nations Henry tries to build at the play's end, a community that includes even nations that, from the Elizabethan perspective, were national and religious enemies. In this especially the play seems to imply that there will be a future beyond Elizabeth, and one that will require wise statesmanship to ensure continued prosperity for England.

Friar Bacon and Friar Bungay was performed by the Queen's Men.[42] A more explicitly laudatory prophecy ascribed to the past that culminates in the reign of Elizabeth appears in another play by the Queen's Men, the anonymously authored *True Tragedy of Richard III*. The strained construction of this prophecy is telling, for it indicates the lengths the author of this play will go in order to flatter the queen. There, the character of the Queen mother steps forward at the close of the play and, along with two other figures, recites a genealogy of the English monarchy from Henry VII to Elizabeth. It is the Virgin Queen, unsurprisingly, who receives the most elaborate and laudatory speech:

> Worthy Elizabeth, a mirror in her age, by whose
> wise life and civil government, her country was defended from
> the cruelty of famine, fire and sword, war's fearful messengers.
> This is that Queen, as writers truly say,
> That God had marked down to live for aye.

This expression of confidence that Elizabeth is immortal—"marked down to live for aye [ever]"—gets around the problem of having to confront Elizabeth's death and the uncertainty of what will follow it. But as the speech progresses, the language becomes more hesitant about expressing such confidence:

> if e'er her life be ta'en away,
> God grant her soul may live in heaven for aye.
> For if her Grace's days be brought to end,
> Your hope is gone, on whom did peace depend.[43]

The passage awkwardly admits the possibility of Elizabeth's death, but it holds out immortality as an option: "*if* e'er her life be ta'en away," and "*if* her Grace's days be brought to an end." The subject of Elizabeth's mortality is phrased in the conditional, and the possibility of her death is presented as an unmitigated catastrophe: "your hope is gone." This sentiment, oddly coming just a few lines after the confident assertion that Elizabeth is "marked down to live for aye" can be said to be a product of poor playwriting or textual corruption. *The True Tragedy* has rarely received a kind word from critics, for its language or for the state of the 1594 quarto.[44] But I think there is something beyond a poet's or a printer's incompetence behind the prevarication of these lines. Here we see a voice struggling to articulate a conundrum for Elizabeth's loyal subjects: how to broach the inevitable succession question, and how to face the political realities it will entail. The author of *The True Tragedy* hedges his bet somewhat, holding out the possibility that the issue of her death might be deferred indefinitely. Greene is more willing to face the reality of Elizabeth's mortality and the uncertainty that will follow her death by simply ending Bacon's prophecy with her.

The shape of the future that could be ascribed to the prophets of the past on the popular stage looked different some twenty years after *Friar Bacon* and *The True Tragedy* were performed (and after *The Faerie Queene* was written). As Shakespeare and Fletcher's *Henry VIII* comes to a close, Archbishop Thomas Cranmer delivers a prophecy that *begins* with Elizabeth, rather than one that ends with her. Inspired by the birth of the princess, he declares: "This royal infant—heaven still move about her— / Though in her cradle, yet now promises / Upon this land a thousand thousand blessings." Cranmer's Utopian vision of Elizabeth's reign is tempered by awareness of mortality: "but she must die: / She must, the saints must have her." This is not cause for despair, though, for as the archbishop explains, despite being a "virgin" she will leave the kingdom in the hands of a capable heir:

> Nor shall this peace sleep with her, but as when
> The bird of wonder dies, the maiden phoenix,
> Her ashes new create another heir
> As great in admiration as herself,
> So shall she leave her blessedness to one
> . . . .
> Peace, plenty, love, truth, terror,
> That were the servants to this chosen infant,
> Shall then be his, and like a vine grow to him.[45]

Shakespeare and Fletcher craft here a new version of the "hindsight masquerading as foresight" motif that we have been considering, one that was unavailable to Greene and his Elizabethan contemporaries. Cranmer, a Jacobean dramatic rendition of a Henrician historical figure, is able to foresee the peaceful transfer of power in 1603 to James I because Shakespeare and Fletcher had witnessed it; they had even benefited from it professionally. By the time *Henry VIII* was performed by the King's Men, James had already lost his oldest son and heir, Prince Henry. If this gave the playwrights pause or made them feel uneasy about the perils of hereditary monarchy, it is not evident here. A second son, Charles, was there to take his elder brother's place in the line of succession. Plus, it has been argued that *Henry VIII* may have been originally written to commemorate the marriage of James's daughter Elizabeth to the Elector Palatine, in which case the play could be celebrating multiple possibilities for the future of the ruling family despite the death of Henry.[46] Whether through Charles or Princess Elizabeth, there is hope for continuity beyond the living king. As Cranmer says of James's fecundity, comparing him to a tree with growing limbs, "He shall flourish, / And, like a mountain cedar, reach his branches / To all the plains about him."[47]

The speech occurs in almost parallel position to Bacon's at the end of *Friar Bacon;* it is delivered at a ceremonial occasion to the king and his court, and it is nearly the penultimate passage of the play. Henry III called Bacon's prophecy "mystical." Henry VIII replies to Cranmer's speech with the words "Thou speakest wonders."[48] Once again, though, what seems mystical or wondrous to the onstage auditors is perfectly clear to playgoers who, like Shakespeare and Fletcher, had additional hindsight with which to work. In 1613, the ascension of James and the "branches" of his progeny were a part of the national consciousness. The vision of the future that can be projected onto the past changes decade by decade, year by year, even minute by minute. It also changes in response to what the future looks like in any given present. The King's Men, serving a generative monarch, could create in

Henry VIII the fiction of a prophecy from the past that accounts for the present and intimates futurity. The Queen's Men, serving a virgin ruler, could only offer, in *The True Tragedy of Richard III,* a confusing idea of what is to come, and in *Friar Bacon and Friar Bungay,* a pragmatic assessment: one that gives to the past the ability to see to the present, but that acknowledges uncertainty about the future beyond that, and in response promotes readiness for and a practical response to the inexorable dynastic rupture that lay ahead.

Notes

I am extremely grateful to Kirk Melnikoff, who generously read a draft of this essay and gave me many valuable suggestions for revision.

1. Marjorie Garber, "'What's Past is Prologue': Temporality and Prophecy in Shakespeare's History Plays," in *Renaissance Genres: Essays on Theory, History, and Interpretation,* ed. Barbara Kiefer Lewalski (Cambridge: Harvard University Press, 1986), 308. For a thick historical elaboration of this idea in terms of the early modern period, see Keith Thomas, *Religion and the Decline of Magic: Studies in Popular Beliefs in Sixteenth and Seventeenth Century England* (Oxford: Oxford University Press, 1971), 423–31.

2. Quotations from Spenser taken from *The Faerie Queene,* ed. A. C. Hamilton (New York: Longman, 1977), Book III.iii.49.6, 50.3.

3. On prospective heirs and general thinking about the succession in the late sixteenth century, see, for instance, David Scott Wilson-Okamura, "Spenser and the Two Queens," *English Literary Renaissance* 32 (2002): 66–67 and Catherine Grace Canino, *Shakespeare and the Nobility: The Negotiation of Lineage* (Cambridge: Cambridge University Press, 2008), 5.

4. Robert Greene, *Friar Bacon and Friar Bungay,* ed. J. A. Lavin (London: Ernest Benn, 1969), Scene XVI.62. All further quotations from the play are taken from this edition, and will be cited parenthetically in the text.

5. Here is a highly selective overview of Spenser critics who have looked at the prophecy and its political connotations: Wilson-Okamura, "Spenser and the Two Queens," Bart Van Es, *Spenser's Forms of History* (Oxford: Oxford University Press, 2002), 165ff., Harry Berger, *Revisionary Play: Studies in the Spenserian Dynamics* (Berkeley: University of California Press, 1990), 129–30, Andrew Hadfield, "Politics," in *A Critical Companion to Spenser Studies,* ed. Bart Van Es (New York: Palgrave Macmillan, 2006), 44–45, David J. Baker, "Historical Contexts: Britain and Europe," in *The Cambridge Companion to Spenser,* ed. Andrew Hadfield (Cambridge: Cambridge University Press, 2001), 47–48, John Watkins, *The Specter of Dido: Spenser and Virgilian Epic* (New Haven: Yale University Press, 1995), 155–56 as well as Watkins's article "'And Yet the End Was Not': Apocalyptic Deferral and Spenser's Literary Afterlife," in *Worldmaking Spenser: Explorations in the Early Modern Age,* ed. Patrick Cheney and Lauren Silberman (Lexington: University Press of Kentucky, 1999), especially 156–63. Ian McAdam does glance at succession issues in *Friar Bacon and Friar Bungay* in "Masculinity and Magic in *Friar Bacon and*

Friar Bungay," Research Opportunities in Renaissance Drama 37 (1998): 42–43 and 57–58.

6. See, for instance, Peter Mortenson, *"Friar Bacon and Friar Bungay:* Festive Comedy and 'Three-Form'd Luna,'" *English Literary Renaissance* 2 (1972): 194–207, Barbara Howard Traister, *Heavnely Necromancers: The Magician in English Renaissance Drama* (Columbia: University of Missouri Press, 1984) 75, and Frank Ardolino, "'Thus Glories England Over All the West': Setting as National Encomium in Robert Greene's *Friar Bacon and Friar Bungay,*" *Journal of Evolutionary Psychology* 9 (1988): 218–22.

7. See David Bevington, *Tudor Drama and Politics: A Critical Approach to Topical Meaning* (Cambridge: Harvard University Press, 1968), 223.

8. Albert Wertheim, in "The Presentation of Sin in *Friar Bacon and Friar Bungay,*" *Criticism* 16 (1974) writes that the "phrases mark a chronological progress from the present backward," 283.

9. Robert W. Maslen observes that *"Friar Bacon* stages a competition between the comic and tragic modes for dominance of its narrative," in "Robert Greene and the Uses of Time," in *Writing Robert Greene: Essays on England's First Notorious Professional Writer,* ed. Kirk Melnikoff and Edward Gieskes (Burlington, VT: Ashgate, 2008), 175.

10. Geoffrey of Monmouth, *The History of the Kings of Britain,* trans. Lewis Thorpe (Middlesex: Penguin Books, 1966), 171, 174.

11. Howard Dobin, *Merlin's Disciples: Prophecy, Poetry, and Power in Renaissance England* (Stanford: Stanford University Press, 1990), 22.

12. Virgil, *Aeneid,* trans. Allen Mandelbaum (Berkeley: University of California Press, 1971), VI.1048–50.

13. *Aeneid,* VI.899–900, VI.1141–1142.

14. Wilson-Okamura, "Spenser and the Two Queens," 82.

15. Watkins, *The Specter of Dido,* 155. See Colin Burrow, "Virgils, From Dante to Milton," in *The Cambridge Companion to Virgil,* ed. Charles Martindale (Cambridge: Cambridge University Press, 1997), 86.

16. Thomas Wilson, in *The State of England A.D. 1600,* ed. F. J. Fisher (London: Camden Miscellany, 1936), third series, lii, 2.

17. While it was illegal by the late 1580s to speculate openly on the royal succession, it was certainly a topic that occupied people's minds. See, for instance, Leonard Tennenhouse's discussion of people preoccupied by the topic in *Power on Display: The Politics of Shakespeare's Genres* (London: Methuen, 1986), 85–87.

18. See *Friar Bacon and Friar Bungay* V.67, 86, VII.48, 53, 64, 104, 115, VIII.84, 112, 124.

19. Greene used the English chronicles as a supplement to his main source, the anonymous prose work *The Famous Historie of frier Bacon;* see Percy Z. Round, "Greene's Materials for *Friar Bacon and Friar Bungay,*" *The Modern Language Review* 21 (1926): 19–23. Deanne Williams writes of the play's cultivation of, and manipulation of, a sense of the Catholic, medieval past. See *"Friar Bacon and Friar Bungay* and the Rhetoric of Temporality," in *Reading the Medieval in Early Modern England,* ed. Gordon McMullan and David Matthews (Cambridge: Cambridge University Press, 2007), 31–48.

20. For instance, in this play Greene also has King Henry refer to his residence as "Hampton House," the Tudor palace constructed by Cardinal Wolsey and given to Henry VIII in 1526 (IV.35), a more glaring error. See note 35 in Lavin's edition.

21. The moments are: IV.13; VII.68; IX.1; IX.105; IX.204; XVI.6.

22. *Richard II,* I.ii.12, quoted from *The Riverside Shakespeare,* second edition, ed. G. Blakemore Evans et al. (Boston: Houghton Mifflin, 1996).

23. See, for instance, Mortenson, "*Friar Bacon and Friar Bungay:* Festive Comedy and 'Three-Form'd Luna,'" 207.

24. Bryan Reynolds and Henry Turner write of the play's "basic homology between magic and the theatre," in "From *Homo Academicus* to *Poeta Publicus:* Celebrity and Transversal Knowledge in Robert Greene's *Friar Bacon and Friar Bungay* (c. 1589)," in *Writing Robert Greene,* 92.

25. See, for instance, *John of Bordeaux, or The Second Part of Friar Bacon,* ed. William Lindsay Renwick (Oxford: Oxford University Press, 1935), TLN 34–36 and 790–92.

26. Christopher Marlowe, *Doctor Faustus,* quoted from *English Renaissance Drama: A Norton Anthology,* ed. David Bevington et al. (New York: W.W. Norton, 2002), 4.1.45–47. Emphasis added.

27. Barbara Traister, in *Heavenly Necromancers,* talks about the scenes with the magic glass as "plays-within-the-play" and likens them to the dumb show tradition, 81–82.

28. See Kent Cartwright, *Theatre and Humanism: English Drama in the Sixteenth Century* (Cambridge: Cambridge University Press, 1999), 225.

29. Scott McMillin and Sally-Beth MacLean comment on the "lushness of dramatic speech" in the play in *The Queen's Men and Their Plays* (Cambridge: Cambridge University Press, 1998), 137.

30. Williams speaks of Bacon as a "figure of temporal break," and argues that certain moments in the play "cultivate a consciousness of historical difference" in "*Friar Bacon and Friar Bungay* and the Rhetoric of Temporality," 37, 39.

31. Canino contends that in the Elizabethan era the Plantagenets could even be viewed as "templates of disaster." *Shakespeare and the Nobility,* 13.

32. C. S. Knighton writes that by the sixteenth century "tourism was already a matter requiring regulation," in the Abbey. *Acts of the Dean and Chapter of Westminster 1543–1609, Part One,* ed. Knighton (Woodbridge, Suffolk: Boydell Press, 1997), liv.

33. On the elaborate arrangements for Eleanor's tomb, for instance, which involved provisions for tapers and the saying of intercessory prayers, see Robert Fabyan, *The New Chronicles of England and France,* ed. Sir Henry Ellis (London: F. C. & J. Rivington, 1811), 393.

34. Holinshed, for instance, writes of Edward II as one "whose disordered maners brought himselfe and manie others vnto destruction." *The Third Volume of the Chronicles* (London, 1586), 318.

35. See, too, Andrew Escobedo, *Nationalism and Historical Loss in Renaissance England: Foxe, Dee, Spenser, Milton* (Ithaca: Cornell University Press, 2004), 79.

36. Rupert Taylor, *The Political Prophecy in England* (New York: Columbia University Press, 1911), 87.

37. Greene himself wrote a pamphlet on the subject of the defeat of the Armada

called "The Spanish Masquerado" that figures the conflict with Spain as a struggle against Antichrist. On Greene and this work, see Anthony Esler, "Robert Greene and the Spanish Armada," *English Literary History* 32 (1965), 314–32.

38. Reinhart Koselleck, *Futures Past: On the Semantics of Historical Time,* trans. Keith Tribe (New York: Columbia University Press, 2004), 14–15, 17–18, 19. See also Koselleck's much more general comments on prognosis in "The Unknown Future and the Art of Prognosis," in *The Practice of Conceptual History: Timing History, Spacing Concepts,* trans. Todd Samuel Presner (Stanford: Stanford University Press, 2002), 131–47.

39. On this point, see Traister, *Heavenly Necromancers,* 74. A number of critics have noted that the play clearly condemns the notion of enclosing the island. See, for instance, Williams, "*Friar Bacon and Friar Bungay* and the Rhetoric of Temporality," 43, and Ardolino, "'Thus Glories England Over All the West,'" 220, 222.

40. This is in contrast to Greene's use of anti-Spanish stereotypes in "The Spanish Masquerado." See Esler, "Robert Greene and the Spanish Armada," 329.

41. Ardolino, "'Thus Glories England,'" makes a similar, or at least complementary, point when he remarks that the marriage of Margaret and Lacy represents the "right balance of court and Country," 223.

42. The 1594 quarto of the play names the Queen's Men on the title page. On this provenance, see McMillin and MacLean, *The Queen's Men and Their Plays,* 90.

43. Cited from *The True Tragedy of Richard III,* ed. W. W. Greg (Oxford: Oxford University Press, 1929), TLN 2225–29 and 2252–55.

44. In *The Queen's Men and Their Plays,* McMillin and MacLean compare the closing prophecies of the two plays in order to make a point about how poetically sophisticated *Friar Bacon* is in comparison (136–37).

45. *Henry VIII,* ed. Gordon McMullan (London: Thomson Learning, 2000), 5.4.17–19, 59–60, 60, 39–43; 47–49.

46. See R. A. Foakes's introduction to his edition of *Henry VIII* (Cambridge: Harvard University Press, 1957).

47. *Henry VIII,* 5.4.52–55.

48. *Henry VIII,* 5.4.55.

Declamation and Character in the Fletcher-Massinger Plays

John E. Curran Jr.

GIVEN the capacity of scholars of English Renaissance drama to disagree over just about anything, the strength of their consensus with regard to one particular issue is virtually astonishing: the superficiality of character within the plays, especially the tragicomedies, of Fletcher and his collaborators and successors. These plays repeatedly have been categorized as the hallmark of late Jacobean theatrical decadence, wherein the playwrights, eschewing with brazen irresponsibility both moral seriousness and psychological sophistication, set forth for the mere titillation of the audience vapid entertainments that rely on artificially contrived plot surprises and hyperemotional rhetorical flourishes, and that thus employ "protean characters," stock types completely conformable to the immediate needs of an isolated scene.[1] Commentators appear unanimous in this condemnation, that, as Madeline Doran says, Fletcher and his fellows always fail though they never really attempt to "show life."[2] The various expressions of this view are many and striking, but my favorite is that of the usually insightful Robert Ornstein:

> The closest parallel to Fletcher's techniques can be found today not in the "coterie" off-Broadway theater but in the daytime radio serial with its stereotyped characters and situations, its improbable melodrama, and its calculated exploitation of the housewife's escapist desire for romance and adventure.[3]

Of course this quote shows its age, but its sentiment has never in my reading been called in question. It is therefore high time for a reappraisal of the Fletcherian plays, and perhaps this as part of a larger reconsideration of our assumptions about characterization in English Renaissance drama. As a recent Forum in *Shakespeare Studies* shows, we have reached the point where we must debate whether Renaissance dramatists, even Shakespeare himself, actually undertook what we could call characterization—the construction, in Alan Sinfield's words, of "continuous selves," personae "able to look forward in self-prediction and backward in self-correction" and "able to signal a consistent sense of their own purposes and motives." Though the weight of opinion for a long time has favored the negative side of this debate, Richard Levin has spoken persuasively for the affirmative in his account of over-protesters. Might Levin's view be further evidenced if we can find that this concept of characterization, with personae exhibiting something like "a sense of continuous selfhood,"[4] applies to the very subset of Fletcherian tragicomedy wherein we would least expect it?

If any group of plays seems vulnerable to the charge of bad characterization, or non-characterization, it is surely the one comprising the Fletcherian plays based on the Controversiae of the Elder Seneca: *The Queen of Corinth, The Double Marriage,* and *The Laws of Candy.* All three though the second is technically a tragedy have tragicomic tendencies, including the wild situations that could conceivably turn in any direction, the preoccupation with noble virtue and honor, and the language of passionate emotion.[5] All three though the third has sometimes been ascribed to Ford[6] are collaborations involving at least two hands, those of Fletcher and Massinger; and, as Robert Kean Turner observes in examining *The Queen of Corinth,* with which Field also helped, collaborations are apt to produce muddled and discontinuous characters.[7] Finally, all three have their supposed excesses abetted by Seneca Sr. The Elder Seneca, often confused with his more famous son the playwright and philosopher, had recorded as models for rhetorical instruction his recollections of and comments on a series of old declamations—mock debates, rhetorical jousting matches. The Controversiae were his digest of the forensic branch of the declamations, the topics of which were often fanciful laws—such as one making ingratitude actionable—with even more fanciful cases applying them.[8] For Eugene Waith and others following his lead, Senecan declamation offered Fletcher and especially Massinger the wildly improbable "hypotheses," the high-pitched, sententious style, and the showcasing of debate that naturally suited and thus did much to shape their dramaturgical practice.[9] The influence of Seneca Sr. would seem to threaten the further attenuating of a dramatic mode that was plenty flat already: to drain from Fletcherian drama what little "life" was potentially in it by inviting the undisciplined playwrights to hurl their cardboard characters into one grossly unnatural scene after another, and thence into gratuitous fits of stilted forensic oratory. Students of the effects of declamation on Renaissance literature have described how rhetorical training imparted a healthy sense of two-sides-to-every-story,[10] but if such a sense, however healthy, contributed anything to characterization, none seem to think it did so for the Fletcherians.[11] What such commentators largely miss, however, is that Seneca's Controversiae by their very nature did have much to add to characterization in Jacobean drama; and in fact, in these three plays the background of Senecan declamation helps the collaborators craft personages individualized well beyond stock type, as they are endowed with psychological depth and with consistency, in terms of both their past and their unfolding lives. Whether these plays manage to "show life" I am unwilling to speculate. But the main characters in *The Queen of Corinth, The Double Marriage,* and *The Laws of Candy,* through their varying kinds and degrees of deviation from an ideal of virtue, are formed with motivations and drives both complex and internally coherent; and the Controversiae stimulate this character-formation because they induce their participating declaimers, and hence our playwrights, to address the motives and drives of specific imagined selves.

That the Controversiae should promote analysis of character is not an obvious point and requires some explanation; after all, no less an authority than Quintilian himself cast a cold eye on just such declamatory exercises, citing especially their lack of realism.[12] But they did so indeed, and this in two important ways.

The first is their manner of often involving, and sometimes even demanding, the practice of ethopoeia, the figure of impersonation: crafting the imagined speech that a certain person might deliver in a given situation.[13] It has been remarked that in theory and practice ethopoeia entailed merely a kind of Theophrastan characterization, in which a representative of a stock type is granted only those touches of vividness that would set off the "notes" marking that type.[14] But the Renaissance understanding of ethopoeia could go well beyond Theophrastanism, as Erasmus's *De Copia* shows. Giving many examples of "variety in characters belonging to the same general type," Erasmus explains that when fashioning characters according to type, decorum (as always) is to be observed, yet individual personalities nevertheless are to be brought forth, by means of personal qualities which while they do not violate the standards of the type do nothing to illuminate them and exist without reference to them.[15] Such qualities instead illuminate the specific personage and exist in reference to him or her alone. The Controversiae of Seneca Sr. encourage just such a process of character-fashioning. They are teeming with types—pirates, heroes, tyrants, cranky fathers, restive sons—but since in each controversia a personage is thrown into such a bizarre situation, often incumbent on the declaimers is to determine the nature of that specific personage, that nature having done so much to give rise to that situation in the first place. Why, in Controversia IX.i, would Cimon, sued for ingratitude by his father-in-law, be grateful enough to his late heroic father to undergo prison as ransom for his body, and yet ungrateful enough to his benefactor, the plaintiff, not to refrain from killing an adulterous wife? What about his constitution or his collection of experiences makes him able to endure prison but not adultery? Each declaimer pretending to speak as or for Cimon or his father-in-law is forced to concoct a believable psychological profile, outlining Cimon's peculiar combination of principled honor and stubborn pride, of strengths and maybe even (what we would call) neuroses. This controversia, which inspired Massinger and Field in *The Fatal Dowry,* is entirely in keeping with the modus operandi of the Controversiae.[16] Although Seneca leaves only skeletons of the actual speeches as they were originally declaimed, the extant fragments being mostly collections of sententiae, it remains clear from what we have that declaimers were commonly bound to imagine something of the characters of their subjects, and thus to practice ethopoeia virtually as a matter of course. This is evident when we observe how *The Orator* of "Lazarus Pyott," a series of cases each assigned both a pro and a con speech, includes a great number of the Controversiae, but in a concentrated form, in a given case arranging select lines of several of Seneca's declaimers into two monologues; rather than bits and pieces of many different declaimers speaking as or for Cimon, we have in *The Orator* one speech on Cimon's behalf, his pro se defense, and another in the voice of the plaintiff, his aggrieved father-in-law Callias.[17] Each Senecan speech in *The Orator* being an amalgam of the points of Seneca's declaimers, we catch a glimpse of what each discrete declaimer was trying to do: make persuasive an imagined person's position in a thorny dispute, often in part by imagining what *that* person would say to be likable and logical within the parameters dictated by the case, and thus producing a kind of miniature dramatic characterization wherein we must learn something of who someone is. Shakespeare's use in *The Merchant of Venice* of Declamation #95 of *The Orator,* "Of a Jew, who would for his debt haue a pound of flesh of a Christian," is an obvious instance of the helpfulness of these speeches to the forging of distinctive characters;[18] a great many of *The Orator*'s Senecan declamations hold the same potential as this non-Senecan one, and hence we see how the Controversiae can contain the rudiments of drama and how they might be exploited for that purpose.

The other way the Controversiae enabled characterization was through their foregrounding of "colores." A declaimer's "color" was a "hook" or "spin" or "angle" he decided to take in working with a case's facts. In Seneca's Controversiae the speeches of the various declaimers are excerpted and many of the colores appear within these excerpts, but to many controversiae are also added Seneca's own remarks on the declaimers' methods and degrees of effectiveness, and this commentary is intently concerned with evaluating colores. A glance at the various colores of a controversia, whether we observe them in the speech-fragments or in the commentary, shows that to generate a color was often to conceptualize the subject's motive for doing something, and thus, by extension, to infer what personality might be indicated by such a motive. For example, Seneca in his commentary mentions that some declaimers disagreed about whether Cimon ought to be envisaged as attacking the character of the father-in-law; should he claim himself not ungrateful on the basis of gratitude being dependent on honor, saying that the father of an adulterous whore ought to welcome her death, or on the basis of Callias's contemptible nature, saying that all necessary gratitude was discharged merely by Cimon's lowering himself to marry into such a family? Did perhaps Callias help Cimon out of prison only for self-serving reasons, seeking to elevate his family's standing with the connection to the noble Cimon?[19] One's slant on these questions would constitute an important color; and we see how determining such a slant would also be at one with determining the basic thought-processes of the two litigants. Perhaps Cimon respects his father-in-law, but this respectfulness makes his wife's heedlessness about honor all the harder to take, for she has wronged them both, and perhaps Callias had the purest of altruistic purposes in freeing Cimon and giving him his daughter, and thus Cimon aware of this had all the more cause to be galled by her betrayal; but then, an altruistic Callias would have all the more cause to deem Cimon ungrateful. In fashioning a color, we have begun to fashion a Cimon and a Callias. *The Orator*'s Cimon gestures at the color impugning Callias's motive, while *The Fatal Dowry* takes a different tack, assuming a respectful "Cimon" (Charalois) and an honorable "Callias" (Rochfort). In what sense are we positing that Cimon is not ungrateful, and if not ungrateful, what was he thinking and why? That construction of colores should lead to construction of character naturally follows from the forensic matrix of the Controversiae. In a forensic context an orator was necessarily dealing with a hypothesis rather than a thesis—a definite and specific rather than an indefinite and general question.[20] In emphasizing this distinction between hypothesis and thesis, Joel B. Altman and Thomas O. Sloane both show that training in rhetoric advantaged the Renaissance writer by teaching him to approach broad human issues indirectly through particular cases—sexuality considered not with "should a man marry," but rather with "is marriage good for *this* man."[21] Such an advantage held for deliberative arguments (like this one) as well as for forensic, but in the latter it was inherent; this we see in the Controversiae, with their constant focus on matters of equity. Through the colores, which Altman calls "highly refined interpretations of motive and cause," the declaimer ventures to answer convincingly the specific questions of equity emanating from the facts, in effect developing and fleshing out the specific hypothesis; hence in every discrete controversia the personages are or can easily become what Altman calls the parties in the trial scene of Sidney's *Arcadia:* "fictional hypotheses."[22] Is a fictional hypothesis so conceived far from being a character?

In these three Fletcher-Massinger plays, the fictional hypotheses and the ethopoeic constructions embedded in the Controversiae are indeed adapted into dramatic characters. Each play includes some Theophrastan types, it is true, but in each case these are only minor figures within the dramatis personae;[23] the main personages in all three plots are of a different species altogether, one whose categories are marked out not by types but by degrees and kinds of moral inadequacy. Helpful here in describing these categories is J. Leeds Barroll's theory linking characterization to Renaissance concepts of humanity's common impulse to reconnect with the transcendent: since under transcendental theory all humans "aspire," it might lead an author to consider what would "serve to differentiate a specific man from the total of human beings on earth"; so the "study of how men really behave, the characterization of human beings, develops as a study of departures from the desirable."[24] A person is what he or she loves; and people are differentiated one from another in how they misconstrue what they love or falter in their aspiration toward it. Characters in these plays are individualized in just such a way, through the conception of a particular imagined person's particular falling short of perfection. In our three plays, four categories of departures from the ideal may be seen to emerge: 1) the depraved and villainous but still somehow vulnerable; 2) the upright and heroic, outstanding in both goodness and greatness, but still somehow compromised; 3) the mostly virtuous and sympathetic but seriously flawed; 4) the mostly contemptible but not basically evil. These categories help set off the complexity and depth of characterization here, as we observe how the personages are grouped according to their mode of aspiration and delusion; but there is additional complexity in how members of each group differ from each other in the nature of their drives. And matters grow even more complex, and characters still further individuated, when we cite a fifth category wherein a personage fits into none of the above-named four, but instead into some blend of two of them. Each play comes equipped with a specimen of this fifth, mixed category: *The Queen of Corinth*'s Merione, *The Laws of Candy*'s Cassilane, and *The Double Marriage*'s Martia. And yet, even with all this complexity, the playwrights' control over the characters remains intact. Martia is never a cipher whose motive is situational, the product of plot-demands; like those of Levin's overprotesters, her reactions to changing circumstance spring from an imagined personality which though not simple maintains its oneness, operating in accordance with its own temperament and with its own recent and distant past. This holds for all the characters examined below: the plots' twists do not produce them; rather, their imagined psyches, patterned with internal cohesion, create the plots. The Controversiae underpin and abet this entire system, but for a great many of these characters—in fact, we find representatives in each category but the first—the source in Senecan declamation directly affects their depth and consistency; motives and drives are envisaged, and shaped to make sense, in light of the ethopoeia in or implied in the Controversiae and of the colores of Seneca's declaimers.

The first category is by far the simplest, but its members are still more than mere monochromatic villains; *The Queen of Corinth*'s Crates, *The Laws of Candy*'s Gonzalo, and *The Double Marriage*'s Ferrand are all evil, but all are differentiated from stock types, and their particular psychological ills establish the principal themes that allow us to understand the other characters. The most sophisticated villain is Crates, who hates and intrigues against his virtuous younger brother, the Queen's favorite Euphanes, and who eggs on the troubled Prince Theanor to monstrous vice, including the horrid rape of Merione. Partly an evil counselor and partly the Theophrastan "Elder Brother" from the Overburian Characters,[25] Crates is actually driven by a much deeper inner turmoil than these types would indicate: obsessive fear of the world's tendency to turn men into toadies who "part with their essence" (I.i.105–7). Horrified at how selves get lost in social convention, what he calls "formes" (II.iv.43), with crime he strikes out through the Prince at all kowtowing, especially at that which he associates with Euphanes, whose polished courtiership wins him huge influence with the Queen. To Crates, who has long felt slighted by his brother (I.ii.155–66), Euphanes has been utterly changed by travel and promotion, "A man drawne up, that leaves no print behind him/Of what he was" (II.iv.33–34), and has subsequently forced an analogous change on the entire country, as all must accommodate themselves to him (III.i.1–14). Crates is reclaimed, realizing both that in being a prince's familiar he has not avoided playing a role, just fallen into a particularly wretched one (IV.iv.25–27), and, as his schemes and then his bitterness are dissolved by Euphanes' eloquence, that courtly acumen does not preclude sincerity (IV.iv.2–8, 99–107). But thus this reclamation, insofar as it is indeed a breaking down of his paranoia about "formes," has been believably prepared and accounted for. Crates proves amenable to a kind of psychological diagnosis, even as through him the play poses an interesting question: is successful social performance ever truly free from suspicion? What is the cost to ourselves of being ingratiating to the powerful? Gonzalo is an ambitious machiavel, a Venetian lord who has infiltrated Candy's inner circle so he can snatch power for Venice and, eventually, for himself; this he plans to do by romancing with striking chutzpah the vain Cretan princess, Erota, and ruining her best man, the old general Cassilane. Like many another stage machiavel Gonzalo is devoid of conscience and in love with his own trickery, but unlike most machiavels he is an odd combination of the menacing and the absurd, insidiously adept at exploiting others' pride, yet in another sense a Politic-Would-Be. His downfall comes about because of his own affliction with that very same failure of empathy and self-criticism which he tries, initially with prospects of great success, to use in others to their destruction; in the process he advances the theme of pride, rendered in the play as an ignorance of others' feelings and of one's own limitedness of vision. Ferrand, too, is a rare mixture of the dreadful and the impotent. English Renaissance drama is quite overpopulated with tyrants, who variously get sunk in pleasure or in murderous insecurity, but few in my reading enjoy their power less and hate themselves more than Ferrand. By his own misery Ferrand is *tortured,* which goes to an idea at the heart of the play. Being confronted with Juliana's courage, loyalty, and defiance as she endures the rack is clearly a torture to him, as derided and "contemn'd" he must finally yield, ignominiously "conquer'd" (I.ii.109, 118, 138). This scene borrows heavily from Controversia II.v and its descriptions of the wife tortured by a tyrant for her rebel husband's sake, and *The Orator*'s wife even claims that "the Tyrant himselfe was tormented at my tortures."[26] But the character of the tyrant is of little concern in Seneca or *The Orator*, so long as it's a given that he is surpassingly cruel; thus the playwrights have departed from the controversia to show us something of who *this* tyrant is, in part so he can help them build up this central theme of torture and what it really means: facing unbearable truth, especially about oneself. With Ferrand, as with Crates and Gonzalo, the playwrights make much more out of a villain than they easily could have made: Ferrand is not just any tyrant, nor Crates just any evil counselor/elder brother, nor Gonzalo just any machiavel.

The portraits of the villains and the themes they bring up have a great bearing on the development of characters of the second category, the excellent but still imperfect heroes: *The Queen of Corinth*'s Spartan Queen and Euphanes; *The Double Marriage*'s Juliana; and *The Laws of Candy*'s Antinous. And in the latter two cases, the Controversiae are a decisive factor in character construction.

The Queen and Euphanes have an extravagant goodness that in itself drives the plot, especially insofar as it brings them into conflict with Crates and Theanor through the aforementioned problem of ingratiation. The Queen and Euphanes both excel at dutiful self-control, and admire this in each other. The Queen rigidly, and commendably, enforces an idea of self-sacrifice for the common good, on her subjects and on herself. She breaks up her own son's love affair for reasons of state and expects his full compliance, for she is capable of the same kind of self-abnegation when she perceives it warranted (I.i.38–39): she automatically takes Euphanes' part over Theanor's during the rebellion, much more concerned for the life of a meritorious servant than for a worthless son's (IV.iii.131–42), and both here and in sentencing the guilty Theanor to death she proclaims her political motherhood much more binding on her than her biological (IV.ii.14–22, V.ii.115–24, V.iv.136–41). For his part Euphanes mirrors her civic piety by being as forgiving and indulgent of Theanor as the Queen is hard on him; she is willing to abjure her ties to her son, while Euphanes is willing to ignore Theanor's insults, profess the obedience he owes to his prince, and refrain from seizing the opportunities for power (and revenge) the Queen's love affords (III.i.185–209). For the sovereign and for the subject alike, personal feelings are magnanimously put aside, including their mutual attraction: Euphanes turns his back on it, and thus too on ambition, to keep faith with his previous contract with Beliza; and the Queen's disappointment, even while her wrath is only feigned, is genuine, but she subdues herself (III.i.320–24). And yet this heroic self-discipline can seem bothersome. In the Queen's promotion of Euphanes and her strangely decisive detachment from Theanor, she is so zealously impartial that she appears partial—swayed by her feelings, of sexual desire for Euphanes, of revulsion for Theanor's weakness, and even of reveling in her posture of and reputation for irreproachable authority. As for Euphanes, he always does the right thing, but always does so in a style that will obviously raise him in others' esteem. In begging the Queen not to retaliate against Theanor's depredations, Euphanes merely increases her favor of himself and her alienation from her son (III.i.252–343). Euphanes is so good at looking good that he looks somewhat amiss. Though he and his Queen are both heroes in terms of virtue, courageous and pure of motive, neither is a paragon, for neither can let down for even a moment their facade of piety, and neither can see how that facade might come across in the eyes of those closest to them, and thus how it might have bad effects. Euphanes' and the Queen's carriage and their treatment of each other enact inherently good but apparently suspicious rituals of ingratiation, and as such do plenty to feed Crates' malcontentedness, and give him plenty of ammunition for his goading of Theanor into crime. It is not that the heroes are "at fault" for anything; but the play's trouble comes about because Euphanes, the Queen, Crates, and Theanor are who they are. If either the Queen or Euphanes were less stubbornly honorable or more sensitive to the fragile psyches of their family members, the plot would never work. The combustion is sparked only by the interaction of these especial ingredients.

Juliana is likewise stubborn in her goodness in a manner which makes her a hero but which also qualifies that heroism; specifically, she is heroically ready to undergo torture for noble causes, and yet a bit too ready to torture herself and hence to torture others. In conjuring her the playwrights have done some delicate work with Controversia II.v, in which the wife, having been physically broken in maintaining her silence to protect her tyrannicidal husband, sues him for ingratitude, now that he has slain the tyrant and tried to divorce her in order to find a new wife in better childbearing condition. In this dispute the plaintiff has a decided advantage, at least in terms of equity; unsurprisingly the surviving excerpts from the declamations are lopsidedly for her. If she is to be attacked at all the declaimers must address two questions, one regarding colores and the other ethopoeia: her level of knowledge of her husband's plotting; and her level of devotion to him. First, we might think that if she knew nothing, we could thereby undermine the praise she earns for her silence; but Seneca tells us otherwise, as he notes approvingly the opinion of Fabianus and Lucius Vinicius that the only way to weaken the wife's position was to assume she knew everything.[27] If the husband had had a plan and told her about it, we can call keeping silence merely the discharging of her wifely duty, and no real boon to him. Second, can we use her stance in her suit of ingratitude to impugn her character? If truly so impeccable, wouldn't she concede her barrenness, and patiently want her husband to enjoy children and the state to gain the children of a tyrannicide? *The Orator*'s husband protests his statesmanlike desire for children, even invoking Cato, and accuses the wife of selfishly placing her own pleasure before the needs of the commonwealth; the wife's speech, meanwhile, gives some ground to the husband's on this point by her self-aggrandizing and spiteful tone: "why would he put me away, to take a richer wife? For one more noble he cannot haue."[28] So perhaps the husband can aid his ill-favored cause at least a bit by holding that true love and pure motive preclude the suit. *The Double Marriage* brings forth a distinctive hero in light of these questions: Juliana does not merely learn all about Virolet's plan to assassinate Ferrand, but persuades her husband to confide in her as his closest adviser and compatriot; and then, tortured for her husband's sake but cast away by him for a new wife, she disputes him not at all, instead viewing him still as "a noble, and an honest Gentleman" (III.iii.263). On both counts, her knowledge and her devotion, Juliana is informed by what would constitute the weakened position of the controversia's wife, but the effect of this is to garner even greater sympathy for her. She is not only more than sage, discreet, and tough enough to be entrusted with her husband's secrets, but she is also heroic enough not to think herself a hero; and she loves him enough to let him go and think the best of him. Another effect, however, is to present us with a lady a little too inclined toward loss and pain.

Juliana is no simple "Virgin Martyr" with a masochistic appetite for self-sacrifice,[29] as she is endowed with desires and passions; but thus she is all the more complex in her penchant for depriving herself of that which is rightfully hers and which she really does want, and thereby tormenting herself and others, especially Virolet. In three episodes this penchant is examined, each playing off Controversia II.v. First, in I.i she enthusiastically embraces her husband's preoccupation with the planned tyrannicide, even though it has been what's kept him from embracing her in their bed. She is driven by no mere death-wish or pathological thirst for honor: her sense of duty and of patriotism-before-pleasure is ingrained, having been impressed upon her by her family (I.i.135–49), and she dearly wants her husband to survive his "glorious enterprize," even urgently advising him to abort the mission when she discovers it is suicidal (I.i.252–83). Her prioritizing of his public cause over her own very strong private yearnings references one of the wife's main points in the controversia, that her failure to conceive a child before her torture, when the shadow of tyranny and her husband's distraction discouraged sex, cannot be held against her;[30] but this reference merely highlights how Juliana seems bound both to deprive herself of pleasure and to forgo any sort of leverage that might come of such deprivation. Here, she expressly pines for her husband's physical "ardour" but *applauds* him for denying it, canceling both her enjoyment and any sense that she is a victim of circumstance. Indeed, at the play's opening she is already offering to give up her claim to Virolet, inferring from his coldness that he is seeking pleasure elsewhere (I.i.23–37); her sincere love is intertwined with an impulse to crush her own spirit, which in turn pains her husband, here inducing him to reveal to her his cares about Naples's suffering and his plans for a coup. The way is paved, then, for the second episode, in which she again concedes to a prospective substitute, this time one real instead of imagined (III.iii), and again tortures her husband and herself with her concessions. Unlike in the controversia,[31] which gives it special focus, Juliana's supposed barrenness after the torture is a nonissue, transparently a pretext forged by the lawyer to secure a divorce (III.iii.254–55); given much greater grounds for dispute than Seneca's wife, Juliana refrains. Nor though she easily could does she dispute the point of Martia, her rival, that (as per the controversia) a wife's not informing on her husband, even under torture, is merely her duty (III.iii.206). Though much more attached to her husband than seems the controversia's wife, Juliana doesn't fight for him. This is another sign of her abundant goodness, but it once again inflicts harm on herself and on Virolet, who responds in the worst way possible: he decides to be cold to Martia. Enraged, Martia scorns Virolet, leading to the third episode: Juliana's unconscionable, but fully characteristic, refusal to enjoy him until they are ceremoniously reunited in marriage. Virolet feels "torments" over the false divorce (IV.iii.35) when she approaches him with the news of Martia's vendetta against him, but after Martia confirms that she now abhors Virolet and releases all claim on him, Juliana is resolved to suppress her urges until a church wedding can sanctify them. She even says that if properly married to him she would deem the rack or any other torture worthwhile so long as she could pleasure him (IV.iii.170–204)—a sharp reminder to us that her rectitude in this her final concession is torturing them both. What the Senecan wife ultimately seems to want is ratification of her status as the true wife, even though she probably cannot physically enjoy it; in this light, it says much about Juliana that, fully ratified as and fully capable of acting as *the* wife, she cannot bring herself to accept her victory. Where the controversia suggests an unusually virtuous wife, the play makes her more virtuous still; and yet the play also gives that virtue a vague dark side. Does Juliana somehow punish herself for desiring pleasure? Does she punish Virolet, latently disdaining his inferiority to her? What unbearable truth is encoded in all her torturous concessions? It's hard to tell. But what's clear is that her character is sufficiently well drawn to repay such speculation about hidden drives, and that her personality has an enormous causal influence on the plot. Everything is different if Juliana is another person, one either less passionate in love or more aggressive in its pursuit.

Antinous like Juliana is a hero derived from the much stronger disputant in a lopsided controversia, and like Juliana's his heroism is, in the play's detailing of his personality, made greater than what the controversia seems to call for, but is also just a bit problematized. In Controversia X.ii, a father and his son have each earned military laurels, but their society can only reward one hero, and the son insists on pressing his claim; when he wins the prize, he requests as his reward that statues be erected commemorating his father, who in a rage disinherits him, hence bringing on the suit. The son is the heavily favored party, having fairly won his reward, tried to use it to glorify his father, and incurred the father's wrath anyway; for the father's side there is only one short excerpt tacked on at the end of Seneca's commentary. But despite this imbalance—or maybe even thanks to it—the scenario very much lends itself to the examination of character, as the case would seem to hinge on the ethopoeic construction of who these two men are and on the colores' ingenuity in divining their intentions. So, why did *this* young man fall into contention with his own father? The declaimers of Controversia X.ii invent many excuses for why the son was prevented from giving way,[32] and in creating Antinous, the play selects from them in a manner which stresses his goodness, especially the profundity of his respect for his father. Antinous initially gains credit by seeming openly and honestly to stand up for his worth against another worthy candidate, and he wins out not because his father, Cassilane, is made a lesser fighter by age, but because the soldiers and senate legitimately judge Antinous's actions in this particular battle to have been the more awe-inspiring. Antinous reveres Cassilane, and tells him firmly that such reverence entails imitating him, and thus accepting the payment earned for valor, no matter who offers to compete for it (I.ii). But as it turns out, this apparent openness and honesty conceal an agenda: after winning, commissioning a statue of Cassilane as his reward, and being met with Cassilane's unquenchable ire, Antinous explains: "What I did, was but onely to inforce/ The Senates gratitude. I now acknowledge it" (I.ii.323–24). Though as admirable in promoting his own cause as Seneca's son could conceivably be, Antinous was not really promoting his own cause at all, but Cassilane's. Thus the play forwards two of the controversia's seemingly contradictory lines of argument—"I contested you because I have a sense of honor befitting your son" vs. "I really did it all for your glory"—subsuming one in the other to the highlighting of Antinous' virtue: set up liking his decorous self-respect, we must finally like his singular filial piety. Moreover, this sense of his virtue is further cemented when we note that, like Juliana, he never engages in the dispute at the controversia's center. As Juliana concedes mournfully but obediently to the outrageous divorce, accusing Virolet of nothing, so does Antinous concede to his outrageously being disinherited, resorting not to law but to humble pleas to the adamantine Cassilane (I.ii.359, III.ii.181–82); and Antinous' love, like Juliana's, abates not at all despite having been rejected.

But also like Juliana's, Antinous's character is not angelic, but human; a hero but no god, he is tinged with that version of pride Gonzalo helps the play to define. Insofar as pride is tantamount to exaggerating one's own greatness, Antinous is guiltless of it, as "far . . . from arrogance" as he claims to be (I.ii.285). But as we learn watching Gonzalo, another form of pride is a failure to appreciate the feelings of others and to examine and check oneself. If the reason Antinous contended with Cassilane for the prize was all along to solidify his father's legacy, he has been loving in his calculations—but also unmindful of his father's sensibility. If we believe that he truly intended to bolster his father's fame in the dispute, on some level he also intended to bolster his own, and in the process he forgot to factor in his father's character. Antinous has evidently inherited his father's thirst for praise, and must know, as Euphanes must know with his shows, how this show is going to play to its audience: all will marvel at his magnanimity. And, unsurprisingly, they do: "Thou art immortall, / Both for thy Son-like pietie, and beauties / Of an unconquer'd minde," says the yet-untarnished Gonzalo, speaking for the assembly (I.ii.296–98). With this gesture the young hero gets the accolades of his entire society—as he must have imagined he would. But Antinous, poised to bask in everyone's laudations, has neglected to account for how his father, being the particular man he is, will likely take all of this. Cassilane reacts very badly, yes; but Antinous knows his father, and should be better able to consider how he'll react. Thus while he earnestly wants his father's approval, he fails to foresee that he cannot obtain it in the same way he can that of everyone else. This is a rather slight and forgivable variety of pride, and certainly much lesser in degree than that of Cassilane; but it is of the same kind: an insularity, a lack of regard for the subtleties of someone else's feelings and a lack of self-scrutiny. He is mortified at being out of Cassilane's graces—"How have I lost a Father? Such a father?" (I.ii.350)—and is so immersed in grief that he cannot even think about Erota's passion for him. But he learns not enough from this mortification and grief, and decides to make a deal with Erota, agreeing to accept her love on condition of her relieving his father's debts and keeping their bargain a secret from Cassilane (IV.i.115–21). Not only is he too caught up in trying to be a good son to do proper justice to Erota's feelings; he is also once again not predicting a predictable catastrophe, given his father's nature. His aid is bound to be divulged to Cassilane, who will then explode in fury. This last error-of-pride sets off a chain reaction, as Cassilane's pride consumes him in vengeance. Soon the combined pride of Antinous, Cassilane, and Erota threatens doom for them all, as they all serve each other with death sentences under the law against ingratitude (V.i),[33] and only Antinous's sister Annophil's improvised solution—indicting the whole world with ingratitude, in a reductio ad absurdum—can save them. A true hero, noble in both his fortitude and his loyalties, Antinous nevertheless has a blemish, his insularity, and he too late discovers this about himself; thus he manifests in his own way the play's concept of pride. The controversia, then, has provided a situation which could only come about because of the personality of a certain young man, one who dishonored his father while he tried to do him honor; in delineating this personality, the play has capitalized on Seneca's dramatic possibilities.

In characters of the third category, blemishes metastasize sufficiently that the basically good are disqualified from hero-status, becoming more a part of the common herd. Erota is one of these. Though a savvy and majestic leader in the tradition of the Fletcher-Massinger queens—*The False One*'s Cleopatra, *The Sea Voyage*'s Rosella, and the Queen of Corinth—Erota's vein of pride, combining insularity with silly haughtiness, causes her to lose the gravitas of these other women. But the best representative of the third category is *The Double Marriage*'s Virolet, whose character owes much to the Controversiae, having been constructed with a method similar to what we saw with Juliana: like hers, his character emerges from contrast with Seneca's ethopoeia and colores; like hers, his character is drawn as a party in a dispute which never arises, because the party does not or constitutionally cannot controvert the case. Virolet, in keeping with the play's title, is composed from the husbands of two different controversiae: the ungrateful tyrannicide husband from II.v and the grateful husband from I.vi, whose marriage to the pirate chief's daughter as payment for her rescuing him alienates his own father and gets him disinherited. This divided provenance would seem to bode ill for Virolet's coherence as a character. But the playwrights have coordinated the two controversiae expertly, extracting from each the makings of a well-meaning man torn apart whenever called upon to decide something. Because of his characteristic inability to make choices when choosing is neccesary, in a single movement he deliberately but unwillingly becomes both husbands at once: he consents to marry Martia. The character of the man who made this very well-intentioned but very poor choice is a peculiar interweaving of the two Senecan husbands; specifically, Virolet is made benevolent but hapless by throwing him into a combination of the husbands' situations, depriving him of their best excuses, and having him then scourge himself for his imprudence. In Controversia II.v the ungrateful husband, who scores some points from his successful tyrannicide, can try to explain himself by claiming that the tortured wife did him no real favor and/or that he cares deeply about becoming a father; Virolet, who remains markedly unsuccessful, never undervalues Juliana's sacrifice, nor does he make any sort of issue out of her supposed barrenness. Meanwhile, the grateful husband of Controversia I.vi, in a far better position for debate, can argue the seemliness of his loving faith to the kind girl who saved him and left her family for him, as well as the unseemliness of his father's prejudice against her;[34] Virolet's faith to Martia, not loving at all, stems from only a regretful sense of obligation, and his father, Pandulfo, is appalled with Martia only because he's wholeheartedly in Juliana's camp. Unlike his Senecan counterpart, Pandulfo wants and expects his son to keep a previously plighted troth; Virolet *shares* his father's attitude, and has no argument to make with him. Faced with the crisis of Martia's offer of rescue, Virolet is stunningly undone: despite his loving gratitude to Juliana he becomes an ingrate toward her, and despite his gratitude to Martia he becomes an ingrate because unloving toward her. He is in a bind, a dilemma much more puzzling than that of either Senecan man; but his lapses of wisdom do much to create that bind and thence to worsen it. The drama comes from his knowledge of this; the forensic dispute preempted, it turns inward, raging within himself, and he cannot but be accused and convicted, and sentenced to torture.

In connection with Virolet's name, connoting virility, some have read the play as a study in the ambiguities of manliness and his character as a study in weakness,[35] but Virolet is weak only in comparison to Juliana; the issue of his emotional strength is not nearly as important as that of his proneness to blundering. When we meet Virolet we are struck by his fervent patriotism and ambition to be an instrument for his nation's freedom, and yet also by his ineptitude. The conspiracy ruined before it begins, Virolet decides to go through with what he knows will be an ineffectual, even suicidal rebellion. As Juliana wakes him up to the folly of this and prescribes hiding, Virolet rebukes his own discomposure: "Thou art constant; / I an uncertain foole, a most blinde foole" (I.i.283–84). Thereafter, his choosing to agree to Ferrand's deal, pardon in exchange for his undertaking a campaign against Sesse, compounds his problem—for would not death at Ferrand's hands be preferable to hunting, in Ferrand's service, Ferrand's enemy? Naturally, brave but inept Virolet loses the battle, and Sesse chides him for this bad decision; Virolet says pointedly, "No more of these Racks; what I am I am," and asks for death (II.iii.37). Lacking neither courage nor principle, he was forced to weigh options, bumbled into the wrong one, and now feels tortured. His defiance of Sesse and philosophical patience in his captivity prove that weakness is not what holds him down; indeed, his Stoic resignation, which must have been what once attracted Juliana, now attracts Martia, and her judgment is sound. The goodness and honor he exudes are really there within, as she perceives (II.iv.123–24). But it is one thing to be unfazed by her threats, and another to handle her fierce love and sudden offer of deliverance—for in the latter case he's pressed into a choice, and so becomes unhinged. Accepting Martia is obviously the worst course; no substantive good for his captive friends in Naples can come of it, and he himself can much more easily endure Martia's torturing of his body (see II.iv.120), and death itself, than he can the torture that will rack his soul upon losing Juliana. At this critical juncture he is given few lines, but the scene nevertheless shores up our sense of his character, for this is *the* decision for him, and he is utterly flabbergasted: "What shall I do?" (II.iv.165), he sputters helplessly. He later tries unavailingly to console himself by noting his good intentions (IV.iii.1–31); his torture *does* come of his moral sensibility, for he *could* simply enjoy both women, if he didn't care about his promise to Martia, didn't honestly love Juliana, and didn't hold marriage in such sanctity. But good intentions cannot prevent his being "tormented" (IV.iii.21); observing his own virtue cannot stanch the pain of knowing that, as is his wont, he opened the very wrong door and is consequently at fault for everyone's misery. And he keeps opening it; having opted to divorce Juliana and adhere to Martia, and having been exposed to the latter's fieriness, he certainly should not choose to be cold to her. Treating her otherwise than as a proper wife is bound to have terrible ramifications, but once again the prudent course eludes him. To keep faith with both women is untenable, and trying to do so, as he does, is ill-advised in the extreme; as before his substratum of good intent collides with an urgent situation demanding a choice, and Virolet is overwhelmed. Each of these missteps brings him, and with him Juliana, closer to death, and her accidental slaughter of him merely culminates the process. Bewildered as Sesse's rebellion erupts around him, and overcome with self-recrimination at his own floundering (V.ii.32–33), he desperately chooses to disguise himself as Ferrand's minion, thinking to gain either access or death, and quickly meets Juliana's dagger. Thus she is, unknowingly but appropriately enough to her character, one final time depriving herself of her desire, hurting herself and him; and they both pay dearly for his incapacity to make a decision, as she soon dies of a broken heart. More prudence or less scruple would serve Virolet well. But then he wouldn't be *this* character, and the plot would never unfold.

While Virolet chooses poorly but feels commendably, characters of the fourth category, though not villains, are laden with base feelings. This category includes Sesse, who as Ferrand's implacable foe is exempt from villain status, but who continually demeans himself with the ways he directs and expresses his merciless wrath. In all his dealings—his exile's origin in an exceedingly petty quarrel (II.i.94–120), his cruelty to all Neapolitans regardless of their attitude to Ferrand (II.i.50–56), but especially his going berserk over his daughter's defection (see II.v.47–57)—Sesse though an aristocrat has about him that savagery with which the declaimers of Controversia I.vi would brand the pirate chief. Another high-born savage is the fourth category's most conspicuous member, the lost soul Theanor. Here the operative source is Controversia I.v, a dispute between two girls who, raped by the same man, demand mutually exclusive forms of restitution, one his death and the other his hand in marriage. This controversia rests on matters of personality to a lesser extent than the others we have examined, as the declaimers are primarily concerned with the logic of fairness; both girls cannot be satisfied, so which one can be denied with the least injustice? This logic slants toward the side of the girl requiring death, for she gets nothing from the other's marriage, while the death sentence grants revenge to both; moreover, a serial rapist should not benefit from redoubled crime. The would-be bride, meanwhile, can only say that if two claims be equally valid, the milder should prevail.[36] Her case might gain ground, however, if a certain line of argument involving motive were more fully developed: a strong mutual love between her and her attacker. While some of the colores would assume him a mere insatiably lascivious beast, there is in others the suggestion that there was already some sort of relationship between him and the girl who would marry him.[37] The play builds its Theanor by taking this premise a vital step further: what if both rapes stem from the man's despair at being deprived of his true love? What if he and his beloved, who now pleads for his life, are meant to be together, but have been kept apart? Such a color could work for the would-be bride, because, in designating the man as her long-ago chosen husband, it would maintain the propriety of her desired marriage, the harshness of depriving her of it, and the extenuating circumstances that twist an ordinary man into doing extraordinary evil. The play, then, generates its own color for this particular case, a color which posits a horrid crime committed by a pusillanimous but less-than-horrid man.

Theanor and Merione, the play establishes, simply belong together, and their separation is at the root of Corinth's distemper. Though this love affair is underwritten, the play does manage to convey it,[38] and so does manage to explain how Theanor is capable of succumbing in such abominable fashion to his feelings of emasculation and powerlessness. We have noted how his mother continually displaces him, such that he is all the more susceptible to Crates' evil advice; though Theanor, absurdly insecure as to his mother's affection and his political stature, is much more receptive than he ought to be to Crates, the Queen's repeatedly casting the Prince aside and favoring Euphanes does much to substantiate the picture Crates paints.[39] But this problem of feeling humiliated and abandoned by his mother in itself cannot account for his seeking an outlet in rape. It is by her specific act of taking Merione away that he is symbolically castrated. The couple were in the final stages of a long and graceful courtship, which the Queen had enthusiastically sanctioned, when Merione was suddenly handed over as a peace-token to Agenor (I.i.24–35). For Theanor the rape Crates proposes is viewed as a kind of "help" (I.i.64): certainly this in the sense of channeling his resentment of his mother, but also, I think, in the sense of getting out his feelings of frustration and agony at being barred by her from his lawful heart's desire. With the plotted rape drawing nigh, he dissimulates in court, feigning to relinquish obediently all claim to "what once / I lov'd above myself" (I.iii.86–93); he seethes beneath this veneer, his trenchant sense of what he's missing palpable.

Theanor is a lowly man whom his marriage would have elevated, and lacking it, he finds perverse solace in descending into an abyss of lowliness, declaring and compounding his now certain ruin by the ruin of what would have saved him. Cut off from her, he enacts a sick parody of the health-giving union that should have been and that now being lost burns him. Hence the gruesome masque-dance around her and the sprinkling water on her after the rape, gesturing to the celebratory bliss, the harmony, and the cleanness of the wedding that should have been;[40] and hence, with his face covered, his silently drawing his dagger in answer to her request that he, to her a mere anonymous thief of her virginity and dignity, marry her (II.i.22–41): they should have married, but now are deadly strangers to each other. The dagger also symbolizes what to each of them is both never-to-be-attained desire and never-to-be-reached salvation: she craves either marriage or death, but he withholds both and consigns her to what is to her a death-like life of shame; just so, he has lost access to marriage and death—he initially thought death a preferable "help" (I.i.64) to this—and been consigned to death-like shame, as this very act stamps him indelibly with that incurable shame she ascribes to herself. The devilish logic of the first rape makes more comprehensible, though no less awful, the second. Everything that is Theanor's has been appropriated by Euphanes, except the shame and guilt for raping Merione; Euphanes having proven immune to Theanor's effort to transfer this guilt onto him, the Prince again seeks "help"—what he here calls "quiet" (IV.iv.19)—in further self-debasement, this time by setting out to spoil what Euphanes is permitted to enjoy but he is not: marriage with the right partner. Raping Beliza at once lashes out at Euphanes, and through him at the Queen, and repeats Theanor's urge to attack marriage, something necessary for but unavailable to him.[41] His final contrition, too, is more understandable on the same basis: kept from acting on this manic, self-loathing impulse to express his despair through his misdeeds, he is capable of genuinely hating them (V.iv.15–17). Thus while the play's comic resolution in the idea that his raping Merione was no crime, in that the two were bound in de facto marriage (V.iv.196–99), is as awkward morally as it is in terms of plot, in terms of Theanor's character it makes thematic sense. They were *supposed* to have been married all along, and his downward spiral came from lacking her; thus his renewal, and the play's happy ending, come with a sense that their union is a kind of inevitability. Tragedy nearly prevailed because of a denial of the truth which at last all must acknowledge: Theanor needs to be with Merione. Theanor is not a mere filler for the controversia's animalistic rapist, so that its plot can be set sensationally on stage.[42] Rather, that rapist is expanded into a particular case-study, such as the more deft and pleasing one Fletcher and Massinger produce with Lisander in *The Lovers' Progress,* of the adverse effects on a man of not having his woman.

Sesse and Theanor, though in much different ways, are bad men who aren't really villains; this is complex enough, but for characters of the fifth category complexity is such that they fit comfortably into no single category, but straddle two. Each character has a unified and stable personality with conflicting dimensions to it, and each, interestingly, is an elaboration of the analogous figure in the Controversiae.

Merione, Theanor's beloved, falls into both the second category and the third, as she appears both heroic and non-heroic, all at once. This double sense of her might be attributable to her anomalous status as a rape-victim who lives,[43] or to bad characterization, but I suggest otherwise: perhaps she is conceived and drawn as a particular woman who defies pat categories. Everything Merione does has a dimension of heroic self-possession and another of non-heroic conformity with protocols—with, that is, the dictates of ingratiation. In this she has moorings in Controversia I.v's victim-who-requests-marriage; to the extent any sort of ethopoeia emerges from her speech in *The Orator,* she appears sympathetic in being a stalwart for both mercy and her own rights, but every point she makes is bound up with honor in some way: the Sabines with forgiveness of and marriage to their ravishers were "no lesse honest but more discreet" than Lucretia and Virginia, and more numerous, and so her own marriage ought to be judged acceptable.[44] Merione too has a seemingly independent spirit but keeps checking herself against society's approval. When we first meet her she simultaneously questions her brother Leonidas's right to marry her off and imposes it on herself (I.ii.15–22). In deferring to him she is also bowing to her society's expectations, showing obedience as a sister and as a subject to the Queen, who pushes for diplomacy's sake the marriage to Agenor; and yet isn't Merione also in a way independent-minded, even heroic here in sacrificing herself for the greater good, which good includes allegiance to her independent-minded, heroic Queen? Merione is basically virtuous, but her virtue consistently walks this tightrope of the headstrong and the compliant, and her response to the rape epitomizes this. She faces down her cowardly attacker with forceful indignation and also with remarkable composure, such that we see how Crates' plan to use spectacle to madden her into shocked silence could not possibly work (II.iii.10–13); but thus composed she seeks marriage with her assailant, pleading that his "foul will" would be made "fair with marriage" (II.i.37)—a rather thorough subordination of self to society, this. Then again, at the same time there is more boldness in demanding marriage than there is in asking the assailant merely for secrecy and abandonment, as in the case of Cervantes' Leocadia.[45]

Being as she is, then, Merione refuses to forgive herself for her "shame" but also resolves to live on with it, which invokes the problems of the Lucretia template, but with twists and particularities. Lucretia martyrs herself for warped standards of female chastity, but is also heroic in that it is she who assumes the right to determine the severity of what she's been through. So when Crates calls Merione "no Lucrece" (II.iii.17–23) he is and is not correct. He thought that obsession with reputation would silence her, but it does no such thing. Like Lucretia she openly declares herself ruined forever, heedless when others implore her to get over it, and enjoins the men around her to avenge her (II.iii.89–123, 154–72). Also like Lucretia, however, she is demonstrating her extreme obedience to the code of virginity. But how does her living on, even lapsing into an inability to speak (III.ii), inflect all this? On the one hand, in living on Merione outdoes Lucretia's heroism, by making her statement in her own way, without dying for it; but on the other hand, perhaps she nullifies any statement, losing a self-assertive protest in a passive, quiet victimhood. Of course, unlike Lucretia's, Merione's attacker is the man who's supposed to be her husband; but even so, what does it mean that she agrees to take Beliza's place and undergo rape a second time?[46] This might be her own unorthodox, very un-Lucretia-like way to seize her happiness as well as save the day, or it might be yoking herself with the most degrading sort of ingratiation to her society—agreement that since the right man has ravished her, she's not really been harmed. Hence while her adaptation in the trial scene of the Senecan woman is only of feigned exigency, it reflects her divided nature: Merione boldly proclaims that her honor should be held as sacred as Beliza's (V.iv.60–62), and that she is as worthy as Beliza to have the Queen grant her wish (V.iv.121–27); and yet in the process she reestablishes honor as the priority, while leaving us no assurance that a life with *Theanor* is what *she* truly *wishes* for. Merione throughout exerts a will that is both singular and common, and her character, with her double-sided reactions to events from start to finish, both moves the plot forward and furthers the play's inquiries into ingratiation.

If Merione both is and is not outstanding in noble self-assertion, Cassilane belongs to both the second category and the fourth. He has a greatness about him commensurate with that of a hero, yet his version of pride does not merely qualify this greatness; it nearly cancels it out. Controversia X.ii contains little from the father's point of view in the extant fragments, but the suggestion about him, from the very structure of the dispute, is that he is a battle-hardened soldier whose honor, which means everything to him, is in a doubtful state because of his age, and he reacts to this doubt with an embittered defensiveness about that honor, which only serves to undermine it. Though it appears he's had a long and storied career, the father holds that only his most recent deeds can be recognized for him not to be disgraced; in fact, to him losing to the son in the contest seems to erase all the honor of that career, as though it must be viewed as never having happened unless validated by glory *now*. The color he is afforded expresses this very thing: so I'll not forget this defeat, boy, you'll cast my ignominy in bronze.[47] Cassilane storms out of the senate striking exactly this note (I.ii.325–33); he is the controversia's father fully embellished, with the liminal state of his honor between past and present a problem hanging over him, which he responds to in so poor a manner as to devolve into a near-villain. The contradiction implied in Seneca is here apparent: Cassilane argues for the prize by citing his fifty-year service (I.ii.152–56, 215–16), as though viewing the celebration of his current deeds as, in large measure, a just reward for all his previous ones; and yet he sees his son's proposed monument to those old deeds as an unendurable slight on them (I.ii.314–19), as though the only honor that counts is the honor which his fresh deeds force Candy to hand over. His confusion about his identity humanizes Cassilane, making him a hero-with-a-blemish; but his cantankerous and unreasonable demand that he be worshiped according to both sides of the equation casts him into another, inferior mold. It is in this that his self-isolating pride is the play's most egregious, for he sees people not as other souls but as mere reflectors of his own glory. His solipsism blinds him to the impossibility of his being satisfied, for if his son gave way the superiority of Cassilane's current deeds could not be authenticated, and so he either wins the prize illegitimately or loses; but he is blind also to the love and goodwill indicated by the efforts to satisfy him. Excuses are offered for Cassilane on general bases—"Old men are chollerick" (I.ii.348)—and on particular ones, as Antinous conjectures that his father's "great heart," never vulnerable to fear through a lifetime of war, is now acutely vulnerable to passions of anger and sorrow (II.i.302–10); these do and do not work for him. He is an old man only just now observing his age and confronting obsolescence, and after so long and so pressured a career, he is understandably touchy about how he's to be viewed, having earned his society's and the audience's indulgence of his foibles. And yet he is at the same time a contemptible, self-centered old misanthrope, as hateful toward loved ones and as emotionally unstable as Sesse or Theanor. This blemished hero/near-villain character while difficult to categorize is crucial to making Cassilane's reclamation understandable and believable. When he learns he's beholden to Antinous for discharging his debts, his enraged pride boils over, shutting out any trace of consideration for his son's intents; not even Antinous' guilty plea to the charge of ingratitude assuages Cassliane in his desire to have his own son killed. Though this madness does not violate his prideful character as we have seen it—we might even say this was ever his trajectory—it is so extreme that his recovery from it is almost necessary for him if he's not to appear radically revised, as though he'd never had a heroic aspect. But even in recovery he overlaps categories. A true hero, one whose fundamental sensibility eschews baseness, must at length overcome such insane pride, and Cassilane does, blessing his son, begging forgiveness, and shaking off his ravenous appetite for "popular applause" (V.i.321–30). And yet, this very appetite helped him to this turnaround, as it was instigated by a chorus of warnings about the infamy that would graft itself onto Cassilane forever should he persist (V.i.293–314); there remains in him an element of that same baseness which started all the trouble—his overweening concern for how he'll be celebrated. With Cassilane the playwrights have enlisted Controversia X.ii to depict, as they do brilliantly with the less heroic, more obstinate Sir John Van Oldenbarnavelt, the psychology of a man whose lust for "popular applause" burdens his old age, such that it threatens to undo all he's worked for over a lifetime.

Finally there is Martia, in whom the third and fourth categories intersect with the utmost intricacy. Never a hero and never a villain, she is somewhere in between, but her level of goodness is very difficult to gauge.[48] She has obviously inherited her father's hot-temperedness and been influenced by him to be overbold in pursuit of desire and to brook no insult; but does this nature and nurture in her background, being beyond her control, make her a mostly forgivable, basically good person, or merely explain her basic badness? Her past life lies behind her falling in love and running away with Virolet—and her thereby altering everyone's destiny—but how so? Perhaps her response to him shows her to be at her core a kindhearted soul who, ignorant and impressionable, and encountering goodness for the first time, falls under its spell; or perhaps, while she purports to love Virolet's virtue, she truly has the spirit of a pirate, whose knee-jerk response to something pleasant is to plunder it. This tantalizing character, whom we get to know well but still find difficult to judge, is a derivation of the Senecan pirate chief's daughter. Though she's not a disputant in Controversia I.vi, the girl's character is of critical import to the case. What drives her? The declaimers, says Seneca, mostly agree that her intentions were not lustful or rebellious, but compassionate. And yet, her upbringing among pirates and her turning on her own father point to a disconcerting wildness in her; Seneca's laurels go to Arellius Fuscus' exposition on how the man cannot love his deliverer, so unpredictable in her temerity.[49] Martia, though she views herself as an aristocrat, and binds herself to what she thinks is aristocratic comportment, has actually been brought up as, and acts the part of, a barbarian. She cheers on her father's worst enormities, his mercilessness and his petty grudge-holding, wrongly understanding them to be noble (II.i, esp. 135–44); she goes to great lengths to prove to Sesse that she shares his values, but they are, with some refinements—humanity toward non-Neapolitans—those of a cutthroat pirate. Hence she comes to the captive Virolet as a practiced torturer, through imitation of her father (II.iv.46–47). That Virolet is unafraid of torture at first amazes, and then excites her; her father's scoffs at dangers and wounds have not prepared her for *this* type of "Noble mind" (II.iv.124). But what is the nature of her amazement? Does she glimpse and admire a more civilized mode of life which beckons to the person she truly is underneath all the bluster? Or is he a kind of rare, new treasure for her to grab, the situational and moral obstacles keeping her from it—he's married—to be rashly dismissed?

We hope for the former but the latter dogs us; she seems to be or to have the potential to be a better person than Sesse, but there's always the suspicion that she's her father's daughter after all. Pressing her claim to Virolet before his shocked wife and father, she holds that for Virolet she has suffered tortures far beyond what Ferrand did to Juliana (III.iii.209–29): this reminds us that she has in fact been victimized, not just in the escape but throughout her hard life; but we must recall that she's in the process here of stealing an innocent woman's husband, and wonder if she's also, at least unconsciously, torturing her victim. We must wonder too about the violence of her anger at Virolet's withholding sex from her, which ends up throwing her into the arms of Ferrand. Perhaps this is best seen as the sad retrogression of a person driven toward good but abruptly deprived of hope; suddenly denied Virolet's civilizing influence, and having given up everything for it, she naturally backslides to her brutal condition. But is she merely perceiving an insult in not getting her way, and reacting with utterly disproportionate vindictiveness—Virolet deserves "no end of torments" (IV.ii.86)—the way her father always does? Is her wildly seeking Ferrand perhaps the equivalent of her father's wildly seeking her, a similar mad dash for revenge? Her savage upbringing surely informs Martia's reactions, but we're not quite sure to what extent, and so, like Sesse's own men (IV.iv.60), we're unsure how much to pity her. At Ferrand's side she is tortured at the sight of the victorious Sesse (V.iii.117–21), and pleased to be killed; does this signal that she has always been Sesse's victim, as the creature of his savagery, or that she is essentially at one with him, and tortured only by their separation? Like Seneca's declaimers, we tread on uncertain ground in approaching her true self.

What is certain is that we are dealing with a coherent character to which we can reasonably apply this type of analysis, and that Controversia I.vi has made such a reading more, not less, practicable. We should note in closing that in not one of these plays is the outcome of the plot hinged on the outcome of the Senecan-based dispute at hand: the dispute in *The Queen of Corinth* is rigged; the parties in *The Double Marriage* refuse to dispute; and the dispute in *The Laws of Candy* is at first rigged, and then refused. These are no frivolous courtroom dramas, wherein the characters exist for the sake of plot. Rather, Seneca's Controversiae are tapped for their value in building characters, from whose particular personalities dramatic situations can grow. This is by no means an infallible dramaturgical formula; no debt to the Controversiae nor anything else can save *The Fair Maid of the Inn* from stupidity.[50] And no one claims our three plays as masterpieces; there are unsightly gaffes in *The Queen of Corinth*, such as Leonidas' forgetting that he's Euphanes' alibi, and his unforgivably inane line: "Such pretty Lawyers, yet / I never saw, nor read of" (V.iv.71–72). Nevertheless, these plays are inhabited by well-wrought characters, ones formed by a process which, helped by declamation, has granted them at least a portion of mimetic inwardness. If this claim be true, perhaps we should revisit our conception not only of the Fletcherians, but also of character in Jacobean drama—of, that is, how, and how well, it works.

Notes

1. Frank Humphrey Ristine, *English Tragicomedy: Its Form and History* (New York: Columbia University Press, 1910), xiv, 111, 115–17; E. H. C. Oliphant, *The Plays of Beaumont and Fletcher* (New Haven: Yale University Press, 1927), 39–44, 60–63; Milton Boone Kennedy, *The Oration in Shakespeare* (Chapel Hill: University

of North Carolina Press, 1942), 170–71; Lawrence B. Wallis, *Fletcher, Beaumont, and Company: Entertainers to the Jacobean Gentry* (New York: King's Crown, 1947), ix, 144–46, 219–20; Eugene M. Waith, *The Pattern of Tragicomedy in Beaumont and Fletcher* (New Haven: Yale University Press, 1952), 9–11, 25, 28, 38–41 ("protean characters" is Waith's); Una Ellis-Fermor, *The Jacobean Drama: An Interpretation,* 3rd ed. (London: Methuen, 1953), 25–26, 201–26; Madeleine Doran, *Endeavors of Art: A Study of Form in Elizabethan Drama* (Madison: University of Wisconsin Press, 1954), 199–201, 217, 369–70; Robert Ornstein, *The Moral Vision of Jacobean Tragedy* (Madison: University of Wisconsin Press, 1960), 163–69; Clifford Leech, *The John Fletcher Plays* (Cambridge, MA: Harvard University Press, 1962), 35–36; Charles Osborne McDonald, *The Rhetoric of Tragedy: Form in Stuart Drama* (Amherst: University of Massachusetts Press, 1966), 28, 267, 285–86; George C. Herndl, *The High Design: English Renaissance Tragedy and the Natural Law* (Lexington: University Press of Kentucky, 1970), 228–59; Arthur C. Kirsch, *Jacobean Dramatic Perspectives* (Charlottesville: University Press of Virginia, 1972), 38–47; Joel B. Altman, *The Tudor Play of Mind* (Berkeley: University of California Press, 1978), 395; Robert Kean Turner, "Collaborators at Work: *The Queen of Corinth* and *The Knight of Malta,*" in *Shakespeare: Text, Language, Criticism: Essays in Honour of Marvin Spevack,* ed. Bernhard Fabian and Kurt Tetzeli von Rosador (Hildesheim: Olms-Weidmann, 1987), 315–16, 325–26; David Farley-Hills, *Jacobean Drama* (Basingstoke: Macmillan, 1988), 164–85; Lee Bliss, "Beaumont and Fletcher," in *A Companion to Renaissance Drama,* ed. Arthur F. Kinney (Oxford: Blackwell, 2002), 536. Discussions finding thematic value in Fletcherian tragicomedy, especially regarding politics and gender, ignore characterization; see Leech, *Fletcher Plays,* 32, 36–38; Mary Beth Rose, *The Expense of Spirit: Love and Sexuality in English Renaissance Drama* (Ithaca: Cornell University Press, 1988), 184–86; Philip J. Finkelpearl, *Court and Country Politics in the Plays of Beaumont and Fletcher* (Princeton: Princeton University Press, 1990), 6–7; Peggy Munoz Simonds, *Myth, Emblem, and Music in Shakespeare's* Cymbeline*: An Iconographic Reconstruction* (Newark: University of Delaware Press, 1992), 29–65; Kathleen McLuskie, "'A Maidenhood, Amintor, at my Years': Chastity and Tragicomedy in the Fletcher Plays," in *The Politics of Tragicomedy: Shakespeare and After,* ed. Gordon McMullan and Jonathon Hope (London: Routledge, 1992), 92–121; Ira Clark, *The Moral Art of Philip Massinger* (Lewisburg: Bucknell University Press, 1993), 15–16. See also three essays in the collection *Renaissance Tragicomedy: Explorations in Genre and Politics,* ed. Nancy Klein Maguire (New York: AMS, 1987): John T. Shawcross, "Tragicomedy as Genre, Past and Present," 24–26; James L. Yoch, "The Renaissance Dramatization of Temperance: The Italian Revival of Tragicomedy and *The Faithful Shepherdess,*" 115–38; William Proctor Williams, "*Not* Hornpipes and Funerals: Fletcherian Tragicomedy," 143–46. For Massinger's moral seriousness detracting from characterization, see John S. Wilks, *The Idea of Conscience in Renaissance Tragedy* (London: Routledge, 1990), 221–22. For the thematic worthlessness of the Fletcher plays see Sandra Clark, *The Plays of Beaumont and Fletcher: Sexual Themes and Dramatic Representation* (New York: Harvester Wheatsheaf, 1994), 156.

    2. Doran, *Endeavors,* 370; see also 233–34. For more recent affirmations of this rather fuzzy standard see Harold Bloom, *Shakespeare: The Invention of the Human*

(New York: Riverhead, 1998), 5; Robin Headlam Wells *Shakespeare's Humanism* (Cambridge: Cambridge University Press, 2005), 27. For problems in discussing characterization see Elizabeth Fowler, *Literary Character: The Human Figure in Early English Writing* (Ithaca: Cornell University Press, 2003), 3–5.

3. Ornstein, *Moral Vision,* 166–67.

4. Forum: "Is There Character After Theory?" *Shakespeare Studies* 34 (2006): 21–74; see Alan Sinfield, "From Bradley to Cultural Materialism," 29; Richard Levin, "Protesting Too Much in Shakespeare and Elsewhere, and the Invention/Construction of the Mind," *English Literary Renaissance* 37 (2007): 352–59, quote 354.

5. On *The Double Marriage* as having a tragicomic structure see Waith, *Pattern,* 132–34; Marvin T. Herrick, *Tragicomedy: Its Origin and Development in Italy, France, and England* (Urbana: University of Illinois Press, 1955), 266–67; Clark, *Moral Art,* 192.

6. For a synopsis of the earlier phase of the debate over the authorship of *The Laws of Candy,* and a guarded though convinced attribution of almost all of it to Ford, see Oliphant, *Plays,* 472–85. But Oliphant does argue, I think rightly, that the inclusion of a play in the Beaumont and Fletcher First Folio (1647) makes for firm evidence that Fletcher had some significant hand in it (468); and this play was so included. For Ford see also Cyrus Hoy's Textual Introduction to his edition of the play (see note 23 below). For *The Laws of Candy* as one of the Fletcher-Massinger declamation plays, see Eugene Waith, "John Fletcher and the Art of Declamation," *PMLA* 66 (1951): 229; and esp. Bertha Hensman, *The Shares of Fletcher, Field, and Massinger in Twelve Plays of the Beaumont and Fletcher Canon,* 2 vols. (Salzburg: Universität Salzburg, 1974), 2:224–38.

7. Turner, "Collaborators," 316–17.

8. For Seneca Sr. and Roman declamation see Michael Winterbottom's Introduction to his edition, *The Elder Seneca,* 2 vols. (Cambridge, MA: Loeb Classics, 1974), 1:vii–xxiv; S. F. Bonner, *Roman Declamation in the Late Republic and Early Empire* (Liverpool: University Press of Liverpool, 1949), 31–43.

9. For scholars who trace Fletcherian drama's links to declamation and at least imply a negative judgment of them see Waith, *Pattern,* 86–98, 187–90, 203–7; Waith, "Fletcher," 226–34; Waith, "*Controversia* in the English Drama: Medwall and Massinger," *PMLA* 68 (1953): 286–303; Donald Lemen Clark, "Ancient Rhetoric and English Renaissance Literature," *Shakespeare Quarterly* 2 (1951): 202–3; McDonald, *Rhetoric,* 28–29, 34–35, 47–65, 262, 267; Leech, *Fletcher Plays,* 37; Brian Vickers, *Classical Rhetoric in English Renaissance Poetry* (London: Macmillan, 1970), 72–73; Kirsch, *Perspectives,* 38; Hensman, *Shares,* 1:174–75, 192–93; Clark, *Moral Art,* 31–32, 36–37, 191–92. For the adverse effects of debate on drama see Kennedy, *Oration,* 7–12; Doran, *Endeavors,* 316–22; on Beaumont and Fletcher plays, Ellis-Fermor, *Jacobean Drama,* 223–24; on Massinger esp., Oliphant, *Plays,* 60–63, 68. For the bad effects of declamation on the drama of Seneca Jr. see Bonner, *Declamation,* 162–67.

10. Sister Miriam Joseph, *Shakespeare's Use of Art and Language* (New York: Columbia University Press, 1947), 203–5; McDonald, *Rhetoric,* 120, 265–66; Walter J. Ong, *Rhetoric, Romance, and Technology* (Ithaca: Cornell University Press, 1971), 65–66; Richard A. Lanham, *The Motives of Eloquence: Literary Rhetoric in the Re-*

naissance (New Haven: Yale University Press, 1976), 1–35; Altman, *Tudor Play,* 3–4, 31–34, passim; Arthur F. Kinney, *Humanist Poetics: Thought, Rhetoric, and Fiction in Sixteenth-Century England* (Amherst: University of Massachusetts Press, 1986), 19–22; Kinney, "Rhetoric and Fiction in Elizabethan England," in *Renaissance Eloquence: Studies in the Theory and Practice of Renaissance Rhetoric,* ed. James J. Murphy (Berkeley: University of California Press, 1983), 385–93; Clark, *Moral Art,* 21–22; Quentin Skinner, "Moral Ambiguity and the Renaissance Art of Eloquence," *Essays in Criticism* 44 (1994): 267–92; Thomas O. Sloane, *On the Contrary: The Protocol of Traditional Rhetoric* (Washington, D.C.: Catholic University of America Press, 1997), 8–11, passim; Neil Rhodes, "The Controversial Plot: Declamation and the Concept of the 'Problem Play,'" *Modern Literary Review* 95 (2000): 609–22; Peter Mack, *Elizabethan Rhetoric: Theory and Practice* (Cambridge: Cambridge University Press, 2002), 158–64. For the advantages of tragicomedy for such multivalency, see Nancy Maguire, Introduction, *Renaissance Tragicomedy,* 6–8.

11. See Altman, *Tudor Play,* 29–30, 53, 104–5, 395; Kinney, *Poetics,* 22–23, 288.

12. Quintilian, *Institutio Oratoria,* 4 vols., trans. H. E. Butler (Cambridge, MA: Loeb Classics, 1920–22), II.x.3–15, 1:272–79, V.xii.17–23, 2:306–11, X.ii.12, 4:80–81, X.v.14–23, 4:120–27. See also Bonner, *Declamation,* 80–82. See also Erasmus, *Ciceronianus,* trans. Betty I. Knott, in *Collected Works,* vol. 28, ed. A. H. T. Levi (Toronto: University of Toronto Press, 1986), 433–34; *Ciceronianus,* in *Opera Omnia* I-2, ed. Pierre Mesnard (Amsterdam: North Holland, 1971), 695–96.

13. For sources see *Rhetorica ad Herennium,* trans. Harry Caplan (Cambridge, MA: Loeb Classics, 1958), IV.l-lii, 386–99; *Aphthonii Progymnasmata,* trans. R. Agricola and J. M. Catanaeus, with notes from R. Lorichius (London, 1616), fols. 128–39; Richard Rainolde, *The Foundacion of Rhetorike,* ed. Francis R. Johnson (New York: Scholars' Facsimiles and Reprints, 1945), fols. xlix–li. On these works and ethopoeia see Joseph, *Shakespeare's Use,* 10, 16–17, 20, 127; Donald Lemen Clark, "The Rise and Fall of Progymnasmata in Sixteenth and Seventeenth-Century Grammar Schools," *Speech Monographs* 19 (1952): 259–63; McDonald, *Rhetoric,* 18–19, 41, 43–46, 75–87; Wilbur Samuel Howell, *Logic and Rhetoric in England, 1500–1700* (Princeton: Princeton University Press, 1956), 140–43; Altman, *Tudor Play,* 45–53; Brian Vickers, *In Defense of Rhetoric* (Oxford: Clarendon Press, 1988), 26–29, 47–49; Kinney, *Humanist Poetics,* 9, 19–20; Mack, *Elizabethan Rhetoric,* 27–29, 42. For a Renaissance account see Thomas Wilson, *Arte of Rhetorique,* ed. Thomas J. Derrick (New York: Garland, 1982), 357–58, 373.

14. Benjamin Boyce, *The Theophrastan Character in England to 1642* (Cambridge, MA: Harvard University Press, 1947), 24–49; Bonner, *Declamation,* 150, 162; Mcdonald, *Rhetoric,* 47–49, 87–88, 94–95; Waith, "*Controversia,*" 288–89; Doran, *Endeavors,* 218–20, 225–28; Sister Joan Marie Lechner, *Renaissance Concepts of the Commonplaces* (New York: Pageant Press, 1962), 219–23; J. Leeds Barroll, *Artificial Persons: The Formation of Character in the Tragedies of Shakespeare* (Columbia: University of South Carolina Press, 1974), 23–26; Christy Desmet, "The Persistence of Character," *Shakespeare Studies* 34 (2006): 50–52.

15. Erasmus, *De Copia,* trans. Betty I. Knott, in *Collected Works,* vol. 24, ed. Craig R. Thompson (Toronto: University of Toronto Press, 1978), 583–84. See also *De Copia,* in *Opera Omnia* I-6, ed. Betty I. Knott (Amsterdam: North Holland, 1988), 208–10. See also Quintilian, *Institutio,* XI.i.39–42, 4:176–79.

16. See *Elder Seneca,* IX.i, 2:214–35; and also *Senecae Rhetoris Suasoriae, Controversiae, Declamationumque Excerpta,* ed. Andrea Schottus (Heidelberg, 1604), 113–16. For Seneca Sr. and *The Fatal Dowry,* see Waith, "Controversia," 296–303; Hensman, *Shares,* 1:49–65; Introduction to *The Fatal Dowry,* in *The Plays and Poems of Philip Massinger,* vol. 1, ed. Philip Edwards and Colin Gibson (Oxford: Clarendon Press, 1976), 3–4; Clark, *Moral Art,* 180–81 .

17. Le Sylvain, *The Orator,* trans. Lazarus Pyott (London, 1596), 185–89. For a list of the Senecan declamations in *The Orator* see Waith, *Pattern,* 203–4.

18. *The Orator,* 400–406. See Rhodes, "Controversial Plot," 615–18.

19. *Elder Seneca,* IX.i.11–12, 2:226–29; Schottus, 114.

20. See Quintilian, *Institutio,* III.v.5–18, 1:398–407; Aphthonius, *Progymnasmata,* fols. 151, 153.

21. Altman, *Tudor Play,* 64–67; Sloane, *On the Contrary,* 95–96.

22. Altman, *Tudor Play,* 29, 101–5. On colores and motive, see Quintilian, *Institutio,* IV.ii.88–100, 2:98–105. On determining motive in forensic cases see also *Ad Herennium,* I.xvi.26, 50–53, II.iii.5, 64–67; Wilson, *Arte,* 193–94.

23. All references to these three plays are from *The Dramatic Works in the Beaumont and Fletcher Canon,* 10 vols., ed. Fredson Bowers et al. (Cambridge: Cambridge University Press, 1966–96): *The Queen of Corinth,* ed. Robert Kean Turner, vol. 8; *The Double Marriage,* ed. Cyrus Hoy, vol. 9; *The Laws of Candy,* ed. Cyrus Hoy, vol. 10. For Theophrastan character in Massinger see Hensman, *Shares,* 2:425–27; on the characters in question here, 1:215–20, 1:180–81, 2:235.

24. Barroll, *Persons,* 80–81, 50.

25. *The Overburian Characters,* ed. W. J. Paylor (Oxford: Basil Blackwell, 1936), 17–18. See also Hensman, *Shares,* 2:426.

26. *Elder Seneca,* II.v.6–7, 1:324–27; Schottus, 82; *Orator,* 264.

27. *Elder Seneca,* II.v.18–19, 1:338–43; Schottus, 83.

28. *Orator,* 264–66.

29. For "Virgin Martyrs" see Simon Shepherd, *Amazons and Warrior Women: Varieties of Feminism in Seventeenth-Century Drama* (New York: St. Martin's, 1981), 179–201, for Juliana 182–83. See also Clark, *Plays,* 74–77. Juliana is also compared to Shakespeare's Portia, Nancy Cotton Pearse, *John Fletcher's Chastity Plays: Mirrors of Modesty* (Lewisburg: Bucknell University Press, 1973), 172–73; Clark, *Moral Art,* 192. But Juliana has a much more active role than Portia's, and more sexual energy.

30. *Elder Seneca,* II.v.16, 1:336–39; Schottus, 83.

31. *Elder Seneca,* II.v.13–15, 1:332–37; Schottus, 83.

32. *Elder Seneca* X.ii, 2:388–407; Schottus, 135–37.

33. For gratitude as the staple of Massinger's moralizing see Clark, *Moral Art,* 23, passim. The preoccupation with gratitude in *The Laws of Candy* is probably internal evidence for its inclusion in the Fletcher-Massinger canon.

34. *Elder Seneca,* I.vi, 1:134–51; Schottus, 58–60; *Orator,* 223–25.

35. Pearse, *Chastity Plays,* 176; Shepherd, *Amazons,* 182–83; Clark, *Moral Art,* 192, 198–99; Clark, *Plays,* 74.

36. *Elder Seneca,* I.v, 1:120–35; Schottus, 56–58.

37. See Cestius Pius, *Elder Seneca,* I.v.1, 1:122–23, I.v.8, 1:132–33; Schottus, 56, 57. Interestingly, this suggestion is used *against* the would-be bride.

38. Merione expresses her attachment to Theanor I.ii.30. Their love is at least hinted at in Pearse, *Chastity Plays,* 159–61; Turner, "Collaborators," 317.

39. For discussions emphasizing the rape as a protection of Theanor's masculinity and an opposition to his mother, see Suzanne Gossett, "'Best Men are Molded out of Faults': Marrying the Rapist in Jacobean Drama," *English Literary Renaissance* 14 (1984): 315–16; Karen Bamford, *Sexual Violence on the Jacobean Stage* (New York: St. Martin's, 2000), 133–43.

40. See Clark, *Moral Art,* 37–38.

41. Perhaps this is something like what Merione is saying in her plea to marry Theanor: he could not enjoy that first rape, and he then fell into a second, because those first "embraces" "were unlawfull, / Unbless'd by *Hymen,* and left stings behind them, / Which from the marriage bed are ever banish'd" (V.iv.99–101). This is cryptic, but it suggests to me the notion that Theanor was plagued by the lack of marriage, and that this is related to both crimes.

42. See especially Bamford, *Sexual Violence,* 133–43.

43. Gossett, "Marrying the Rapist," 316–17.

44. *Orator,* 256.

45. This is only one of the salient differences between the play and the novela; another is the absence in the novela of a relationship between rapist and victim, the rape prompted here by sheer impetuosity. For Leocadia's speech see Miguel de Cervantes, "La Fuerza de la Sangre," in *Exemplary Novels,* vol. 2, ed. B. W. Ife, trans. R. M. Price (Warminster: Aris & Phillips, 1992), 106–7. For the novela as a source see Hensman, *Shares,* 1:204–6.

46. I maintain that the bed-trick here is no real surprise to the audience; the drift of Euphanes' mentioning of plotting it with Merione (V.i.1–2, V.ii.11–17) must be clear to anyone familiar with the conventions of the drama of this time. See also the remarks on how Fletcherian tragicomedy, including *The Queen of Corinth,* prepares us with clues for the finale's reversal(s), of Verna Foster, "Ford's Experiments in Tragicomedy: Shakespearean and Fletcherian," in *Renaissance Tragicomedy,* 99–100.

47. *Elder Seneca,* X.ii.19, 2:406–7; Schottus, 137.

48. Martia has been read as though the playwrights intended her to be unambiguously bad; see Pearse, *Chastity Plays,* 174–75; Shepherd, *Amazons,* 182–83; Clark, *Moral Art,* 194–95, 200–202; Clark, *Plays,* 74–77.

49. *Elder Seneca,* I.vi.10–11, 1:146–49; Schottus, 59.

50. For the Senecan source here see Hensman, *Shares,* 2:363–64.

Reading Orlando Historically: Vagrancy, Forest, and Vestry Values in Shakespeare's *As You Like It*

Chris Fitter

IN pursuing the original meaning(s) of *As You Like It*—recuperating the drama as *they* liked it—we should seek, by conventional imperative, the historicities of the local level.

Ros.   Then shall we be news-crammed.
Celia. All the better; we shall be the more marketable.

(1.2.89–90)[1]

Yet we should also, less conventionally, search within the text for discernible structural implications to the truism that drama is crucially incomplete in its written form. Having recognized, that is, that this play of 1599 is responsive to conditions and events specific to the late 1590s, we should investigate it also, *qua* script, as designed for a self-completionary meaning achieved through interactive performance before a specific and generically familiar target audience, at the new Globe. It will be the contention of this paper that, when approached through this dual methodology—grasped in its topicality, and scrutinized for constructed performance latencies—*As You Like It* becomes discernibly a protest play; and that its indictments of an emergent ideology unfold substantially through surprise operations upon the figure of its supposedly lovable young hero, Orlando, which work at the level of stagecraft. Literary criticism has not always taken the drama's political measure, sunnily asserting, for instance, as recently as the 2005 Penguin edition that from the moment it escapes the world of Duke Frederick, "all the rest of the play is one long celebration of benign comic freedom";[2] or even concluding that Shakespeare's Arden "seems to have only one definitive attribute: an exclusion of contemporary reality."[3] Yet *As You Like It,* with its cast of malnourished cottager, bankrupt gentleman, starving vagrants, scathing malcontent, and assorted political refugees, takes pains to foreground anti-Arcadian perspectives, evoke political ills, and countervaluate harsh contemporary attitudes. Sparkling as the play often is, its tonal range and nuances, as well as its targets of hilarious political mockery, have yet to be fully identified. This essay will accordingly seek to demonstrate the play's responsiveness, at both textual and performance levels, to two particular historical conditions, each escalating at the *fin de siècle* under pressure of fresh legislation and royal proclamation: the demonization of vagrancy, and the intensification of what we might dub vestry values. And in examining (for reasons of length) the presentation mainly of Orlando, it will uncover a number of political "performance secrets," as we might term them: mechanisms that, seeking to outflank mounting censorship pressures, could activate on the stage transformative dimensions of meaning preserved invisible on the page.

In the opening of act 4, Rosalind, debating Jaques, refers suggestively to those who "betray themselves to every modern censure" (4.1.6). Her words point to a climate of indictment fissuring the national culture in the 1590s; and in so doing, they pinpoint for us a missing link, I suggest, in literary criticism's connection between *As You Like It* and that "freedom" of medieval carnival values which the play is often noted to celebrate. For there is more to this transmission than a broad matter of folk festivity as generally bequeathed to London's new professional theaters (Barber), or of the state continuing to license a temporary, politically cathartic revolt by anarchic bodily values (the Bakhtin school), let alone of an undiscriminating conflation of carnival and popular culture with riots and crime (Richard Wilson).[4] Though there is some truth in all these models, the connection between *As You Like It* and carnival values must also be grasped at the level of political topicality, as the drama's response to a nationwide *institutional* development: the authoritarian alliance of the state church with divisive parish oligarchies—a union legislatively empowered, distinctively repressive, and expressed above all in an intensifying campaign to exalt local hegemonies by extirpating folk revels. Blessed by the crown, the new authoritarianism of local government with its suppressive agenda grew notably harsher through the 1590s, to the point of detonating explosions of protest from parliament itself, shortly before this play was written, in 1598. Critical to *As You Like It,* and hitherto unrecognized in studies of the drama, is the absolute centrality of this hardening prosecutorial climate driven by oligarchic vestries.

Certain features of this pattern were not new. Central government's alliance with local officers had been long-standing in Tudor England. Crackdowns on the poor were routine in periods of economic distress, suppressing alehouse keeping, promiscuity, and traditional parish revels. Reformation zeal had long stigmatized calendary festivals as pagan and was phasing out community drama as papist. Yet by the end of the century, a new level of censoriousness had developed, born of a now extraordinarily tight embrace between central authority and local elites. Officers in town and village were flooded with new directives (for road maintenance, provision of militia weapons, regulation and relief of the poor), and became proportionately more highly empowered by the late Elizabethan state. "Having to a very large extent functioned outside the state system," observes Steve Hindle, "the parish now changed its character, becoming to an unprecedented extent a local expression of state authority."[5] Simultaneously, parish self-representation had disengaged itself from a broad-based local franchise to establish the self-perpetuating rule of elite "select vestries." As Christopher Hill long ago noted, "From the mid-sixteenth century we find groups of richer parishioners formally agreeing to exclude 'the rest of the common people', although not the leading families of the parish, who would be consulted on important matters even if not members of the vestry . . . Select vestries from about 1590 onwards aspired to have their authority confirmed by a faculty from the bishop. They appealed to the bishops' dislike of democracy, against the 'great confusion' which would result 'if the whole parish should be electors' . . . and 'excite the ruder sort to extreme liberty.'"[6] This late sixteenth-century secession of the prosperous notables of town and village from the community at large generated a new severity of class-control: an almost adversarial, policing relation to social inferiors, aggressively seeking to enforce, as a reformation of manners, substantially "Puritan" values of industrious abstinence and righteous sobriety.

There thus emerged in early modern England a distinctively postmedieval structure of feeling, whose ingrained Victorian familiarity perhaps disguises its emergence in the sixteenth century: the "bourgeois" attachment of snobbery not to wealth or to rank but to staid civic respectability. These vestry values, as we shall call them, imposed on community by the bureaucratic regimentation of reforming oligarchies, established a monied authoritarian primness, a new snobbery of sanctimonious repressiveness, that rejoiced in scapegoating the poor and prohibiting their folk celebrations. The old feastings, ales, and merry-makings had comprised "shared recreational activity," expressing "communitarian sentiments"[7] and fostering "a strong sense of neighborly identity":[8] one in which the poor had had their rightful place. But now, in the name of public order, anything perceived as popular disorder, scandalizing the godly, was to be extinguished: a project pointedly extending to festal pastime.

The result was a clash of cultures, fought out in village and parish across late Elizabethan England, in bitter local wars over civic control and the *mores* of Christian neighborhood, that escalated through the 1590s and would reach its fiercest point in the first decade of the seventeenth century. "Swearing, tippling, sexual irregularities, 'night walking', absence from church, feasting and merry-making, and general idleness: these were the common targets of reformers everywhere."[9] Thus clergy fulminated that after Sabbath revels of bearbaiting, dancing, and drunkenness, "men could not keep their servants from lying out of their houses the same Sabbath day at night."[10] The curate of Winsley in Wiltshire, infuriated by midsummer feasting, thundered in

1602 "that all women and maids that were singers and dancers were whores, and as many as did look upon them no better than they." "The phallic maypole," notes Hill, "was for the rural lower class almost a symbol of independence of their betters": so that opposition to the strict rule of city fathers might express itself in the erection of maypoles and playing of May games (e.g., Lincoln 1584–85). At Shrewsbury in 1588 prohibition of the maypole saw protestors jailed.[11]

Late Elizabethan class conflict thus pitched "emergent ideology" against "residual" through rival ideals of community.[12] Feudalism's superstructure had promoted, in David Underdown's words, "the traditional concept of the harmonious, vertically integrated society," whose bonds of paternalism and good neighbourliness were expressed in "familiar religious and communal rituals": a scheme rebuffed by the vestrymen's emergent ideology, with its accent upon "the moral and cultural distinctions which marked them off from their poorer, less disciplined neighbours."[13] Ian Archer writes similarly of the new oligarchic values being imposed in London: "the expression of the social bond [as] a much more hierarchically articulated one than the older practices of commensality among neighbors," the emergent model emphasizing "the extraction of deference in return for patronage, in particular through the exercise of poor relief."[14] The 1590s, argues Peter Clark, "unstopped a cascade of internal community vendettas . . . the new machinery of the poor law allowed parish busy-bodies to victimise any poorer villager whose face they happened to dislike."[15] In Underdown's summative words, "Whether initiated by county JPs or borough corporations, by village notables or reforming ministers, the campaign against popular festivals was almost invariably divisive. In that campaign Puritans naturally took a leading part. Puritan insistence on the distinction between the elect and the reprobate made the idea of all-inclusive parish harmony unrealizable . . . Examples of urban conflict can be culled from every part of England."[16]

Church ales—festivals of wassailing (or pledging one's neighbors) used to raise money to pay the parish clerk and support the parish poor—were becoming replaced by the fun-free cash demands of parish rating. In Somerset, Wiltshire, Worcester, Berkshire, Devon, and other cloth-counties, we find church ales prohibited from the 1590s on grounds of order: a suppression fomenting bitter county disputes, and even fistfights in church.[17] Zachary Some, of Sandon in Essex, reviled his parson in 1592 as "a prattling fool, for preaching against drunkenness," and hurled hassocks at the sexton.[18] The power of churchwardens, moreover, was now escalating. The churchwarden, as Eric Carlson records, had thirteenth-century origins, but his duties were standardized under the Tudors as the upkeep of church property and valuables.[19] It was important that he be a man of some prosperity, as he would have personally to outlay expenses in advance; and from the 1580s on, his social status rose further, as more gentry, moved by a "desire to enforce their own social attitudes," held the office.[20] Elected in church after evensong, the churchwarden was powerful as the crucial arbiter of fluctuating social status in the parish: for nearly everywhere it was he who allocated seating positions in the church, pinpointing the hierarchic location of each member of the congregation. Those who paid the highest church rates ranked supreme; but with local fortunes rising and falling, accusations of bias and favoritism grew commonplace.[21] Parish snobbery's Master of Ceremony, all too often deference was his exaction and abasement his métier.

For the churchwarden's duties extended to breaking into alehouses to haul off roisterers to church, and presenting moral offenders to the ecclesiastical courts. It thus lay with him to report and prosecute the culture of revelry—men and women caught drinking, dancing, fornicating, even harboring pregnant women.[22] And it was upon the state's elevation of these formidable powers of suppression and chastisement to a yet higher level that the countercultural riposte of *As You Like It* was written: for by act of the 1598 parliament, churchwardens were made also Overseers of the Poor. As such, they now, universally, assessed their fellows for the poor rate, and placed paupers and their children in work. Classifying the poor as deserving or undeserving, they enjoyed discretionary powers to supplement—or otherwise—the income of workers paid too little to survive: a brutally substantial number. For as Paul Slack has noted, records in Essex in 1598–99, for instance, show that twenty per cent of those *in work* were "not able to maintain themselves and their charge by their labour."[23] The most recent book-length study of poor law legislation, Steve Hindle's *On the Parish,* reveals that Elizabethan statutes did not in themselves confer entitlement on the poor: though about 20 percent of the early modern population were in need, only about 5 percent received relief, and this was mainly through granting such makeshifts as rights of pasturage, gleaning, and fuel gathering, not through financial payment. Parish officers, Hindle insists, "negotiated" relief with the paupers—making eligibility depend upon criteria of social respectability such as sobriety, deference, and church attendance.[24] "Vestries are found removing disorderly pensioners from their almshouses or temporarily depriving them of poor relief in hope of 'amendment' of their behaviour."[25] Furthermore, the same parliament now granted powers of summary justice to constables. In consequence, as has long been noted, parish officers—self-appointing vestrymen "recruited almost exclusively from the upper stratum of village society"[26]—now came to use poor relief as a means of social control. The "urban oligarchs and village notables who dominated local government" had "the authority to police their inferiors almost at will."[27]

The campaign against folk revelry utilized church courts: another institution that had become explosively controversial by the late 1590s. Over two hundred and fifty of these existed in Shakespeare's day, and to these "bawdy courts" men and women might be taken not only for failure to attend church regularly or pay the poor rate but for drunkenness, swearing, ribaldry, whoring, "wickedness of life" or defending allegedly "popish" ways. "Mean persons," it was complained in parliament in 1598, had to appear in these "for small causes" whilst there was "a toleration of offences in great persons" (266). The church, conversely, was turning a handsome profit from what was increasingly viewed as a scam. Such was public anger that even parliament expressed outrage, proposing in 1598 "a roving commission on ecclesiastical abuses," only to see it suppressed by royal intervention as encroaching on crown prerogative. "An extensive literature of denigration [emerged] in which the church courts were characterised as oppressive, unjust, corrupt and inefficient."[28]

When *As You Like It* was written, then, a counter-traditionalist order of disciplinary vestry values that was tightening a noose round the neck of popular culture was receiving fresh support and consolidation from state and church, despite widespread protest. Abetting through select vestries the interests of a disenfranchising, newly domineering parish elite; sermonizing upon an industrious and killjoy godliness; suppressing church ales; prosecuting merrymakers and calendar festivity through church courts; functioning through churchwardens to arbitrate parish status and regiment the desperate poor: by 1599 a kind of usurping cultural totalitarianism was being clamped in place and contentiously policed—the snobbish new authoritarianism of "every modern censure" (4.1.6).

"Hot and rebellious liquors in my blood" (2.4.49): *As You Like It*

By contrast, "the place of the stage" as recent criticism has shown, was in "the margins of the city," where "forms of moral incontinence and pollution were granted license to exist." In the Liberties, "license shades into licentiousness without even the trace of a seam."[29] The topographically mediated impetus to transgressive autonomy of official culture suggests a framing "politics of the playhouse" that conditioned reception of any individual play; so that criticism needs, as Jean E. Howard suggests, "to take account of the potential consonance or conflict between the ideological import of a drama and of the material conditions of its production."[30] In the closed-off, licensed other world of the Globe playhouse, its appetitive hubbub placed among brothels and close to a bearbaiting house, its pleasures sequestered by the bought privacy of forty-two-foot high walls, wherein alcohol was on sale and whores swaggered their allure, there was no raising of a curtain or dimming of lights to subdue the boisterous audience mood as Elizabethan plays began. It is into the midst, therefore, of exuberant carnival forces that the haughty young gentleman walks who opens *As You Like It;* and this impeccably dressed figure, "point-device in [his] accoutrements, as loving [himself] than seeming the lover of any other" (3.2.372–74), commences with a familiar torrent of class snobbery. He is, he insists, through to his exit near the end of the first scene, a "gentleman of birth." He seeks "Gentleman-like qualities," and "exercises as may become a gentleman" (69, 72). He invokes his "gentle condition of blood" (45), and his quarrel with his brother is that he "mines my gentility with my education." He aspires, he says, to "good education"—hardly an exciting prospect in the carnival world, as *Love's Labour's Lost* underlines—and he laments being "marred with idleness." Since the rebuke of 'idleness' was a staple invective of anti-theatrical discourse, the term sets him further at odds with audience values, and the high-minded disgust may have been received as auditorium insult. (Contrast the celebration of idleness elsewhere in the drama: Charles on the banished Duke's men who, like Robin Hood's men "fleet the time carelessly as they did in the golden world," 1.1.118; and Amiens's song praising pastoral *otium* "Under the greenwood tree," 2.5.1–9.) For Orlando is correspondingly abusive of the lower classes. "You have trained me like a peasant," Orlando complains to his elder brother. He must "feed with hinds." "Shall I keep your hogs" he protests (35), as the climax to his lofty scorn.

Most tellingly of all, Orlando is shrill with self-pity because he is not rich enough. He has, he blurts before an audience packed with servants, laborers, apprentices, tradesmen, and ex-soldiers, "but poor a thousand crowns" (2). He insists again on the sum as minuscule at line 73 ("the poor allotery my father left me"). Though no critic seems to have remarked on it, a thousand crowns (£250) was in fact the approximate equivalent of £125,000, or around $200,000 in today's currency.[31] The groundlings must have wept for him. In that period, when Orlando pronounced £250 inadequate to his gentility, an unskilled laborer earned £7 per year, a schoolteacher only £20 per annum, and Shakespeare may have paid only £60 for the second largest house in Stratford. A contemporary playwright of good standing would receive only £5 for a new drama. To be considered a true gentleman, one needed to spend at least £60 per year: and at this rate, Orlando was set up for over four years without having to breakfast before noon.

Orlando, it seems clear, and through him, gentlemanly self-pity, are being set up by Shakespeare for what we might call carnival targeting. Adam the hind will not return the class contempt, remaining so sympathetically in ideological complicity with overclass scorn that Orlando confidently includes him in a trick on Oliver: "Go apart, Adam, and thou wilt hear how he will shake me up" (1.1.26–27).

It turns out to be the elder brother who channels at Orlando the latent carnival targeting, initiating a deixis that renders Orlando the butt of audience mockery through very much of the drama. When Oliver crosses the groundling-encircled Globe stage, he asks Orlando in startled tone—as well he might—"Now sir, what make *you here?*" (italics mine). "Nothing," replies

Orlando snobbishly, for he is "not taught to make anything," but is being "marred," "with idleness." As Orlando rails, Oliver responds with horror— and a presumable glance at the thousands of people watching— "Know you where you are, sir?" When Orlando replies in deictic naivety, "O sir, very well: here in your orchard," he must have been met by audience laughter. Yet still Oliver persists, with a gesture perhaps at the groundlings, "Know you before whom, sir?" "Ay, better than him I am before knows me" counters Orlando, in catastrophically haughty deictic ignorance. In a piece of brilliantly scripted stage ambiguity, then, Orlando's ideological posture, defined through his loud class superciliousness, is being punished as misfit through a pattern of unknowing audience interaction. Where other characters, we will see, acknowledge or tease the Globe community, Orlando is apparently unaware of the spectators' (presumably often vocal) existence. He inhabits the drama as a deictic outsider. In a pastoral play, he complains from the outset against being kept "rustically" (7); and, disapproving of the forest as "desert," he will hang tongues on every tree "That *civil* sayings show" (3.2.113, 116, emphasis mine). In contrast to the Duke's description of the happily sequestered life "exempt from public haunt," Orlando defines himself contrariously as "inland bred" (2.7.97): a phrase evoking, perhaps, the realm across the water from the Globe, beyond the Liberty. He belongs to London city, officialdom's realm, subject to the gentlemanly authority of the Puritan city council.

Orlando, then, is sequestered from us, marooned inside the fiction amid a lapping sea of spectators. In Shakespeare's theatrical targeting of Orlando, the kind of deictic lobotomy that excises his auditorium consciousness, irreparably rendering his vision not strictly sightless but site-less, will become a politically strategic privation.

Yet this stagecraft-punished overweening gentility is but one aspect of a crucially ambiguous and ideologically destabilized Orlando, in whom thwarted pretension to class superiority becomes paradoxically articulated through a discourse that smacks of underclass rebellion. Orlando insists that he is treated like an animal—precisely as were the poor. "Hounds were better fed than servants, and they were sometimes better housed," records historian Keith Thomas. He cites a Stuart commentator who noted masters to care so much more for their dogs than their servants, that "you may see in some men's houses fair and fat dogs to run up and down and men pale and wan to walk feebly."[32] In More's *Utopia,* Hythlodaeus similarly judges that the poor, who "never stop working like cart-horses," "get so little to eat, and have such a wretched time, that they'd almost be better off if they *were* cart-horses."[33] One of the leaders of the 1596 Oxford Rising held that "servants were so held in and kept like dogs that they would be ready to cut their masters' throats."[34] Accordingly, Orlando is on familiar ground for many in the audience when he complains that his condition at the hands of Oliver "differs not from the stalling of an ox" (10): a perspective that goes some way to explaining Adam's apparent sympathy, as a servant who anticipates how poorly he will be treated "When service should in my old limbs lie lame / And unregarded age in corners thrown" (2.3.41–42). Orlando persists with "His animals on his dunghills are as much bound to him as I" (14–15), and wonders whether he will have to share husks with the hogs (37). His bitter claim that "his horses are bred better" (10–11) is a standard plaint of class resentment: found in Jack Cade (*2 Henry VI*) who, arraigning Lord Saye, declares "thou oughts't not to let thy horse wear a cloak, when honester men than thou go in their hose and doublets" (47–49).

Orlando's conclusion is likewise politically charged. His spirit, he claims, "begins to mutiny against this servitude. I will no longer endure it" (22–23). He will rebel against what sarcastically he terms "the courtesy of nations"—an angry indictment of social convention that anticipates the explicitly subversive intentions of another wronged younger brother, Edmund in *King Lear,* who cheerleads groundling mutiny against "the curiosity of nations" (1.2.4). ("Why brand they us / With base? With baseness? Bastardy? Base? Base?" 1.2.9–10.) True to his word, Orlando erupts into violence when insulted (or perhaps struck) by his elder brother, with a deftly immediate success, pinioning Oliver into pain and concession, that must have won a gust of admiration from the crowd. "Wert thou not my brother, I would not take this hand from thy throat until this other had pulled out thy tongue for saying so" (59–61). Yet even here, the offense is to have been termed low-born (villain/ villein, 55).

In the context of the populist theater, then, its carnivalesque orientation still close to the surface in the play's opening minutes, Orlando will be received as an arrestingly contrary figure. Alienating in his shrill class contempt, offensive in his whining genteel insistence on the insulting insufficiency of the wealth bequeathed him, comically hapless in his deictic sightlessness, he yet echoes the language of underclass resentment, and embodies the exciting spirit of active resistance: that cocktail of ideological contrarieties can become almost a Molotov cocktail. This Elizabethan Angry Young Man also possesses street-smart combat skills of the kind that might prove very handy in London's back-streets, as he will demonstrate a second time against Charles the wrestler; yet the charismatic masculine potency, we will see, is cross-grained by sermonizing self-obsession, and he will prove for nearly the length of the drama the dupe and doting puppy of overmastering Rosalind. Punished by duping, targeted by comical deictic unknowingness, and mocked in the allocation of execrable verse, his sneering hubris is humbled: and the ideologically conflicted Orlando of the play's opening, already destabilized by his ambiguous class position, becomes incorporable into the playhouse's community of revelers.

For Orlando resembles many in Shakespeare's carefully appraised audience, victims of the severest form of primogeniture practiced in Europe, who are thus appropriable by a politically disaffected and skeptical theater. Louis Montrose has aptly noted that, since "Shakespeare's audience must have included a high proportion of gentleborn younger sons" acquiring law at the Inns of Court, as well as large numbers of apprentices and servants, consequently "Youths, younger sons, and all Elizabethan playgoers who felt that Fortune's benefits had been 'mightily misplaced' (2.1.33–34) could identify with Shakespeare's Orlando."[35] Yet Montrose misses the strident negatives in Orlando's early characterization, like almost all critics (a recent editor, for instance, pronounces Orlando "a thoroughly likeable and good-natured young man," and thinks his opening speech on "but poor a thousand crowns," to "establish immediate sympathy for young Orlando").[36] Conversely, the rare voice of percipient repulsion, trumpeted in Bernard Shaw, discerns only the "safely stupid and totally unobservant young man."[37] But to miss either the supercilious misfit, stuffy fall-guy to carnival values, or the stirring martial mutineer, is to miss the crucial political redirection of Orlando's development from intense ambiguity toward the telos of *As You Like It:* the play's triumphant incorporation of deflated genteel resistance, the ludic rout of vestry values.[38]

Initially, however, the preponderantly outsider status is reprised in the scene where Orlando and Adam resolve to flee on Adam's savings (2.4.39–62). Announcing to Orlando his brother's murderous intentions, the hitherto near-silent Adam breaks out into fourteen lines of a curiously exclamatory homage to Orlando. Commencing, tellingly, in reiteration of Oliver's opening and deictically fraught question, "Why, what make you *here?*" (2.3.4, italics mine), Adam continues "Why are you virtuous?" and eventually concludes "Know you not, master, to some kind of men / Their graces serve them but as enemies? / No more do yours. Your virtues, gentle master, / Are sanctified and holy traitors to you." The strong possibility of deixis here, Adam indicating the groundling sea early antagonized by Orlando's hubristic self-pity, looks clinched by Adam's concluding lines:

> O *what a world is this,* when what is comely
> Envenoms him that bears it!
> (emphasis added; 2.3.14–15)

"This" is a habitual deictic pointer in Shakespeare, and the Globe theater as "the world"—its motto was *totus mundus agit histrionem,* The entire world moves the actor—would, many critics assert, become a self-referential commonplace.[39] It is frequently taken so where Jaques's "All the world's a stage," 2.7.139, is concerned. It is not commonly read so in this passage, however, even though Adam's melodramatic staccato "This is no place! This house is but a butchery! / Abhor it! Fear it! Do not enter it!" (27–28) would be consonant with the earlier audience estrangement, and produce hilarious targeting.[40] These deictic histrionics are precisely consonant, too, with what follows: for Adam and Orlando now launch into an enthusiastic Puritan sermon traducing carnival joys.

Traditionally construed ahistorically, in terms of noble old man and compassionate youth, the values of this scene in 1599 were wholly different in tone. First, Adam lauds his own "thrifty" lifestyle (39) that made possible his savings. Thrift was of course a cardinal virtue of Puritanism and of vestry values, and by definition antagonistic to the priorities of the pleasure-seeking, theatergoing crowd. (Jaques's speech on the seven ages of man indeed fires the riposte, when Adam is carried in, in the "youthful hose well saved, a world too wide / For his shrunk shank," 2.7.160–61.) Next, the sermonizing tone becomes explicit, with "He that doth the ravens feed / Yea providently caters for the sparrow / Be comfort to my age" (43–45). If the Almighty however will provide for Adam in age, what need the lifetime of thrift? The contradiction swells the surreal unease of the moment, as Adam discloses himself to be startlingly wealthy, the possessor of five hundred crowns (£125 or over $100,000 by today's measure), yet begs Orlando to maintain him in servility ("Let me be your servant. / Though I look old, yet I am strong and lusty," 46–47). The moment must surely have been close to incomprehensible to many of the humbler spectators, whether servants, apprentices, or laborers, as the very reverse of their own attitudes and aspirations: particularly in an age when apprentices, as historians tell us, "were exposed to an almost limitless sadism from their masters."[41] Adam's gesture looks less like Christian generosity than potentially suicidal recklessness, coupled with bizarre preference for abasement over personal freedom. The London underclasses who flocked to liberatory wish-fulfillment in *Tamburlaine* would find Adam's will-to-servitude a hard sell. Indeed, it will be populist Iago, exuberantly bonding with the groundlings (for the first two acts) through beer-swilling, drinking songs, direct address, lewd jokes, patriotic compliment, and the engineering of exciting sword fights, who utters the perspective of the rowdy, carnivalesque playhouse upon the ideal of indefeasible servility. And it will sound almost like a reminiscence of old Adam.

> You shall mark
> Many a duteous and knee-crooking knave,
> That, doting on his own obsequious bondage,
> Wears out his time much like his master's ass,
> For naught but provender, and when he's old, cashiered.
> Whip me such honest knaves.
>
> (*Othello*, 1.1.44–49)

So large a sum of money as Adam possesses required, moreover, an enviably fat and bulging super-purse. (One authority estimates that it would have to have weighed close to one and a half kilograms, "more than a bag of sugar.")[42] As Adam holds out to Orlando that clinking, mesmerizing bag—"Here is the gold. / All this I give you" (45-46)—the groundlings, so close to this numinous object, must have suspended their collective breath in envy of Orlando's fortune.

Climaxing the estrangement, Adam now plunges into pointedly antagonizing homiletics.

> In my youth I never did apply
> Hot and rebellious liquors in my blood,
> Nor did not with unbashful forehead woo
> The means of weakness and debility.
>
> (48-51)

Delivered to a pit of cheery youthful swillers, located in a notorious red-light district, and in the midst of a comedy, the chances of success for such sentiments look unpropitious. "Just Say No" was a message that, here, did not exactly sing. These godly imperatives of meek teetotalism and retiring chastity summed up, of course, the coercive regime of the new vestry values, inflicted on the socially inferior, the poor, and where possible, the young. Adam, neocon, is specifically assailing youth culture ("In *my youth, I* never did . . ."; emphasis added), whose heartland lay in the riotous freedoms of Liberties such as Southwark, and the pleasures of the playhouse. In 1600, perhaps half of England was under twenty years old, as was much of the theatergoing public.[43] The number of apprentices in London had doubled between 1580 and 1600, rising to some thirty thousand—two to three times the normal proportion—and the number of servants became possibly even greater.[44] To the authorities such figures posed an alarming threat, particularly as London apprentices developed their own, rowdy subculture. "At any sign of general disaffection, the city's first precaution was always to order a curfew for apprentices and servants, and to close the alehouses where they would loiter with intent."[45] As Roger Manning records, even though "these discontented younger sons of the gentry added an articulate and politically sophisticated leaven to the London crowd," "To contemporaries, gentlemen apprentices were associated with riotous living."[46] Adam's charge, moreover, that sexual and alcoholic license "woos . . . weakness and debility" echoed the refrain of local elites and parish officers (noted by historian Keith Wrightson) that drinking and alehouses ruin a man, thus raising the local poor rate.[47] Pitched into Elizabethan culture wars, then, thrifty Adam, censorious gerontocrat, far from comprising the elevated exemplar for which Shakespearean criticism has always sentimentally mistaken him, would have commanded at a public theater much the same reception that a TV evangelist might expect from an inset cameo sermon in *The Rocky Horror Picture Show*.

Further suggestive for the concerns of this drama was the fact, noted by historians, that since in this, the golden age of flogging, many apprentices ran away, and servants were often laid off at short notice, youth culture tended to overlap with the vagrant population.[48] *As You Like It* surely maps just this confluence, its political stance thus both compassionate and commercially astute. Indeed an almost precisely contemporary tract (first edition 1603) articulates just this conjunction, the fate dreaded by Adam "When service should in [his] old limbs lie lame" (2.4.41):

> It is the custom of most men nowadays (so wretchedly covetous are they grown) that they toil their servants while they can labour, and consume their strength and spend them out: and when age cometh, and the bones are full of ache and pain, they turn them out of doors, poor and helpless into the wide world to shift for themselves as they can; and they must either beg or steal or starve, for any relief they shall receive from their masters . . . and thus it cometh to pass that many become thieves and vagrant beggars through their master's niggardliness that would not do his duty in bestowing some proportionable and competent relief upon them.[49]

Yet as out-of-touch, gentlemanly Orlando responds to Adam's words, he completely misses the injustice of his own class so accurately foreseen by Adam, projecting instead the denigrative authoritarianism visited by the well-born on servant and vagrant alike:

> O good old man, how well in thee appears
> The constant service of the antique world,
> When service sweat for duty, not for meed.
> Thou art not for the fashion of these times,
> Where none will sweat but for promotion,
> And having that, do choke their service up
> Even with the having.
>
> (56–62)

Presented, in Adam's crowns, with an immediate instance of astounding subaltern loyalty and magnanimity, Orlando perversely attacks underclass shiftlessness. The true note of ideology ("In the sphere of ideology, concrete particular and universal truth glide ceaselessly in and out of each other, bypassing the mediation of rational analysis")[50] is sustained as his tirade sketches an almost demented extreme of patrician deserving. Indifferent to the harshness of sixteenth century treatment of elderly servants (More, in *Utopia,* 1516, had made the same point)[51] Orlando lauds laboring dutifully, apparently forever, with no thought of wages (devoted or "constant service," that will "sweat for duty, not for meed").

Furthermore, the unctuous antimaterialist sermon contradicts his own aching self-pity on inheriting "but poor a thousand crowns" (1.1.2). The tranquil self-contradiction forms another instance of that blind, self-pitying plaint of the well-born, tellingly juxtaposed to the desperate plight of commoners, articulated and targeted in Henry VI, in Romeo, and in Henry V—all of them "superfluous and lust-dieted men" in the words of *King Lear,* who "will not see / Because [they] do not feel" (*King Lear,* 4.1.66–68).[52] Finally, Orlando's reproach of material self-interest in the lower orders establishes, in a principle pervasive in Shakespeare, the sly spectacle of dominant ideology's fervent theory dealt demolition by actuality: had servants indeed been heedless of pay, Orlando would not have had those crowns to aid him.

If Adam's rectitude of abstinence was dear to the heart of every churchwarden, Orlando's ideology of underclass fecklessness came straight from the tightened lips of Overseers of the Poor. Adam and Orlando embrace in a tender duet of vestry values: unconquerable servility in a joyless work ethic kneels to hierarchism's calm deserving of feeless underling duty. The self-congratulatory duo of the dour Puritan work ethic unite proudly against the scandal of the lower classes: vice-ridden ("unbashful forehead[s]"), ignobly concerned about their wages ("sweat . . . for meed"), and disrespectful to their betters (swilling "hot and rebellious liquors"). They are oligarchy's newlyweds, melting into a marriage made in the very heaven of early capitalist accumulation.

Then Orlando swiftly pockets the chunky bag of coins proffered by Adam.

The moment, rich in satiric potentiality, suggests, at the very least, the double standard of those who deplored lower-class cries in their parish for financial help while making hefty sums themselves. It may even have hinted at the widespread contemporary suspicion of embezzlement by vestry officers. The 1601 parliament, for instance, saw one MP object to a bill compelling churchwardens to resume levying shilling recusancy fines against the very poor, for fear that churchwardens might instead compile a secret list, and "take fourpence for themselves and dispense with the rest."[53] Indeed, in the very parish in which this play was being performed (the Globe was located in St. Saviours, Southwark), an intense resentment gathering against restriction of the traditionally universal parish franchise was being buoyed by accusations that the vestrymen were spending the monies gathered for poor relief upon "private feasting." An appeal to parliament was eventually launched, in 1607, and a 1608 ruling restored traditional voting rights. (These circumstances are normally related by critics only to *Coriolanus.*)[54] Generally, however, "Before Laud the Church seems to have had no 'social justice' policy which would challenge the rule of local oligarchies," so that "embezzlement by town and parish oligarchies of funds intended for poor relief proceeded apace in the century between the Reformation and Revolution."[55]

"I blush, and hide my sword" (Orlando, 2.7.119)

Given Adam and Orlando's embrace of the anti-populist discourse of handwringing self-righteousness, and Orlando's double standard on cash, it is no wonder that Orlando's incorporation into the drama's community of revelers is *purgatorial,* proceeding by both personal suffering and stage humiliation. Personal expropriation disrupts his genteel fantasia, disorienting him in the inbreaking of cold realism.

> What, wouldst thou have me go and beg my food,
> Or with a base and boisterous sword enforce
> A thieving living on the common road?
> This must I do, or know not what to do
>
> (2.3.31–34)

Despite immediate, appalled disavowal ("Yet this I will not do, do how I can"), Orlando's despairing cry defines what he *will* do, commanding the men he encounters to share, at point of sword, their food with him. As he is driven, flinching, to the common road, the play's opposition to state authoritarianism embraces a second front, in the humane counter-valuation of the condition of vagrancy. For, wandering without master, lacking work and wielding a sword, Orlando is in Elizabethan legal terms both a "sturdy beggar"—capable of work yet without it—and precisely the category of vagabond against whom Elizabeth had just issued a proclamation in 1598: Orlando is a man "wandering in the common highways" who possessed "forbidden weapons" and attempted armed robbery. Establishing martial law for the summary lynching of such disorderly vagrant persons, the proclamation could not but have been in the minds of audiences in 1599–1600. Indeed the crown issued another in January 1600, renewing the command to all officers to suppress and punish "rogues and vagabonds wandering up and down this realm idly and insolently."[56]

Vagrancy was, as *As You Like It* shows, a problem more for the desperately trekking unemployed themselves than for the Tudor state which endlessly vilified them and hysterically exaggerated their numbers, as wandering, dispossessed folk, criminalized per se by legislation, sought forest and commons wastes where they might elude the further catastrophes of bloody lashings, ear-boring, branding, incarceration in bridewells, impressment, summary execution under martial law, or even the penal slavery twice legislated by parliaments.[57] "No-one could guess, by reading this Act [of 1597], that there was any lack of employment in England as the century drew to its close."[58] The parliamentarians of 1597–98 even decreed that the wandering destitute should be dispatched to the galleys. No evidence has been found, however, that suggests this barbarism was enforced.[59] "It is difficult", writes historian

J. A. Sharpe, "to draw any real distinction between the vagrant and the unstable poor of the parish, the migrant workers, servants or poor laborers who had no real stake in the community, and who were terribly vulnerable to the economic crises of the period."[60] In 1590, some counties saw the whipping and branding of vagrants at the rate of a new one every day; and an alarmed contemporary in the early seventeenth century estimated the vagabond horde at eighty thousand.[61]

Shakespeare's treatment of rural refugees and the dispossessed is a politically charged departure from both political and literary norms. That outlaws holed up in the forest seek "sermons in stones and good in everything" (2.1.17), proving morally superior to the court, which banishes and seizes at whim, has some basis in pastoral convention and Shakespeare's source, Thomas Lodge's *Rosalynde.* Yet Lodge's greenwood is studiedly a courtly paint-job: the entire confection is a bravura gentlemanly fantasy into which no reality intrudes. The actuality of Elizabethan patrician attitudes consisted in a well-nigh pathological hatred of the roaming and propertyless as "vagabonds," whether in forests or on the roads. Best-selling contemporary literature claimed to profile their true nature as "cony-catchers and bawdy baskets": professional criminals freely choosing a life of pleasurable wandering over decent Christian labor, their fleshly sores and emaciation mere self-inflicted tactics to fleece gullible citizenry.[62] Thomas Harman's *Caveat for Common Cursitors,* an early classic of the emergent genre of rogue literature, claims to survey at first hand a worthless and predatory "fraternity" organized into criminal specializations (rufflers, priggers, palliards, Abraham men), armed with a horrifying repertoire of stratagems, and protected by an arcane language of its own. Harman, who delights in recounting anecdotes of harassing and even torturing vagrants, appears to have invented the term "rogue," from the Latin "rogare", to ask: thus eliding a plea for bread with criminal status. Thereby popularized, the term became, as Linda Woodbridge has noted, "elevated to the status of a legally defined technical term in a statute" in the 1572 Poor Law act.[63] Reprinted in 1573 and 1592, Harman's writings on the "scelerous secrets" of the "rowsey, ragged rabblement of rakehells" spawned many imitators, most notably in the pamphlets and plays of Robert Greene and Thomas Dekker multiplying through the 1590s and the early Jacobean period.[64] Welcomed by the propertied classes, and helping drive the penal legislation of branding and ear-boring, of bloody floggings across country to houses of correction, rogue literature furnished a legitimative discourse. "Rarely has any culture fashioned so wily and powerful an enemy out of such degraded and pathetic materials," comments William Carroll.[65] Conveniently repealing the medieval sanctity of poverty and mendicancy, and displacing the passionate tradition of Christian distributivism urged by the Commonwealthmen, the rogues gallery of cheerily cunning parasites ideologically anesthetized guilt over re-enserfing victims of enclosure, depopulation, and ill-chance in the ghastly new proletariat.

As sword-wielding hunger, Orlando figured a commonplace of Elizabethan England. A letter to Lord Burghley speaks in 1596 of rebellious men who "stick not to say boldly 'they must not starve, they will not starve,'" and who protest "that the rich men have got all into their hands, and will starve the poor."[66] The parliament of 1597–98 had considered no less than fifteen bills to remedy poverty and vagrancy, in what Bacon called "a feast of charity."[67] But so incorrigible proved gentry self-interest that parliament diluted the bill to suppress enclosures. To the anger of the queen herself, it actually rejected such antipoverty bills as that to enforce the provision of hospitality (thus failing to heed, as the bill's sponsor put it, "the lamentable cry of the poor, who are like to perish"), as well as a bill criminalizing those practices of forestalling and regrating ("odious to the commonwealth") that inflated food prices.[68] For the impoverished of England, consequently, little was to change, as a Digger pamphlet (1650) would show.

> We have spent all we have, our trading is decayed, our wives and children cry for bread, our lives are a burden to us, divers of us having five, six, seven, eight, nine in family, and we cannot get bread for them by our labor. Rich men's hearts are hardened, they will not give us if we beg at their doors; if we steal, the law will end our lives. Divers of the poor are starved to death already, and it were better for us that are living to die by the sword than by the famine.[69]

These are the realities by which Orlando and Adam will be rapidly transformed. In terms of theatrical sympathies, act 2 scene 5 unfolds as the transitional scene. Freshly displaced from gentlemanly hauteur, Orlando is subjected to a final, purgatorial targeting, even as his desperation figures a condition of pathos. Thus the scene has the Duke's forest lords deck a table with food—yet the Duke is absent and his men leave to find him. Stage directions, and commonsense probability, suggest the loaded table did not leave with them: and indeed that laying of the table, enforced by the script, was needless to the scene. A feast set for a Duke thus remains onstage (I would bet center stage) throughout the following scene, in which a starving Orlando and collapsing Adam totter at the brink of death. Critics have noted with puzzlement the near-certain presence of the table in 2.6, but failed to recognize the deducible political effects.[70] First, the spectacle of a laden board juxtaposed to terminal starvation must have formed a graphic, visually dominant tableau of contemporary social injustice. And it is probably no accident that when, in the ensuing scene, Orlando returns to steal food, Jaques and the Duke, laughing amid plenty, are debating the propriety of satire, and bourgeois transgressions of courtly dress codes (2.7.42–87). Aristocracy and bourgeoisie are thus locked cheerfully in ethical contention, while the Third Estate, desperate and indigent, roam famished as complete outsiders to the political conversation. Second, as Adam collapses from hunger and Orlando begs him not to die, promising desperately to find food—somewhere, somehow—the Duke's stacked table sits just feet away: and Orlando never sees it. That complex stage moment serves not only to emblematize Elizabethan inequity but to make Orlando look something of an idiot. Our gentleman protagonist, alienatingly censorious and moralistic, is metaphorically and literally unseeing, missing what exists literally almost under his nose. Orlando the unseeing is perpetuated at the deictic level, too: his language is conspicuous once more for comical auditorium misprision: "If this uncouth forest yield anything savage, I will either be food for it or bring it food for thee . . . thou shalt not die for lack of a dinner if there live anything in this desert" (2.6.6–7, 16–17). Invisible on the page but stark on the stage, such performance dimensions disclose a mordant populist politics, often pointed through hilarity.

When in 2.7 Orlando discovers the Duke's company and demands food at sword point, he becomes the deictic fall-guy once again. "Speak you so softly? Pardon me, I pray you. / I thought that all things had been savage here" (2.7.106–7). The moment can be played for a thrilling turn of high adventure, or can be keyed into another instance of Orlando the audience-insulting and impercipient; especially as he then launches into what sounds like unconscious audience address, conceiving the community of the Forest / Globe as godless idlers—just the view, of course, that Perkins and Puritanism held of vagabonds.

> whate'er you are
> That in *this desert inaccessible*
> Under the shade of melancholy boughs
> *Lose and neglect the creeping hours of time;*
> If ever you have looked on better days;
> If ever been where bells have *knolled to church* . . .
> (2.7.109–14; italics mine)

That the Globe was situated very close to St. Mary Overbury, so that her knolling bells must have been regularly audible in the roofless theater, introduced yet another ironizing instance of auditorium cluelessness on the young gentleman's part. Further, the machismo credentials of tough-guy Orlando, destroyer of the Duke's wrestler, now bursting in with sword brandished, are successfully mocked by languid Jaques:

Orl.	Forbear, and eat no more.
Jaques.	Why, I have eaten none yet.
Orl.	Nor shalt not till necessity be served.
Jaques.	Of what kind should this cock come of? . . .

Orl. But forbear, I say.
He dies that touches any of this fruit,
Till I and my affairs are answered.
Jaques. And you will not be answered with reason, I must die.

(2.7.88–91, 98–101)

Yet with Orlando humiliated, the scene then modulates into an intense poignancy. The play grants the audience delicious "punishment" of these misfit sneerers, then under the power of a crafted intensity of pathos, relents to forgive and include them. Just as swordsman Orlando suffers comical humiliation by Jaques's aristocratic contempt, so Puritanical Adam, vaunting his toughening by abstinence from sex and booze—"Though I look old, yet I am strong and lusty" (2.4.47)—has been reduced to whimpering for death: "O I die for food. Here lie I down and measure out my grave" (2.6.1–2). Act 2 scene 7 then progresses to a moving hospitality, as "an old poor man" (129)—all bravado drained and no crowns in sight—now wordless, broken, slumped helpless on Adam's shoulder, becomes cared for, fed, and respected ("Good old man, thou art right welcome . . . Support him by the arm," 200–201, 202). The tonality is heightened by the delicate, paradoxically stately lyric poetry of Orlando's imploration, echoed by the Duke:

> True it is that we have seen better days
> And have been knolled with holy bell to church
> And sat at good men's feasts and wiped our eyes
> Of drops that sacred pity hath engendered.
>
> (120–23)

The lines summon movingly an older tradition, aligning Christian duty with hospitality, whose stage effect of large and beautiful compassion traduces the meanness of Elizabethan ruling discourse. This is, in effect, indiscriminate almsgiving of the kind urged by the church fathers, at odds with the unwearying Tudor discrimination between the deserving and undeserving poor. As Duke Senior, menaced at sword point, freely grants to the armed vagrant Orlando his fill at the banquet—"Sit down, and feed, and welcome to our table" (2.7.105)—his calm and remarkable mercy works as humanitarian rebuke to the hardened heart of Elizabethan officialdom, adamant in parliament and proclamation.

The effect is at once poetically deepened by Jaques's poignant Seven Ages of Man speech, and the reentry of Orlando with the aged Adam in his arms—in his helplessness close to "second childishness and mere oblivion" (165)—which together infuse the graphic, transforming pathos of a common humanity into the perception of vagrants, the reviled terrorists of official discourse. When the two Masterless Men fall ecstatically upon nourishment, sympathy is further overlaid by the power of song, supplied by Amiens.

> Blow, blow thou winter wind
> Thou art not so unkind
> As man's ingratitude

The song may hint at another topical grievance to which the 1598 proclamation had alluded: the presence of multitudes of discharged or deserting soldiers among England's penniless wanderers. The proclamation gestured angrily at vagrants "colouring their wandering by the name of soldiers lately come from the wars"; but the reality was the discharge of many servicemen with little or no pay, in many cases unable to work through injuries incurred in the defense of their country: grievances discussed in *2 Henry VI*, and later hinted in the death of Jack Cade.[71] Shakespeare presented the condition again, almost simultaneously with *As You Like It,* in the case of Pistol (*Henry V*), whose crucial defense of a bridge against the French made him, in Fluellen's admiring words, "as valiant a man as Mark Anthony" (3.6.15), yet who ended up friendless, wifeless, unrewarded, and cudgeled by the very officer who so fulsomely had praised him. "Figo for thy friendship!" exclaimed Pistol (3.6.58): whom the drama's close found gloomily resolving "To England will I steal, and there I'll steal" (*Henry V,* 5.1.91).

> Freeze, freeze, thou bitter sky
> Thou dost not bite so nigh
> As benefits forgot.
> Though thou the waters warp
> Thy sting is not so sharp
> As friend remembered not.
>
> (*As You Like It,* 2.7.184–89)

In a striking prefiguration of *King Lear,* where Lear, Gloucester, and Edgar each plummet from comfortable privilege into the humbling strokes of eye-opening poverty, Adam and Orlando, pitched into the desperate paths of "bare distress" (2.7.96), have found that sermonizing snobbery cannot survive the experience of unaccommodated man. Exposed themselves to feel what wretches feel (*Lear,* 3.4.34), discovering in the acid of their own bellies a society heedless that "distribution should undo excess / And each man have enough" (*Lear,* 4.1.69–70), they follow, respectively, the terminal options of either broken-spirited death ("O I die for food," 2.6.1) or of robbery with violence. Unaccommodated Orlando, stumbled upon the banqueting Duke, now redefines in desperate hunger what it means to be a gentleman. It is no longer a matter of scorning servants as "hinds," disparaging their concern for adequate wages, or pining for "such exercises as may become a gentleman" (1.1.72). "If you," he begs the Duke, have

> ever sat at any good man's feast,
> If ever from your eyelids wiped a tear,

> And know what 'tis to pity and be pitied,
> Let *gentleness* my strong enforcement be.
>
> (2.7.115–18; emphasis added)

The personal experience of starvation and outcast status have dissolved, it seems, the brusque class haughtiness. ("O how bitter a thing it is to look into happiness through another man's eyes," 5.1.42.) Following this scene, Puritanical Adam disappears from sight, and Orlando ceases to be a disapproving, anti-carnival figure, becoming puppet instead in Rosalind's playful subversions. Invited hereafter by Jaques to "rail" satirically against the world, Orlando's answer is remarkable.

> I will chide no breather in the world but myself,
> against whom I know most faults.
>
> (3.2.275–76)

He continues to be something of a gull, however, twisted around Rosalind's transvestite finger, his poetry mocked (in sharp contrast to Lodge's original), and his somewhat wan residual personality easily upstaged by perfervidly passionate Silvius. Pitifully duped until the very denouement, it is Orlando, when Duke Senior seems close to rumbling Rosalind's identity, who reiterates her preposterous lies in a burst of heartfelt naivete:

> But good my lord, this boy is forest born,
> And hath been tutored in the rudiments
> Of many desperate studies by his uncle,
> Whom he reports to be a great magician
> Obscured in the circle of this forest.
>
> (5.4.30–34)

If the fortunes, then, of Adam and Orlando present vestry values fusilladed by carnival targeting, and a subsequent movement into chastening, diminishing forgiveness as suffering dissolves their pusillanimous righteousness, the values of Rosalind and Celia are substantially those of *As You Like It* itself. It was overwhelmingly the women who were "As They Liked It," bouncing into the Globe's enclave of exuberant misrule as the bearers of carnival values. When in act 1 Le Beau announces a wrestling match imminent and Touchstone suggests this scarcely "sport for ladies" (1.2.129), Rosalind calls out, in terms very strange if her only audience is Celia, "But is there any else longs to see this broken music in his sides? Is there yet another dotes on rib-breaking?" (131- 33). Clearly deictic, the cheerleading appeal (and presumable enthusiastic response) heighten the carnival bonding that Rosalind's exuberant transgressiveness will sustain right through to the epilogue.

Moreover where Orlando had sneered at underclass concern about wages, the women are prompt to rescue from poverty. "Buy thou the cottage, pasture and the flock / And thou shall have to pay for it of us," Rosalind immediately promises Corin. "And we will mend thy wages" adds Celia (2.4.90–92). Little noted by literary critics today, such sympathy must have stolen the breath away from poorer audience members, for wage complaints from the propertyless were currently pouring in to justices of the peace. Cottagers wholly dependent on wages, often in the western forests, were petitioning magistrates for relief, Buchanan Sharp records; and in 1595, for instance, come bitter complaints of wage-cutting.[72]

Celia shares occasionally in the deixis. Arrived in Arden, she slyly opines, with approving audience survey, "I like this place, / And willingly could waste my time in it" (2.4.92–93). Chiming with the drama's numerous pastoral endorsements of fleeting the time carelessly as in the golden world, the merry response contrasts again with Orlando's [initially] disapproving line on forest dwellers who "Lose and neglect the creeping hours of time," 2.7.112.

The word "forest" in fact occurs no less than twenty-three times in this play, though never more than three in any other.[73] Yet as these deictic instances cumulatively suggest, a master motif of this drama is that the "forest"—so lovingly scrutinized by generations of critics for its environmental details, so lauded for its clarifying, therapeutic effects as a sanctuary in great creating nature—this forest is in fact no more sylvan than mustard and pancakes. "The circle of this forest" (5.4.34) denotes the theater itself.

Christopher Hill noted that "London was for the sixteenth century vagabond what the greenwood had been for the medieval outlaw—an anonymous refuge."[74] Our play confirms the shrewdness of this insight, since on a primary level its forest—safely sequestered from the world of courtly authority, a place of idleness, free speech and pleasure, often egalitarian in tone, and full, we are told, of horned creatures (cuckolds)—proves manifestly to signify the Globe and its creatures. "Now my co-mates and brothers in exile," the Duke exultantly introduces the theme, "Are not these woods / More free from peril than the envious court? / Here feel we not the penalty of Adam" (2.1.1, 3–5): a sly congratulation on escaping the world of ingrate hierarchism.

Deictic elision of forest with playhouse abounds in the play, its success facilitated by the apparent absence of stage props to install a separate world. "Well, this is the forest of Arden," says Rosalind, gazing around, mischievous and appraising. "Ay, now I am in Arden the more fool I" mocks Touchstone (2.4.12–13). When Rosalind and Touchstone debate Orlando's execrable verse, Touchstone resolves, with sweeping democratic gesture, "Let the forest judge" (3.2.120). "Here we have no temple but the wood," he later jokes, "no assembly but horn-beasts" (3.3.43–44). Audrey hopes "it is no dishonest desire, to desire to become a woman of the world" (5.2.4–5).

The Duke's praise of "this our life, exempt from public haunt" clarifies the purpose of this running deixis. Jokes about "the circle of this forest" (5.4.34), reversing pastoral's customary *urbs in rure* for *rus in urbe,* serve not only to raise laughter, define character, and promote a commercially shrewd audience-actor bonding, but to define or christen the theater and its constituency. For the Globe has recently opened: this is perhaps only Shakespeare's second play there. And it has been carefully located across the water from the regulated city of London, in a traditional "Liberty" where the city authorities lack jurisdiction. (Rosalind's "Now go we in content / To liberty, and not to banishment," 1.3.133–34, possibly winks at this in pun.) The identification of the new theater with merry greenwood refuge thus underscores its chosen political identity: a realm of countercultural freedom and flourishing satire, of antiauthoritarian populism. The forest identification baptizes impunity, sparking the encircled Globe community of players and spectators alike into collective self-celebration as holiday outlaws. Laying on (with a trowel) the transgressive, carnival roistering suppressed by the vestrymen, its gregarious hilarities restore that lost experience of neighborliness and community, rebuilding, like medieval festivity in Bakhtin's words, "a second world and a second life outside officialdom."[75]

In conclusion, Shakespeare can be seen to infiltrate subtexts of subversion through a stagecraft of stealth. Primary among his performance shibboleths, we have seen, is that form of what we might call determinate or constructed latency (as opposed to the generic and indeterminate openness of dramatic form per se when transferred to the stage) which often works through deixis and the distribution of deictic effects. Orlando the unseeing, on the stage a figure of punitive ridicule, does not exist on the page. In the new stronghold of the Globe Theatre, however, where the Lord Chamberlains' Men possess finally a home of their own, the play as performed announces the continuity of the company's perspective ("As You Like It"), celebrates the impunity enjoyed in the liberty of Bankside, and consolidates its constituency, to sure commercial advantage, through the potent spell of deictic revel.

Notes

1. All quotation of *As You Like It* is from the Arden edition, ed. Agnes Latham (London: Methuen, 1975).

2. Katherine Duncan Jones, introduction to the Penguin *As You Like It* (London: Penguin Books, 2005), xxiii.

3. Edward Berry, *Shakespeare and the Hunt* (Cambridge: Cambridge University Press, 2001), 171.

4. C. L. Barber, *Shakespeare's Festive Comedy* (Princeton: Princeton University Press, 1959); M. M. Bakhtin, *Rabelais and His World,* trans. Helen Iswolsky (1968;

rpt. Bloomington: Indiana University Press, 1984). Richard Wilson aligns the transgressive carnivalesque energies of *As You Like It* with "the felonies associated with forest rioters," and popular ritual with specifically criminal activities such as poaching, in "Like the Old Robin Hood: *As You Like It* and the Enclosure Riots" in *Will Power*), 63–82; quotation from 76.

5. Steve Hindle, "The Political Culture of the Middling Sort in English Rural Communities c. 1550–1700" in Tim Harris, *The Politics of the Excluded, 1500–1850* (Basingstoke: Palgrave, 2001), 137.

6. Christopher Hill, *Society and Puritanism* (London: Secker and Warburg, 1964), 374.

7. Archer, *Pursuit of Stability*, 92–93.

8. Underdown, *Revel, Riot and Rebellion*, 94.

9. Ibid., 52.

10. Hill, *Society and Puritanism*, 152.

11. Ibid., 152–53.

12. For theorisation of ideological process into residual, dominant and emergent formations see Raymond Williams, *Marxism and Literature* (Oxford: Oxford University Press, 1997), 121–27.

13. Underdown, *Revel, Riot and Rebellion*, 40.

14. Archer, *Pursuit of Stability*, 96, 93.

15. Peter Clark, *English Provincial Society from the Reformation to the Revolution: Religion, Politics and Society in Kent 1500–1640* (Hassocks, Sussex: Harvester, 1977), 249. See esp. 155–57.

16. Underdown, *Revel, Riot, and Rebellion*, 53–54. On sixteenth-century reform of popular culture see also Burke, 207–34.

17. Hill, *Society and Puritanism*, 156–57, 367–68; Underdown, *Revel, Riot, and Rebellion*, 60.

18. David Cressy, "Mocking the Clergy: Wars of Words in Parish and Pulpit" in *Travesties and Transgressions in Tudor and Stuart England* (Oxford: Oxford University Press, 2000), 148–49.

19. Eric Carlson, "The Origin, Function, and Status of the Office of Churchwarden," in *The World of Rural Dissenters 1520–1725*, ed. Margaret Spufford (Cambridge: Cambridge University Press), 164–207.

20. Hill, *Society and Puritanism*, 372; quotation from Carlson, "Churchwarden," 194.

21. Underdown, *Revel, Riot, and Rebellion*, 31–32.

22. Carlson, "Churchwarden," 174; Underdown, *Revel, Riot, and Rebellion*, 59. Moral lapses might also be prosecuted in the quarter-sessions and assize courts. It is notable that in these culture wars, churchwardens in some places outside London chose not to present church absentees to church courts. "It was very tempting to report *omnia bene* in order to defend the community's liberty against the inquisitorial central power": Hill, *Society and Puritanism*, 337; compare Carlson, "Churchwarden," 172–74, 200–206.

23. Paul Slack, *Poverty and Policy in Tudor and Stuart England* (London: Longman, 1988), 65–66 ; cit. Woodbridge, *Vagrancy, Homelessness*, 270.

24. Steve Hindle, *On the Parish: The Micro-Politics of Poor Relief in England c.1550–1750* (Oxford: Clarendon Press, 2005).

25. Archer, *Pursuit of Stability,* 97–98. In the 1601 parliament, Sir Walter Raleigh opposing a bill, narrowly defeated, compelling churchwarden collection of recusancy fines deplored "what quarrelling and danger may happen, besides giving authority to a mean churchwarden!" Cit. Raleigh Trevelyan, *Sir Walter Raleigh* (New York: Henry Holt, 2002), 345.

26. J. A. Sharpe, "The People and the Law," in *Popular Culture in Seventeenth Century England* ed. Barry Reay (London: Croom Helm, 1985), 256; cit. Carlson, "Churchwarden," 193.

27. Beier, *Masterless Men,* 157. "Overseers were authorized to pry, with demeaning thoroughness, into poor people's lives": Woodbridge, *Vagrancy,* 275.

28. Martin Ingram, *Church Courts, Sex and Marriage, 1570–1640* (Cambridge: Cambridge University Press, 1987).

29. Steven Mullaney, *The Place of the Stage* (Ann Arbor: University of Michigan Press, 1995), 43.

30. Jean E. Howard, *The Stage and Social Struggle* (London: Routledge, 1994), 73, 83.

31. We need, as Charles Nicholl suggests, to multiply by five hundred to gain an approximate contemporary equivalence to Elizabethan prices: *The Reckoning: The Murder of Christopher Marlowe* (London: Jonathan Cape, 1992), 1.

32. Keith Thomas, *Man and the Natural World: Changing Attitudes in England 1500–1800* (London: Allen Lane, 1983), 103–4.

33. Thomas More, *Utopia,* trans Paul Turner (Harmondsworth: Penguin, 1977), 129.

34. *Calendar of State Papers Domestic, 1595–97,* 317.

35. Montrose, "The Place of a Brother in *As You Like It:* Social Process and Comic Form," in *Materialist Shakespeare,* ed. Ivo Kamps (London: Verso, 1995), 45.

36. Katherine Duncan-Jones, introduction to *As You Like It,* ed. H. J. Oliver (London: Penguin, 2005), xxi–xxii.

37. George Bernard Shaw, quoted in James Shapiro, *A Year in the Life of William Shakespeare: 1599,* 212, who does not reference the observation.

38. Richard Wilson, it is true, refers to Orlando's "combination of rebelliousness and conservatism," yet he misconstrues Orlando as simply a Robin Hood stereotype. Quoting Eric Hobsbawm's definition of the "social bandit" — "His role is that of a champion, the righter of wrongs, the bringer of justice and social equality. His relation with the peasants is one of solidarity and identity" — Wilson judges this to be "an identikit picture of Orlando"; and he goes on to associate Orlando with the Midland rioters. *Will Power,* 69, 77.

39. For the adoption of this motto by the new playhouse see Richard Dutton, "*Hamlet, An Apology for Actors,* and the Sign of the Globe," in *Shakespeare Studies* 41 (1989): 35–44.

40. The punctuation of these lines varies from edition to edition. I have given more exclamation marks than usual, to highlight the melodramatically exclamatory tone I read here.

41. Lawrence Stone, *The Family, Sex and Marriage in England 1500–1800* (Harmondsworth: Penguin, 1977), 120.

42. D. M. Metcalf, cit. Alan Brissenden, Oxford Classics edition, 1993, note to 2.3.39.

43. D. V. Glass and D. E. C Eversley, eds., *Population in History: Essays in Historical Demography* (Chicago: Aldine, 1965), 207, 212.

44. Manning, *Village Revolts* (Oxford: Oxford University Press, 1988), 191–93.

45. Susan Brigden, "Youth and the English Reformation," in *Rebellion, Popular Protest and the Social Order in Early Modern England,* ed. Paul Slack (Cambridge: Cambridge University Press, 1984), 88.

46. Manning, *Village Revolts,* 193.

47. Keith Wrightson, "Alehouses, order and reformation in rural England," in *Popular Culture and Class Struggle 1590–1914,* ed. Eileen and Stephen Yeo (Sussex: Harvester, 1981), 16–17.

48. Stone, *The Family, Sex and Marriage,* 116–120.

49. John Dod and Robert Cleaver, *A Plain and Familiar Exposition of the Ten Commandements,* 1603 (1662 edition, 199); cit. Hill, *Society and Puritanism,* 237.

50. Terry Eagleton, *Ideology: An Introduction* (London: Verso 1991), 20

51. "They'd [the lower classes] almost be better off if they *were* cart-horses. Then at least they wouldn't have to work such long hours, their food wouldn't be very much worse, and . . . they'd have no fears for the future. As it is, they're not only ground down by unrewarding toil in the present, but also worried to death by the prospect of a poverty-stricken old age . . . The climax of ingratitude comes when they're old and ill and completely destitute . . . [Society] repays them for all the vital work they've done, by letting them die in misery." *Utopia,* trans. Turner, 129.

52. *3 Henry VI,* 2.5.21–54; *Romeo and Juliet,* 5.1.80–84; *Henry V,* 4.1.213–266. All references here are to *The Norton Shakespeare,* ed. Stephen Greenblatt et al. (New York: Norton, 1997).

53. Neale, *Elizabeth and her Parliaments,* 398. The bill was defeated, by one vote.

54. See the introduction by R. B. Parker to *Coriolanus* (Oxford: Oxford University Press, 1994), 40.

55. Hill, *Society and Puritanism,* 375. See also page 250 on later Leveller pressure to redirect embezzled charitable funds to the poor. Hill quotes a John Davenant character in *News from Plymouth* who boasts of building himself a house on misappropriated income when a Collector for the Poor.

56. Proclamation 800, Hughes and Larkin, *Tudor Royal Proclamations,* 3.204–9.

57. On Tudor penalties for vagrancy, see A. L. Beier, *Masterless Men: The Vagrancy Problem in England 1560–1640* (London: Methuen, 1985), 146–170. Paul Slack's appendix in *The English Poor Law* (Cambridge: Cambridge University Press, 1990) lists the changing statutory inflictions. William C. Carroll discusses these in the wider context of Tudor "discourses of poverty" in *Fat King, Lean Beggar: Representations of Poverty in the Age of Shakespeare* (Ithaca: Cornell, 1996), 21–69. C. S. L. Davies has argued that the slavery provisions of the 1547 act were never in fact enforced, but that much the same condition existed under different names: as when Henry VIII had condemned vagrants to serve in "galleys, and other like vessels" in his wars. See Davies, "Slavery and Protector Somerset: the vagrancy act of 1547," in *Economic History Review* 19 (1966): 533–49.

58. Joyce Youings, *Sixteenth Century England* (Harmondsworth: Penguin, 1984), 283. Kelly indeed suggests that the Tudors probably "planned to use the pretense of [adequate] assistance as an excuse for passing restrictive measures of social control

... Suppression of public disorder was the major reason for Tudor concern with poverty." J. T. Kelly, *Thorns on the Tudor Rose* (Jackson: University Press of Mississippi,1977), x, 56.

59. Beier, *Masterless Men,* 161.

60. J. A. Sharpe, *Crime in Early Modern England 1550–1750* (London: Longman, 1999), 146.

61. Christopher Hill, *Society and Puritanism in Pre-Revolutionary England* (London: Secker and Warburg, 1964), 243; *Liberty Against the Law* (London: Allen Lane Penguin, 1996), 52. Contemporaries wildly exaggerated the numbers of vagrants, which probably were around fifteen thousand in the Elizabethan period, expanding in periods of economic distress and returning military campaigns: see Beier, *Masterless Men,* 14–16, and Carroll, *Fat King,* 31–32. In London's Bridewell prison, however, though in the 1560s only 16 percent of the inmates had been convicted for vagrancy, by 1600–1601 the figure had climbed to 62 percent: Paul Slack, *Poverty and Policy in Tudor and Stuart England* (London: Longman, 1988), 93.

62. A convenient gathering of such texts is Gamini Salgado's *Cony-Catchers and Bawdy Baskets* (Harmondsworth: Penguin, 1972). For widespread belief that the homeless bloodied or mutilated themselves and their children to win sympathy when begging, see Carroll, *Fat King,* 48–51, 193. Paola Pugliatti, *Beggary and Theatre in Early Modern England* (Aldershot: Ashgate, 2003), 102–5, records kindred instances from contemporary Italy and France. For the counter-factual topos romanticizing the free and merry beggar, see Carroll, *Fat King,* 63–67, 181–82, 209–15; Woodbridge, *Vagrancy,* 239–48.

63. Woodbridge, *Vagrancy,* 41–43.

64. "Scelerous secrets" quotation from Thomas Harman, *A Caveat for Common Cursitors* in *Cony-Catchers,* 81–82. On Harman, see most recently Patricia Fumerton, *Unsettled: The Culture of Mobility and the Working Poor in Early Modern England* (Chicago: University of Chicago Press, 2006).

65. Carroll, *Fat King,* 47.

66. Quoted by Hill, *Puritanism and Revolution,* 219.

67. Cit. Neale, *Elizabeth and her Parliaments,* 347.

68. See Neale, *Elizabeth and her Parliaments,* 349–50, 366–67.

69. Anon., *A Declaration of the Grounds and Reasons why we the Poor Inhabitants of the Town of Wellingborrow . . . ,* cit. Christopher Hill, *Winstanley: the Law of Freedom and Other Writings* (Harmondsworth: Penguin, 1973), 25.

70. Agnes Latham registers perplexity in her Arden edition, Appendix A, 132–33. Alan Dessen has noted that the visibility to the audience of the groaning table would condition audience sympathy for Adam and Orlando, but has neither explored the politics of this perception, nor perceived the targeting effect of Orlando's obliviousness to the board: *Cambridge Companion to Shakespeare Studies,* ed. Stanley Wells (Cambridge: Cambridge University Press, 1986), 98.

71. Chris Fitter, "'Your Captain is Brave, and Dares Reformation': Jack Cade, the Hacket rising, and Shakespeare's Vision of Popular Rebellion in *2 Henry VI,*" in *Shakespeare Studies,* ed. Susan Zimmerman (Madison: Fairleigh Dickinson University Press, 2004), 32:173–219.

72. Buchanan Sharp, *In Contempt of All Authority* (Berkeley: University of California Press, 1980), 164.
73. Berry, *Shakespeare and the Hunt,* 167.
74. Hill, *The World Turned Upside Down* (Harmondsworth: Penguin, 1975), 40.
75. Bakhtin, *Rabelais and His World,* 6.

Rereading the Side Panels in
The View of London from the North

June Schlueter

UNTIL Herbert Berry's 2000 essay in *Shakespeare Survey 53*,[1] analyses of *The View of the Cittye of London from the North towards the Sowth,* which pictures a Shoreditch playhouse, accepted the Utrecht impression as unique. But in 1998, Ralph Hyde, in *Print Quarterly,* announced the discovery of a second copy,[2] found in 1996 by Clive and Philip Burden tipped into an early edition of John Speed's *Theatre of the Empire of Great Britaine,* first published in 1611.[3] The Burden copy differs from the Utrecht copy in one respect: it contains side panels, each featuring a man and a woman, presumably of London.[4] Berry, who offers a detailed analysis of the topography and the geometry of the *View* as well as commentary on its relationship to John Norden's *Civitas Londini* (1600) (which shows London from the south looking north),[5] concludes that the *View* was drawn sometime between 1600 and 1613 and engraved in about 1610 or later. The side panels, he claims, which are integral to two of the three copper plates that produced the engraving, validate his conclusion: the figures on the left panel (see figure 1) are in Jacobean costume and are, perhaps, King James and Queen Anne; those on the right panel (see figure 2) are in Elizabethan costume and are, perhaps, Queen Elizabeth and a Lord Mayor.

Berry's analysis of the *View,* which concludes that the pictured playhouse is the Curtain,[6] is sophisticated and sound, and, except for a few parting caveats, I do not presume to take issue with it. Rather, I wish to revisit Berry's reading of the side panels of the *View*. For although he has done important work in presenting them, his (tentative) conclusions about the represented figures neither acknowledge nor consider the rich visual vocabulary reflected in the border art of early modern maps. When the side panels are viewed in relation to such images, it becomes clear that Berry is right about one panel and mistaken about the other.

Berry's identification of the figures in the *View* begins with the observation that the couple on the right panel appear older than the couple on the left panel. He assesses their clothing: the pair on the left are in fashionable, even extravagant, Jacobean habit, the pair on the right in "Elizabethan clothing of

REREADING THE SIDE PANELS IN *THE VIEW OF LONDON FROM THE NORTH* 143

Fig. 1. Left side panel of *The View of the Cittye of London from the North towards the Sowth*. Courtesy of the Burden Collection.

two decades or so earlier."[7] Noting the similarity of the pair on the left panel to portraits of King James and Queen Anne by Marcus Gheeraerts, Renold Elstrack, and others, Berry decides that the figures could represent the royal pair—or at least a Jacobean couple. The woman on the right panel, in Elizabethan clothes, is, he proposes, Queen Elizabeth, her hairstyle and neckware as they appear in the many portraits of the Tudor queen. For the man on the right panel alongside Elizabeth, Berry is guessing: "He may be a lord mayor of London, or the idea of one."[8] Underpinning his four identifications is the reasonable assumption that the figures are illustrations "mainly of the government of the country."[9]

Berry is correct in noting that the figures embellishing early modern maps and views were not only decorative but informative, intended to say something about the area represented. At times, the information conveyed fed the imagination, as in maps of exotic parts of the world—the Americas, Asia, Africa—picturing Anthropophagi and others as cannibals, giants, animal-men, and men with heads beneath their shoulders. But, as Willem Janszoon

Fig. 2. Right side panel of *The View of the Cittye of London from the North towards the Sowth*. Courtesy of the Burden Collection.

Blaeu's maps of *Americae* (1617), *Asia* (1618), and *Africae* (1619)[10] show, the exotic did not necessarily equate to the monstrous. For though their sea creatures are sensational—and probably contributed to the maps' saleability—the pictures across the top of each portray, respectively, cities of the New World, Asia, and Africa, and those along the sides present realistic American, Asian, and African natives—or the mapmaker's understanding of them.

Early seventeenth-century world maps, especially, preserved the exotic through creatures occupying the seas, no doubt to create the sense of a dangerous journey to undiscovered parts. But in the cartouches that often lined the borders of such maps were familiar allegorical or mythological figures, vignettes of major cities, and full-length portraits of the inhabitants of various countries. Blaeu's *Nova Totius Terrarum Orbis Geographica ac Hydrographiva Tabula* (1606),[11] for example, engraved by Jasua van den Ende, has side borders with depictions of the four elements and the four seasons, a top row of cartouches with representations of the sun, moon, and planets, and a lower border picturing the seven wonders of the world. John Speed's *A New and Accurat Map of the World* (1626),[12] probably engraved by Abraham Goos, features not only allegorical figures at the edges of the hemispheres but also portraits of Sir Francis Drake, Ferdinand Magellan, Thomas Candish, and Oliver van der Noort (the choice of circumnavigators suggesting that, despite its issuance only in English, the map was marketed both in England and on the continent). And Claes Janszoon Visscher's *Novia Totius Terrarum* (1639)[13] presents twelve Roman emperors across the upper and lower borders and, along its sides, cities and people from various parts of the world.

Maps featuring such regular, paneled borders on two, three, or four sides became known as *cartes à figures*,[14] and, in the first half of the seventeenth century, the golden age of mapmaking, they were plentiful. Jonathan Potter describes the development of map art, particularly the paneled border:

> Until this time [the 1590s] any decoration on maps was stylized, taking the form of clouds, strapwork, windheads and, very occasionally, figures or portraits. From now on, vignette illustrations and border decorations were used to add copious information to the basic cartographic content.[15]

Those who performed maps of individual countries or regions, particularly the Dutch, often used the convention of the *carte à figure*. Blaeu's *Europa* (1617),[16] for example, depicts nine European cities across the top and couples representing ten countries along both sides. His *Germania* (1606)[17] presents eight cities of the Holy Roman Empire across the top, flanking a portrait of the Emperor Ferdinand II, and rows of ecclesiastical and lay electors along the sides. Visscher's *Novissima, et accuratissima Leonis Belgici* (1611),[18] which styles the Dutch Republic as a lion (at peace during the Twelve Year Truce), is bordered on the left and right with vignettes of its cities and, along the top, with coats of arms of the provinces. In England, Speed's county maps (1611), though not formal *cartes à figures,* embellished the work of Christopher Saxton and others not only with informative text (front and back) but also with insets of cities, battles, heraldry, and other identifying signs, at times lining up the shields in border cartouches. Speed's *America* (1627), engraved by Goos, and *The Turkish Empire* (1627),[19] as well as several maps engraved by Jodocus Hondius in *The Theatre of the Empire of Great Britaine,*[20] makes full use of the form: *America,* for example, presents major cities of the two continents at its top border and, along its sides, five vignettes of natives of North America (Speed includes Greenland) and five of natives of South America. Clearly, images forming a map's decorative borders—artwork that added to the document's attractiveness, its informative value, and its saleability—were intended to complement and enhance the cartographic content through pictorial references to the political, historical, and cultural character of a particular place.

146   JUNE SCHLUETER

But the border figures in many of these maps—Speed's *America,* for example—are identified by the text beneath them. The images on the side panels of *The View of the Cittye of London from the North towards the Sowth* have no legends; the figures simply stand on ground discontinuous with that of the *View,* showing a few flora. How can we tell whether the figures on the left panel are King James and Queen Anne, as Berry proposes? Speed's *The Kingdome of Scotland*[21] (see figure 3), published in *The Theatre of the Empire of Great Britaine,* may provide the answer, for it places full-length, labeled images of the royal couple in cartouches on either side, with the princes, Henry and Charles, beneath them. When one compares the King James figure in the Speed map (see figure 4) to the male figure on the left panel of the *View,* one immediately sees their similarity. Each is in doublet and hose, with a full knee-length cape; each sports a trimmed, medium-length beard and wears a sword, ribbon garters, a large linen "band" or collar, lace-edged cuffs, and a high-crowned broad-brimmed hat, though the hat in the *View* does not have the feather. Similarly, Speed's Queen Anne (see figure 5) and the female figure in the *View* each wears a fashionable décolleté bodice, a dress spread by a wheel farthingale, a large lace-trimmed starched

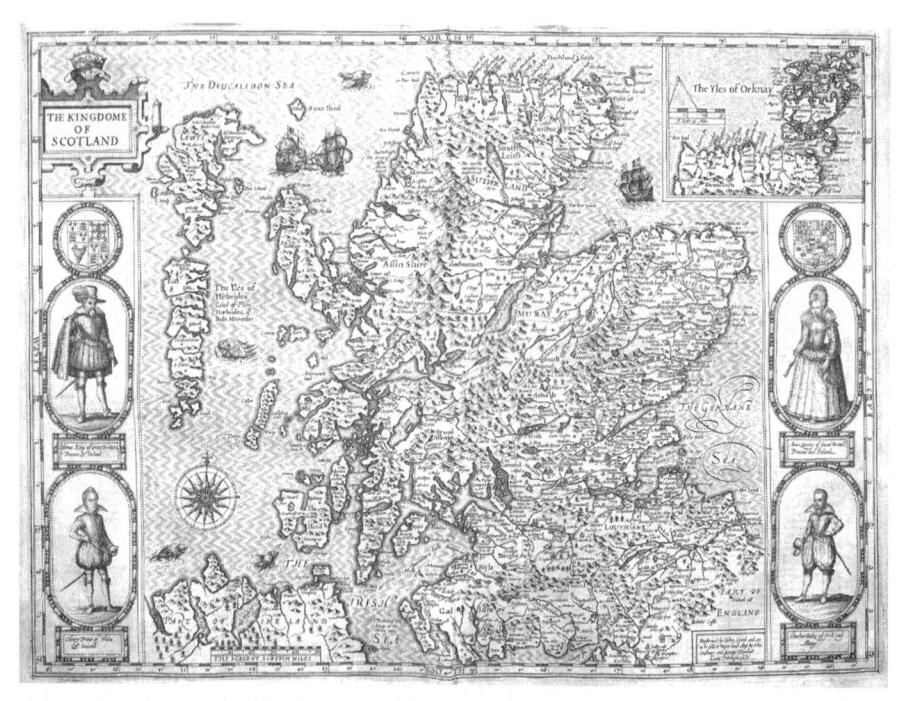

Fig. 3. John Speed, *The Kingdome of Scotland.* From *The Theatre of the Empire of Great Britaine* (London: John Sudbury and George Humble, 1611). Watkins Library, Trinity College, Hartford, Conn.

Fig. 4. King James. Detail from John Speed's *The Kingdome of Scotland*. Watkins Library, Trinity College, Hartford, Conn.

Fig. 5. Queen Anne. Detail from John Speed's *The Kingdome of Scotland*. Watkins Library, Trinity College, Hartford, Conn.

band, lace-edged cuffs, a double row of neck pearls, and a high head-tire; each holds a handkerchief in her left hand, and each carries a fan, though that of Speed's noblewoman is not the feather fan of the woman in the *View.* The artistic relationship between the figures in the Speed map and the *View* is strong, suggesting that Berry may be right in identifying the couple on the left panel as King James and Queen Anne.

Before concluding that they are the royal couple, however, one must look to a particular application of *cartes à figures,* in which formal paneled borders are devoted not to individual monarchs and rulers, as in *The Kingdome of Scotland,* but to generic inhabitants, presented in national costume. Often, in maps, views, and town plans (the latter usually bird's eye perspectives) not using panels of border art—*Londinum Feracissimi Angliae Regni Metropolis* (1572), for example[22]—a disproportionately large male and female figure (in this case, two) are prominently positioned in the landscape. But in maps and views decorated with border art—a frequent practice from the 1590s—the cartouches often contain people of various social classes. Jan Jansson's *Nova Helvetia Tabula* (1630),[23] engraved by Jodocus Hondius II, shows major cities of Switzerland along its top and bottom borders and, along the left and right borders, three couples: "Nobilis Helvetus" and "Nobilis foemina," "Mercator Helvetus" and "Virgo Basiliensis," "Rusticus Helvetus" and "Rustica Helveta." In 1634, after acquiring the copper plate, Claes Janszoon Visscher added border art to Arnold and Hendrick Florenzoon van Langren's *Comitatus Flandria* (c. 1595),[24] placing Flemish cities across the top and bottom, round cartouches in the top corners for Archduke Albert VII and Infanta Isabella Clara, and, on the sides, couples representing various strata of society, labeled "Nobilis" and "Nobilis Uxur," "Civis Uxur" and "Cives," "Rusticus" and "Rustica," and "Piscat. Uxur" and "Piscator." Speed's *The Kingdome of Irland*[25] and *The Kingdome of England,*[26] both published in *The Theatre of the Empire of Great Britain,* are also in this tradition. The first pictures three couples, labeled "The Gentleman of Ireland" and "The Gentlewoman of Ireland," "The Civill Irish Woman" and "The Civill Irish man," and "The Wilde Irish man" and "The Wilde Irish Woman."[27] The second shows four couples, each representing a distinct stratum of society. Indeed, in 1653, when, after multiple runs, the copper plate of Speed's *Kingdome of Scotland* deteriorated, the royal family was replaced with such generic figures, dressed in Scottish costume.

Perhaps the best measure of the figures on the left side panel of the *View* is Speed's *The Kingdome of England* (see figure 6), which presents, on opposite sides and labeled, "A Lady" and "A Noble-man," "A Gentleman" and "A Gentle Woman," "A Citizens Wife" and "A Citizen," and "A Countryman" and "A Country Woman." Interestingly, although the map is contemporaneous with *The Kingdome of Scotland,* Speed's noble couple (see figure 7, upper) are less like the couple in the *View* than his gentle couple (see figure

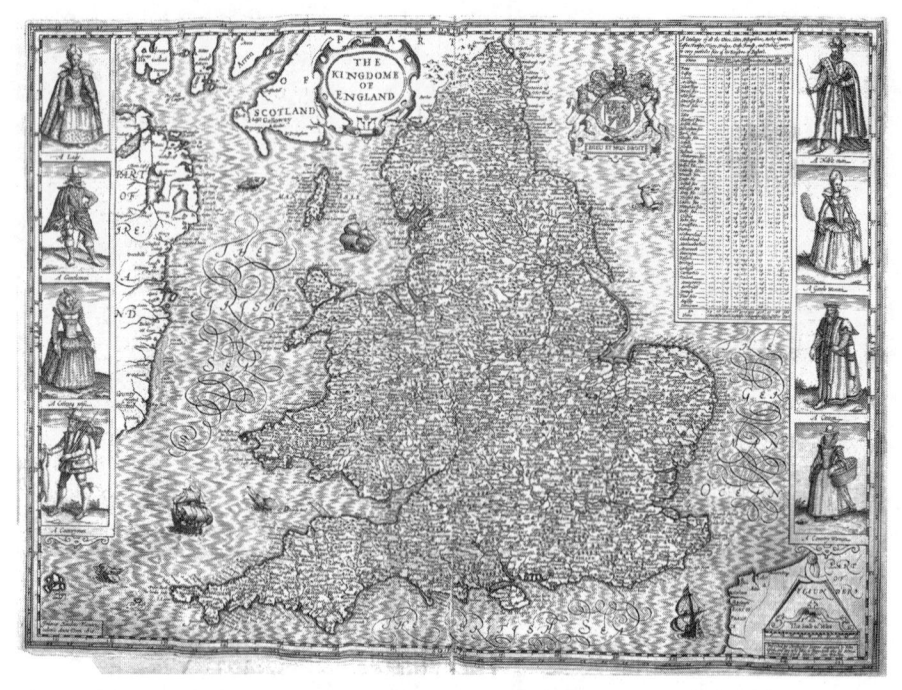

Fig. 6. John Speed, *The Kingdome of England*, 1611. From *The Theatre of the Empire of Great Britaine* (London: John Sudbury and George Humble, 1611). Watkins Library, Trinity College, Hartford, Conn.

7, lower) are. Indeed, there is little difference between the lady in the top cartouche of the Speed map and the gentlewoman in the second tier, other than a long cape for the lady and a plumed fan for the gentlewoman. Notably, it is the gentlewoman, not the lady, that most resembles the female figure on the left panel of the *View*. Berry's caution that the royal couple may only be a Jacobean couple is well taken, for, absent labels, there is little in the conventions of map art to distinguish them.

But what about the right side panels of the *View*, those that Berry believes may be Queen Elizabeth and a Lord Mayor? In assessing the images of these supposed representations of the older government of London, we need only look to the third couple in Speed's *The Kingdome of England*, "A Citizens Wife" and "A Citizen" (see figure 8).[28] Here is a female figure who, like the woman on the right panel of the *View*, wears an older style but still fashionable wired ruff, a moderately hooped dress, slashed shoulder edging, lace-trimmed cuffs, and a brimmed bonnet with a dip over the forehead. And here is a male figure who, like the man on the right panel of the *View*, wears a long robe with cap sleeves, a small ruff (that blends with his beard), and a narrow-brimmed bag hat, and he clutches a pair of gloves. From this compar-

Fig. 7. A Lady, A Noble man; A Gentleman, A Gentle Woman. Detail from John Speed, *The Kingdome of England.* Watkins Library, Trinity College, Hartford, Conn.

A Citizens wife   *A Citizen*

Fig. 8. A Citizen's Wife, A Citizen. Detail from John Speed, *The Kingdome of England.* Watkins Library, Trinity College, Hartford, Conn.

ison alone, one can readily conclude that the female figure on the right panel of the *View* is *not* Queen Elizabeth in outdated clothes but, merely, a citizen's wife. And the "Lord Mayor" is, merely, a citizen.[29] Clearly, the maker of *The View of the Cittye of London from the North towards the Sowth,* or its engraver, knew the conventions of the social class *carte à figure* and, to complement the noble or gentle figures on the left panel, presented a citizen's wife and a citizen on the right.

But can we move beyond the visual likenesses of the people in Speed's maps and in the *View* to determine whether it is more or less likely that the Jacobean couple are the King and Queen? What more does the visual vocabulary of Speed's border art suggest? Speed's *Theatre of the Empire of Great Britaine* (also published in a Latin edition as *Theatrum Imperii Magnae Britanniae,* 1616) is dedicated to King James, who, notably, attempted to unify the kingdoms of England and Wales, Scotland, and Ireland. Speed pays homage to the King's efforts through adjustments to Saxton's maps that give visual coherence to the "Empire" and through pictures of the royal family in *The Kingdome of Scotland,* with James, originally James VI of Scotland, labeled "King of Great Britain, Fraunce & Ireland," Henry "Prince of Wales & Ireland," and Charles "Duke of York and Albany." However, as Bernhard Klein points out in *Maps and the Writing of Space in Early Modern England and Ireland,* the title of Speed's *Theatre of the Empire of Great Britain* "announces a conceptual redirection."[30] Individually and collectively, the maps in his atlas

> promoted the concept of a land-based nation and thus deflected attention from the monarch as the sole focus of national loyalty. In Speed's atlas this process is most clearly visible in the elaborate heraldic presence of the gentry which marginalizes the royal coat of arms and breaks down the hierarchical concentration on the insignia of the ruler. Despite its explicitly royal agenda Speed's cartographic imagery thus contributed to the emergence of a conception of England defined not exclusively in relation to its monarch, but to all the leading families of the gentry.[31]

Klein, who sees Speed's project not only in geographic terms but also in social and cultural terms, notes that in this chronicle of England's contemporary identity, the King is displaced onto the map of Scotland, where he was born, and the comparable spaces in *The Kingdome of England* are occupied by residents of England, arranged by social class. These portraits, he observes,

> turn English topography into a social script that gives the land a voice and a narrative structure: though the narrow scope of these eight portraits suggests a rigid and intransigent society—structured hierarchies, a natural order of heterosexual couples, limited social mobility—the introduction of a "popular" element into the map design constructs the prosopopoeic image of a national space performed by its "users" and shaped by the continuous, daily effort of its loyal inhabitants drawn from various social ranks, belonging to urban or rural spheres, but all mythically united in the vanishing point of the national.[32]

Klein's analysis is consistent with that of Richard Helgerson in *Forms of Nationhood: The Elizabeth Writing of England,*[33] who observes that in maps issued in the first decade of James's reign, the land itself garnered more attention than royal insignia. Speaking of Norden's county maps, he notes that, in 1604, the royal arms that had figured prominently in 1598

> fail to appear on his manuscript map of Cornwall, and they occur on only eleven of the fifty-six county maps added to Camden's *Britannia* in the edition of 1607.... Apparently this feature, so prominent in Saxton's atlas, no longer mattered much to either Norden or Camden.[34]

He continues with this commentary on Speed:

> John Speed may have cared a little more. Thirty-six of the forty-two maps of the English counties in his *Theater of the Empire of Great Britain* (1611) still display

those arms, but in doing so they inflict another sort of displacement. In Speed the royal arms are usually much reduced in scale and always joined by a whole array of other features—arms of local gentry, colleges, or guilds; plans of cities and castles; scenes of battle; pictures of buildings, monuments, and local heroes—features that direct attention away from the king and toward the country.[35]

We do not know who drew *The View of the Cittye of London from the North towards the Sowth.* But if it was an Englishman—Norden, for example (given its apparent connection to *Civitas Londini*), or Speed (given his intense interest in mapping England)—we may see the construction as a reflection of the mapmaker's desire to present not only a static record of the topography of London but also a dynamic cultural instrument of civic, and national, pride. Little is omitted from this expansive, detailed *View:* there are churches, public buildings, houses, windmills, the theater. There are roads and footpaths leading to the city crossing fenced and open fields in the north. And within the landscape, there are people performing a variety of activities, forming a living panorama: men on foot and on horseback, driving a pack horse, leading and following a horse-pulled wagon; horses grazing; a couple walking, preceded by a dog; a group of men engaged in the sport of archery. The images announce the vibrancy of London, which the *View* celebrates as a people's city, its imposing urban outline and adjacent fields testimony to the people's industry and power.

Those who bought and displayed the *View,* which, in the early seventeenth century, would have included growing numbers of the "middle" class, must have spent hours locating familiar structures and marveling at the sweep and the detail of the panorama. But the early modern eye would also have lingered over the *View*'s pictorial embellishments, noticing not only the figures in the landscape but also those prominently displayed couples on its sides. It would have been difficult for such a reader not to connect personally with the *View,* not to experience a sense of the identity of the space he inhabited, not to feel stirrings of civic, and national, pride.

The View of the Cittye of London from the North towards the Sowth is unique in both orientation and layout: no other extant Elizabethan or Jacobean view presents the city from this perspective nor features side panels embellished with outsized human figures. Yet those human figures are reminiscent of the earlier figures in George Braun and Franz Hogenberg's city maps. And when the *View* is considered in relation to maps of the early seventeenth century, it becomes clear that it, too, participates in the then fashionable style of the social class *carte à figure.* Indeed, if the *View* is in sympathy with the "conceptual redirection" Klein and Helgerson describe, then one would not expect royalty to appear on its panels: the borders of the *View* would be reserved for the people of the city.

The 1996 discovery of the Burden impression of the *View* with side panels intact securely places the engraving in Jacobean times. Does it follow, then, as Berry argues, that the pictured playhouse is the Curtain? The Curtain was, after all, the only theater standing near Holywell when James I ascended the throne, the Theatre (erected in 1576) having been dismantled in 1598–99 and rebuilt on the south Bank as the Globe. If the figures on the left side panel are, indeed, Jacobean, then Berry's conclusion would seem inevitable. But there are cautions. For one, we must assume that the engraving was done shortly after the drawing. (Even though the panels are integral to the copper plate and could not have been added after the engraving, it is possible that the engraver added them, even years after the drawing was taken.) For another, we must assume that, even granting its relationship to *Civitas Londini*, the *View* was drawn from life, reflecting the cityscape in its then-present form. (Maps copied from earlier views sometimes retained structures that no longer stood.) Third, we must assume that Berry's geometry is correct and that it points to the place in the *View* where the Curtain, not the Theatre, stood. (Sidney Fisher's geometry produced a different result.)

Unfortunately, even with its side panels accurately annotated, the Burden copy of the *View* does not reveal the date of the drawing. The primary hope now would appear to rest with the Museum of London's archeologists, who, following an August 6, 2008, announcement that a polygonal brick foundation has been discovered in Shoreditch,[36] may be able to test Fisher's and Berry's competing geometries in relation to the *in situ* structure. For now, however, there is little more that *The View of the Cittye of London from the North towards the Sowth* can tell us about the pictured playhouse.

Notes

1. Herbert Berry, "The View of London from the North and the Playhouses in Holywell," *Shakespeare Survey 53* (2000): 196–212.

2. A contact-size reproduction may be found in the pocket of *Tudor London: A Map and a View*, ed. Ann Saunders and John Schofield (London: London Topographical Society Publication No. 159 in association with the Museum of London, 2001). For an informative analysis of the print, see Schofield, "The View of the City of London from the North," 33–57.

3. Ralph Hyde, "A New View of London," *Print Quarterly* 15.1 (March 1998): 63–65. The Burdens are dealers in maps, prints, and books, doing business as Clive A Burden Ltd, in Rickmansworth, Hertfordshire, U.K.

4. The Burden copy measures 1039 mm in width and 96 mm in height. The left panel adds 125 mm, the right panel 131 mm, making the *View* with side panels 1295 mm (approximately 4 feet 2 inches) wide. There is evidence that the side panels were also present originally in the Utrecht copy but were removed.

5. John Norden, *Civitas Londini*, 1600. Reprinted in Ralph Hyde, *Gilded Scenes and Shining Prospects: Panoramic Views of British Towns 1575–1900* (New Haven:

Yale Center for British Art, 1985), 42–43, plate 4. Here and in other references to maps that are available in several sources, I cite readily accessible or high quality reproductions. Many can be found online as well, e.g., http://historic-cities-huji.ac.il, the website of the Historic Cities Center of the Department of Geography, the Hebrew University of Jerusalem and the Jewish National and University Library.

6. Since its discovery in the 1930s in the seventeenth-century journal of Abram Booth (University of Utrecht library, MS. 1198, Hist. 147), scholars have attempted to date the Utrecht *View* (University of Utrecht library, formerly MS. 1108, f. 83, now Gr. Form. 12), the date being key to the identification of the pictured playhouse. Leslie Hotson, "The Wooden O," *The Times* (London), March 26, 1954, pp. 7, 14, and *Shakespeare's Wooden O* (London: Rupert Hart-Davis, 1959), 304–9, Appendix B, argues that it is the Curtain. Those who accept Hotson's argument include Arthur M. Hind, *Engraving in England in the Sixteenth & Seventeenth Centuries,* 3 vols. (Cambridge: Cambridge University Press, 1952–64), vol. 2 (1955), 12–14; Gerald Eades Bentley, *The Jacobean and Caroline Stage,* 7 vols. (Oxford: Clarendon Press, 1941–68), vol. 6 (1968), 131–32; and Rosemary Linnell, *The Curtain Playhouse* (London: Curtain Theatre, 1977), 37–39. Sidney Fisher, *The Theatre, the Curtain and the Globe* (Montreal: McGill University Library, 1964), 2–6, argues that it is the Theatre. Those who accept Fisher's argument include Richard Hosley, "The Theatre and the Tradition of Playhouse Design," in *The First Public Playhouse: The Theatre in Shoreditch 1576–1598,* ed. Herbert Berry (Montreal: McGill-Queen's University Press, 1979), 47–79; John Orrell, *The Human Stage: English Theatre Design, 1567–1640* (Cambridge: Cambridge University Press, 1988), 28–31; and James P. Lusardi, "The Pictured Playhouse: Reading the Utrecht Engraving of Shakespeare's London," *Shakespeare Quarterly* 44 (1993): 202–7.

7. Herbert Berry, "The View of London from the North and the Playhouses in Holywell," 201.

8. Ibid.

9. Ibid., 198.

10. Willem Janszoon Blaeu, *Americae,* 1617; *Asia,* 1618; *Africae,* 1619. Reprinted in Jonathan Potter, *Country Life Book of Antique Maps: An Introduction to the History of Maps and How to Appreciate Them* (London: Country Life Books, 1988), 47, 117, 114.

11. Willem Janszoon Blaeu, *Nova Totius Terrarum Orbis Geographica ac Hydrographiva Tabula,* 1606. Reprinted in Ashley and Miles Baynton-Williams, *New Worlds: Maps from the Age of Discovery* (London: Quercus, n.d.), 58–59.

12. John Speed, *A New and Accurat Map of the World Drawne according to the truest Descriptions latest Discoveries & best Observations that have beene made by English or Strangers,* 1626. Reprinted in Ashley and Miles Baynton-Williams, *New Worlds,* 72–73.

13. Claes Janszoon Visscher, *Novia Totius Terrarum,* 1639. Reprinted in Jonathan Potter, *Country Life Book of Antique Maps,* 15.

14. See Jonathan Potter, *Country Life Book of Antique Maps,* 26.

15. Ibid., 55.

16. Willem Janszoon Blaeu, *Europa,* signed "Janssonio" (before Blaeu changed his name), 1617. Reprinted in Jonathan Potter, *Country Life Book of Antique Maps,* 99.

17. Willem Janszoon Blaeu, *Germania*, 1606. Reprinted in Ashley and Miles Baynton-Williams, *New Worlds*, 60–61.

18. Claes Janszoon Visscher, *Novissima, et accuratissima Leonis Belgici*, 1611. Reprinted in Ashley and Miles Baynton-Williams, *New Worlds*, 68–69.

19. John Speed, *America*, 1627; *The Turkish Empire*, 1627. Reprinted in Jonathan Potter, *Country Life Book of Antique Maps*, 136–37, 119.

20. John Speed, *The Theatre of the Empire of Great Britaine* (London: John Sudbury and George Humble, 1611). Reprinted, from the Latin edition, *Theatrum Imperii Magnae Britanniae*, 1611, as *The Counties of Britain: A Tudor Atlas by John Speed*, introduction by Nigel Nicolson, county commentaries by Alasdair Hawkyard (1988; London: Pavilion, in association with the British Library, 1995).

21. John Speed, *The Kingdome of Scotland*, 1611. Reprinted in *The Counties of Britain*, 266–67.

22. *Londinum Feracissimi Angliae Regni Metropolis*, picturing London c. 1558, was probably drawn by Georg Hoefnagel and engraved by Franz Hogenberg. It was published in *Civitates Orbis Terrarum*, ed. Georg Braun, 6 vols., 1572–1617 (Cologne), vol. 1 (1572). Reprinted in Carl Moreland and David Bannister, *Antique Maps* (London: Phaidon Press, 1993), plate 3.

23. Jan Jansson, *Nova Helvetiae Tabula*, 1630. Reprinted in Carol Moreland and David Bannister, *Antique Maps*, 237.

24. Claes Janszoon Visscher, *Comitatus Flandria*, c. 1595, re-engraved with side panels, 1634. Reprinted in Ashley and Miles Baynton-Williams, *New Worlds*, 52–53.

25. John Speed, *The Kingdome of Irland*, 1611. Reprinted in *The Counties of Britain*, 270–71.

26. John Speed, *The Kingdome of England*, 1611. Reprinted in *The Counties of Britain*, 26–27.

27. For commentary on the English conceptualization of Ireland as wilderness, see Bernhard Klein, *Maps and the Writing of Space in Early Modern England and Ireland* (New York: Palgrave, 2001), 61–75.

28. A single print of the citizen, identical to the citizen in Speed's map, is held in the Guildhall Library Print Room (Pr.L25.1, Catalogue no. p7515701), available as Record 26997 in the Guildhall's online database: http://collage.cityoflondon.gov.uk.

29. I am resting my argument with the border art of Speed's *The Kingdome of England*. In a book, in preparation, on *alba amicorum*, I present watercolor paintings of Lord Mayors, done in London picture shops, that support the identification of the figure on the side panel as a citizen.

30. Bernhard Klein, *Maps and the Writing of Space in Early Modern England and Ireland*, 105.

31. Ibid., 107–8.

32. Ibid., 109.

33. Richard Helgerson, *Forms of Nationhood: The Elizabethan Writing of England* (Chicago: University of Chicago Press, 1992).

34. Ibid., 114, 116.

35. Ibid., 116.

36. Fiona Hamilton, "Dig at New Theatre Site Reveals Shakespeare's First Playhouse," *The Times* (London), August 6, 2008, p. 18.

Reviews

Aliens and Englishness in Elizabethan Drama, by Lloyd Edward Kermode. Cambridge: Cambridge University Press, 2009. Pp. xi + 202. $99.00.

Reviewer: CHARLES R. FORKER

We live in a world, especially in America, where a secure sense of national identity is constantly threatened by elements perceived as alien to a superior native heritage, political, economic, linguistic, or religious. Some fear universalizing health care as a socialist and therefore foreign program; others resent illegal immigrants as competing unfairly with native workers, as unwelcome intruders who, at the very least, should be required to learn English; still others are suspicious of persons who fall outside familiar patterns of Judeo-Christian worship, perceiving them as potential terrorists. Popular anxiety about invasive foreignness emerges in bumper stickers that read "Buy American" or in the need to rename french-fried potatoes "freedom fries." Once the feared imports have become sufficiently assimilated, however, Americans tend to accept them as aspects of a traditional melting-pot diversity—a diversity fundamental to, and definitional of, the culture. Kermode considers such issues in Elizabethan England, proposing to analyze them as reflected in a range of plays dating from the 1550s to the close of the century. His organization is chronological. Two early chapters discuss allegorical plays: the anonymous *Wealth and Health,* Fulwell's *Like Will to Like,* Wapull's *The Tide Tarrieth No Man,* and Wilson's *The Three Ladies of London* with its sequel, *The Three Lords and Three Ladies of London.* Brief consideration of *Sir Thomas More,* in which Shakespeare had a hand, leads to a chapter on the bard's second tetralogy, which in turn is followed by a concluding analysis of three very different comedies from the 1590s—Haughton's *Englishmen for My Money,* Dekker's *Shoemaker's Holiday,* and Marston's *Jack Drum's Entertainment.*

Although generically diverse, all these plays, in the author's view, contribute to an ongoing debate about the nature and quality of Anglo-foreign relations in the period. Kermode sees the English as initially vindicating their sense of superior national selfhood by contrasting it with foreignness, usually as manifested by residents or visitors from Holland or France, but also by cultures psychologically closer to home—the Welsh, Scottish, and Irish. Continental residents are seen as contaminating English morals by taking advantage of Christian hospitality and by corrupting native generosity to make profit at all costs the dominant imperative. Jewishness additionally enters the mix since stereotypes of the usurer, the moneylender, and the dealer in foreign trade often influence dramatic characterization. Kermode's principal argument, however, is that the sense of Englishness that progressively develops in these dramas moves quickly beyond a simple antithesis of the self versus "the other" by incorporating and eventually even celebrating the foreignness that it had begun by rejecting. As he writes, "The English are a people rife [ripe?] for alien confusion, resisting the alien but subject to absorbing the habits of others, afraid of foreignness but needing (to understand or contain) the foreign to bolster and inoculate the self against what they fear" (64). Thus the theater can function not merely as a mirror of national identity; it actually constructs that identity performatively by absorbing and selectively reshaping elements of the alien to project a heightened self-definition of Englishness. Paradoxically, the process of constant mutation over time becomes the only constant, a conclusion too predictable, one might think, to justify the laborious superstructure of theoretical excogitation erected to support it. This is not to gainsay the impressive amount of historical research on political and social background that informs Kermode's discussion.

His summary of the relevant demographics is helpful, since burgeoning concentration of foreigners in urban centers (particularly London) was a significant factor. Norwich, the second city, was only one-sixteenth London's size, and the English capital became the largest urban center in Europe after Paris, numbering about 200,000 by 1600. "Strangers" came to London not only from overseas but from rural areas within the country and from Scotland and Wales. Overcrowding was endemic. Tens of thousands of continental migrants flowed into England for commercial and religious reasons although there was a falling off as the century neared its end. Turbulence in the Netherlands under the tyrannous Duke of Alva and events such as the Saint Bartholomew massacre in France produced a flood of Protestant refugees who clustered in particular neighborhoods, formed their own non-liturgical congregations in competition with the Anglican establishment, and, as "denizens," often shared the halfway status of legal residents uncertainly located between the full rights of "true born" native citizenship and the limbo of stateless transients. Trade with the Levant, authorized in 1581, expanded English horizons, and contributed to the increasingly international character of the capital, which was awash with foreign travelers. The situation for outlanders in England was complicated by those born of English parents abroad, by second-generation children of strangers born in England, by the brief restoration of Catholicism under Queen Mary, whose marriage to Philip II was seen by many as a threat (Mary's reign of course precipitated Protestant exiles in the opposite direction), and of course by the febrile xenophobia aroused by the Armada and its aftermath. Naturalization, although permissible by application to the Crown, was costly and time-consuming, but many continental visitors settled in Britain nevertheless. Landlords profited by charging high rents to strangers, who were often resented because they traded goods or kept shops despite not being freemen of guilds, and who brought with them alien clothing styles, customs, habits, and languages. English was increasingly regarded as "a hodge-podge of tongues" (5), its readiness (unlike French) to absorb foreign words an obvious symbol of the cosmopolitan undertow affecting the national self-image. But frustrations borne of cheek-by-jowl living conditions, of economic and religious friction, inevitably resulted in the scapegoating of "aliens" to produce a cultural environment and a sense of English identity for which Kermode repeatedly invokes the term "confusion."

The confused and confusing matters that the author manfully addresses in this work are inherently interesting and important. Unfortunately their handling here makes for a daunting challenge to readers. So many strands and meanings of the term "alien" tangle in Kermode's prose that stable definitions become impossible, categories keep collapsing upon each other, and clarity vaporizes in a cloud of theorizing abstraction. The mentality of English culture is at once insular and expansionist. Foreignness can be inside or outside of the nation, objective or subjective, a dimension of the adversary or of the self, a denigratory or accepting designation, fantasized or real, conscious or unconscious, an idea staged on the boards or merely conceived in the eye of the beholder. Kermode conveys the impression, perhaps unintentionally and owing to the high level of abstractness to which he constantly levitates his discourse, that English national identity somehow got amalgamated and focused into something approaching a norm or unitary concept which a group of diverse playwrights gradually and communally built up over a half a century. Surely it is not unlikely that dramatists as differently gifted as Wilson and Shakespeare or as tonally dissimilar as Dekker and Marston would betray contrary or widely varying notions of Englishness—notions resistant to all-encompassing generalization and dependent, at least to some extent, on individual talent, mood, personality, genre, or intended audience. The familiar ideological markers of class, race, and gender are frequently invoked but provide few uncluttered avenues to lucidity. Complexity itself tends to become the subject rather than the elucidation of plays in which complexity can be profitably discerned. One has to remind oneself every three or four pages that the supposed subject is plays—professional entertainments and works of art conceived by dramatists to move and please audiences. One would hardly guess from this discussion that in Shakespeare and Dekker, for example, the sense of Englishness, foreignness, and at some level their supposed fusion (or "confusion") were created in the service of stimulating emotion, giving pleasure, and expanding popular awareness.

Kermode confesses unguardedly that his book took "a long time to write. And rewrite. And rewrite again" (xi). One could wish that the arduous revisions had done more to clear up the fogginess of sentences such as "... 'Englishness' constitutes an absent presence, a core that is a space, a performative centre to be displayed on the surface of the dramatized body" (15). Nor do irritating puns in the treatment of Dekker's delightful comedy ("Putting on Eyres" [135]; "Working with your Hans" [137]; "'Hans'-eatic" as applied to Lacy disguised as a Dutchman [141]) lighten the ponderous style.

Tragicomic Redemptions: Global Economics and the Early Modern English Stage, by Valerie Forman. Philadelphia: University of Pennsylvania Press, 2008, Pp. 288. Cloth $59.95.

Reviewer: INEKE MURAKAMI

Many have affirmed Jameson's insight that genre is a "proto-political act" that responds to historical dilemmas, but few have explored a particular genre's historical activities with the kind of protracted, lucidly theorized inquiry found in this book. Forman's primary concern is to show how the often maligned dramatic genre of tragicomedy served as a vehicle for thinking through socioeconomic problems raised by English involvement in the new international markets of the seventeenth century. Specifically, she puts Levant and East India Trading company records, mercantilist treatises, and sermons into dialogue with *Twelfth Night* (1600), *The Merchant of Venice* (ca. 1596), *Pericles* (1607), *The Winter's Tale* (1609–11), *The Island Princess* (1623–24), *The Renegado* (1624), and *The Devil's Law Case* (1617), to analyze how theological concepts ultimately derived from Anselm's satisfaction theory of redemption, are tapped and repurposed to foster new, more modern ways of conceptualizing loss and profit. In the tradition of Jean-Christophe Agnew, Douglas Bruster, Scott Cutler Shershow, and David Hawkes, this book demonstrates how early modern drama and the ostensibly unrelated market reciprocally constituted one another. Forman's commitment to historical formalism lends a salutary boost to the evidentiary value of literary structures identified in diverse mercantile forms, from captivity narratives to royal letters promoting trade.

Global and postcolonial studies should also find this book of interest. Its explication of genre's characteristic work—sometimes mystifying, sometimes identifying or analyzing cultural contradiction—considerably broadens the possible range of inquiries into how, say, characters articulate, foster, or resist cultural fantasies about marginalized social types. Perhaps more important, this book does the fundamental work of historicizing the tendency of tragicomedy to depoliticize contemporary racial and religious conflict as a *strategy*. This approach, which has implications for other "conservative" genres, in no way dismisses the exploitation and suffering tragicomedy attempts to mediate—on the contrary, one of the book's pleasures is its trenchant debunking of how, say, the "balance of trade" theory rhetorically veils the promotion of overbalance (English profit) by disingenuously invoking ideals of equity and moderation (151). Similarly, Forman's insight that the seventeenth-century turn to redemption was motivated by economic valences already present in the theological concept of redemption, writes a suggestive prelude for today's global capitalism in which reactions to socioeconomic inequity are often expressed in religious terms.

The second part of this two-part volume shows the work at its best, with room to explore juxtapositions of a variety of noncanonical texts. Chapter 4 is particularly strong in this respect, with its impressive exploration of the pecuniary motives for England's promotion of "free" trade, and the related ideological work "liberty" performs through captivity narratives and *The Island Princess*. Equally cogent is the discussion in chapter 5 of how *The Renegado* explores diverse economic models through characters including a pirate whose redemption overturns Catholic doctrine in order to integrate the anxiety-provoking excess of profit (178–79). Readings of Shakespeare in part 1 occasionally show the strain of engaging too many powerful readers, but this does little to detract from the force of arguments that link a closely read element, like Perdita's "fardel," to generic resolution, and beyond that, to a cultural contradiction—in this case, the need to reconcile loss as a necessary expenditure, a deferral of profit now normalized in the modern concept of "investment" (94).

More worrisome in a book focused on genre is the slipperiness of generic terms like "tragicomedy" "romance," "romantic comedy," and "comedy." There is, as Forman notes, a tremendous amount of generic overlap in the period, but she rejects tragicomedy's putative hybridity with the claim that tragicomedy is "a genre about the transformation of genre" (7). Genre theory suggests that all genres are always in a state of transformation; to imply that tragicomedy is intrinsically more self-reflexive than, say, Marlovian tragedy, seems a stretch.[1] Also puzzling in the face of excellent criticism on city comedy's interrogation of early modern economics is the repeated assertion that comedy is a genre that "can't fully engage with the [economic] problems it raises" (55). The book's breadth of knowledge sometimes falls short of its grasp of synchronic detail. Jonathan Coldewey's "Some Economic Aspects of Late Medieval Drama" is only one early iteration of the current understanding that neither "theater" nor indeed Shakespeare, waited until 1609 to discover that "there is profit to be made from spectacle-effects" (108). Similarly, it is unfortunate that the timing of this volume did not permit Forman to make use of Richard Kroll's book on tragicomedy and the "Circle of Commerce." It might have been useful to consider how, or if, the theme of redemption linked economic to generic problem-solving in tragicomedy of the Restoration, which is where Kroll posits the genre's strong form.

A related matter arises in the book's narrative. Tragicomedy emerges in "medieval" forms, but is "resurrected" in the seventeenth century to work through the conundrums of economic flux (7). It is not at all clear that tragicomedy was in need of resurrection, or that the socioeconomic dislocations of the sixteenth century precluded serious engagement with the tragicomic form. Given the book's emphasis on the narrative arc of the Christian redemption story, the omission of the morality play—whose narrative typically follows this pattern (i.e., the universal character's innocence, fall, and redemption), not to mention its episodic, double-plot structure and length that place it closer to tragicomedy than to the biblical cycles mentioned—is surprising. Arguments for the continuity of moral plays with Tudor interludes have been made often (and successfully) enough to render the absence of a century of moral drama problematic.[2] Intriguingly, the book's epilogue evokes the tenor and purpose of the moral drama elsewhere overlooked. A polemical epilogue is not a fault—Marxian-inflected criticism often self-historicizes through reflections on its own political commitments—but the book's tight focus on the first twenty years of the seventeenth century might have been better served by exploration of one of the adjacent periods rather than a shift to the present.

The book's alignment with Marxian reading, and numerous citations of Marxian readers, raises an expectation of an extended discussion of class. The decision to make tragicomedy the book's protagonist may be responsible for this absence, but a genre said to engage discourses might be imagined to have a broader "social life." Was there something, for example, about tragicomedy's mixture of gods, kings, and servants that alluded to the political structure of joint-stock companies, or that suited tragicomedy to the emergent discourse of republicanism? It seems unlikely that all early modern viewers of *The Winter's Tale* were equally delighted with tragicomedy's democratic aim to make "precious winners all," or that Webster's critical rejection of tragicomic resolution articulated a universal skepticism in 1617 (105); to whom were these messages directed? The book's otherwise careful elucidation of the economic theories of Mun, Misselden, and Malynes curiously smoothes the tension (in all but notes) of class-inflected, competing polemics, that were as much about sovereignty as sovereigns. Ultimately, these issues do not negate the book's strengths. *Tragicomic Redemptions* stimulates thinking, furnishes ample evidence of the abiding importance of economic criticism, and goes admirably far in its (only partly) tongue-in-cheek aim of redeeming genre criticism.

Notes

1. On genre's tendency to change to accommodate historical conditions Fredric Jameson is in basic agreement with Alastair Fowler and Rosalie Colie.

2. Book-length examples include David M. Bevington, *From Mankind to Marlowe: Growth of Structure in the Popular Drama of Tudor England* (Cambridge: Harvard University Press, 1962); Robert Potter, *The English Morality Play: Origins, History and Influence of a Dramatic Tradition.* (London: Routledge & Kegan Paul, 1975); and W. A. Davenport, *Fifteenth-Century English Drama: The Early Moral Plays and their Literary Relations* (New Jersey: D. S. Brewer, Rowman & Littlefield, 1982).

Shakespeare and the Economic Imperative: "What's aught but as 'tis valued?", by Peter F. Grav. New York and London: Routledge, 2008. Pp. viii + 208. $100.00.

Reviewer: ERIC V. SPENCER

Offering his book as an exercise in historically contextualized New Formalist close reading, Peter Grav argues that "Shakespeare's view of how economic determinants influence and shape humanity seems to progressively darken," so that "what is a benign condition in *The Comedy of Errors* becomes . . . a malignant disease in *Timon of Athens*" (2). After an introduction establishing methodological, cultural, and literary contexts, Grav offers chapters on *Errors, The Merchant of Venice, The Merry Wives of Windsor, Measure for Measure,* and *Timon,* all chosen because they make thematically central "what might be termed 'the monetary mindset'" (2). This mind-set, for Grav, made its sinister ascent to cultural supremacy in the decades around 1600, encouraging those under its influence to objectify or commodify human beings, and to subordinate affective to commercial bonds. In Grav's reading, Shakespeare perceived this encroaching evil and criticized it with increasing ferocity as he aged.

Grav's brief methodological discussion distinguishes his "formalism-of-sorts" (4) from (a) "much literary criticism in the last few decades," which, he claims, tends "to extract and concentrate on select portions of text in order to divine overall meaning," while he, by contrast, puts the plays, "in their entirety, under a microscope with a focus on close readings" (3); (b) "a belief that the meaning of texts is endlessly indeterminate," against which he claims that "the consideration of a text in its entirety, coupled with intuitive common sense," can yield adequately probable interpretations; and (c) the "narrow tenets of New Criticism," which treats literary works as "closed, autonomous systems," while Grav acknowledges the necessity of "historical contextualization in the search for meaning" (4). What results is a "hermeneutic" approach that purports to reveal what Steven Mailloux calls "operative intention," that is, "the actions that the author, as he writes the text, understands himself to be performing in that text and the immediate effects he understands these actions will achieve in his projected reader" (4). The resulting treatments of specific plays find such an operative intention in Shakespeare's opposition, variously reflected in different plays but conceptually invariable, to the corrosive effect of "marketplace" values on "humanistic" values (6).

Grav deserves credit for producing the first book I'm aware of devoted specifically to economic themes and situations in Shakespeare.[1] In addition, his straightforward presentation and reiteration of an unequivocal thesis will make it agreeably easy for future contributors to the conversation to locate their positions relative to his. And he avoids the unnecessary complexity and obscure theoretical idioms that reviewers so frequently (even, these days, stereotypically) deplore.

But there is also *necessary* complexity, and Grav's rigid oppositions, dependent on imprecise definitions, drain his argument of nuance. Methodologically, he relies on widely circulated but reductive caricatures of competing approaches. For example, he announces that he intends to "eschew the bread and butter of new historicism," namely, Gallagher and Greenblatt's "'the single voice, the isolated scandal, the idiosyncratic vision [and] the transient sketch'"(5), so that he may pursue more holistic readings. But by thus reducing New Historicism to the hermeneutically dubious reliance on idiosyncratic fragments, and without pausing to ask why, even if this assessment were fair, New Historicists would adopt such methods, Grav sidesteps rather than engages the real methodological issues at stake.[2] Grav's dismissal of the belief that that "the meaning of texts is endlessly indeterminate" (presumably he has deconstruction in mind) is similarly reductive and imprecise. Whatever its merits or weaknesses, deconstruction is more than such a simplistic belief (and again Grav doesn't bother to ask why anyone would so believe), just as New Criticism is more than the blinkered insistence on treating texts as "closed, autonomous systems." In short, with stunning nonchalance, Grav consigns twenty-five hundred years of debate about interpretation to irrelevance; all we need to do is consider the whole text and use "intuitive common sense."

That said, I could forgive an unconvincing theoretical discussion if, in the following chapters, such common sense paid high enough dividends. But oversimplification hobbles his interpretive efforts as well. Nothing is allowed to cross the yawning gulf between "humanitarian" and "monetary" values (neither of which Grav carefully defines). Characters represent either the former or the latter, and are accordingly either Good or Bad. Too often, moreover, close reading seems to serve this scheme, rather than the scheme developing out of scrupulous attention to the text, as Grav seemed to intend. Thus, when Antipholus of Syracuse woos Luciana, calling her a siren and asking her to spread "o'er the silver waves thy golden hairs" so he can lie on them and say he "gains by such a death," Grav argues that his words demonstrate how he privileges the intangible over the material (making him Good): "while the materiality of gold is ever-present in *Errors,* here its cash value is transfigured through metaphor into a romantic one" (48). But when, in *Merry Wives,* Fenton says to Anne that "I found thee of more value / Than stands in gold or sums in sealed bags," Grav claims that by evaluating her in "blatantly economic terms" and failing to separating her from images of wealth, he "commodifies her" (making him Bad) (70). Although Grav rightly points out that two characters in different contexts may use similar words differently (3), too often his readings of a character's use of economic tropes seem simply to confirm a moral evaluation made on other, unspoken grounds.

Similar oversimplifications hinder Grav's efforts at historical contextualization. He considers *only* economic contexts, and is highly selective even there; he never seriously addresses, for example, the commercial milieu of the London theaters. Thus, in order to facilitate his argument about Shakespeare's critique of "monetarist values" (35) in *Errors,* he points out that Ephesus was "a renowned commercial trading center" (29). Fair enough. But he ignores the arguably more pronounced biblical resonances of Ephesus, and, more importantly, the entire tradition of economic tropes in the language of Christianity. As a result, when Antonio tells Bassanio that he "repents not that he pays your debt; / For if the Jew do cut but deep enough, / I'll pay it instantly with all my heart," Grav can argue that the "figurative has become literal as Antonio views the sacrifice of his heart as the currency to free Bassanio from all debt" (making Antonio Bad) (102). To be sure, the play gives us reason to pause over such language, but by Grav's relentlessly dualistic logic, according to which reducing the intangible or figurative to the material or literal is Bad, we must condemn the Incarnation, much of the New Testament, and the use of such words as "redemption."

It begins to feel, in fact, as though Grav's right hand doesn't always remember what his left hand has done. Having invoked Mailloux's operative intention, he never mentions it again. Having implicitly distanced himself from "politically-driven criticism" (2–3), he takes throughout the book an intransigently anticommercial position. Perhaps most perplexingly, having noted that "certain aspects of [Shakespeare's] life bear at least brief mention, such as his father's involvement with usury, his accumulation of wealth and land and his professional life" in the commercial theater (15), Grav never mentions any of this again, and goes on to construct a Shakespeare who savages the commercial mentality,[3] without ever attempting to make Shakespeare the aspiring bourgeois gentleman inhabit the same universe as Shakespeare the enemy of "cash and exchange values" (7).

I do not mean by all these criticisms to suggest that Grav's reading of the plays as critical of commerce and its consequences is simply wrong; indeed, much evidence does point to Shakespeare's profound concern with the ethical and emotional dimensions of economic institutions and relationships. But the situations Grav discusses are consistently more complex than his categories, his choices of evidence, and his handling of language suggest. This avoidance of complexity makes the book read, in many places, like a competent but undistinguished dissertation overhastily prepared for publication.[4] Readers new to the discussion of economic themes and thinking in Shakespeare and early modern England may discover useful avenues for further reflection, but they will also subject themselves to persistent oversimplifications which more seasoned students of the topic will have trouble swallowing.

Notes

1. Fine volumes from the twenty-five years or so by Jean-Christophe Agnew, Douglas Bruster, William Ingram, Lars Engle, Theodore Leinwand, Lorna Hutson, Melissa Aaron, and others address many of the issues Grav addresses, but cast a wider net than he does.

2. Whether or not he mischaracterizes New Historicism here, the problem would remain that without a careful definition of "hermeneutic," his earlier distinction between a criticism that relies on "select portions" of text and one that treats texts "in their entirety" is at best imprecise and at worst naïve, for even the closest close reading necessarily privileges some "portions" of the text above others, as Grav himself does by paying almost exclusive attention to economic tropes and situations.

3. Indeed, Grav offers, as "the epitome of . . . how a commercial mentality had supplanted traditional . . . values" (110), James I's selling of knighthoods. And yet the Shakespeare who, for Grav, deplores such supplantations purchased a coat of arms for his father in 1596.

4. At the beginning of his conclusion, Grav even refers to the book as "this dissertation" (157). Perhaps this is not an unedited remainder from a prior incarnation of the project, and Grav simply means by "dissertation" a sizable academic treatise, forgetting that the word's more familiar and narrow definition might distract academic readers. If so, it would not be the only evidence of an occasional tin ear for usage. He tells us, for instance, that "engrossers . . . converted arable land to grazing pasture" (9) (presumably he meant "enclosers"), that the first scene of *Errors* "is not sourced in *Menaechmi*" (34) (I don't think even a liberal definition of "source" as a verb can make sense of this construction), that *Merry Wives* reveals an "overreaching thematic concern with money" (71) ("overarching"?), that the final line of a quoted passage "appears to juxtapose what precedes it" (102) (?), and that Lucio is guilty of "downloading . . . his own monetary responsibility onto Mistress Overdone" (118) ("unloading"? "offloading"?). I'm not trying to be a pedantic nitpicker here. When you stake your claim to a reader's attention on your commitment to close reading, you open yourself to judgment on how carefully you register linguistic nuance.

Work and Play on the Shakespearean Stage, by Tom Rutter. Cambridge: Cambridge University Press, 2008. Pp. x + 205. Hardcover $90.00.

Reviewer: C. BRYAN LOVE

In the last twenty years or so, scholars have paid special attention to the business of playing in early modern England; the result has been a steadily increasing collection of informed speculation concerning the operation of the London-based theater companies, including detailed analyses of the repertory system and the competitive and/or cooperative relationships between the different companies. Tom Rutter's contribution to this conversation is *Work and Play on the Shakespearean Stage* (2008), which explores ideas about "work" and "play" in early modern England and their ramifications for both those in the business of playing and playgoers; more specifically, Rutter employs close analyses of play-texts to illustrate the ways in which labor and idleness were represented on the stage to address specific segments of the socially conscious play-going public.

In the first chapter, "Work in Sixteenth Century England," Rutter offers an extremely concise but well-supported and carefully nuanced case for the sociocultural forces that inform his literary analyses. After the obligatory establishing of terms, including the expected, essential exploration of the history of the word "work," Rutter lays out the theoretical underpinnings of social class in England with regard to concepts of "labor" and "idleness." Rutter explains by way of David Aers that in the medieval period the concept of society involved "the tripartite division into those who pray, those who fight and those who labour to maintain fighters and praysters" (11). According to this theoretical framework, elites' military duties excused them from any kind of labor. However, Rutter explains that "[b]y the Elizabethan period . . . [the medieval] model of society appears to have lost much of its currency" (14): not only were the "fighters" doing little fighting, but the Reformation brought to the fore the idea that idleness was a sin, a rejection of God's commandment to postlapsarian man. Rutter explains that these and other complicated social factors and cultural influences led social elites to begin to adopt the language of work to describe their mental occupations in governing and other responsibilities; yet, Rutter explains, the idea that gentlemen were supposed to be idle persisted. This apparent contradiction, in combination with factors such as the emergence of an increasingly wealthy and politically powerful laboring citizen class, led to an extremely vexed understanding of the relationship between labor and social standing.

Rutter's next move is a sharp turn to the business of playing and drama. As Rutter would have it, the problematic nature of the theatrical enterprise made the stage a place especially attuned to and involved in the larger debate over work and play: at the theaters, players of at best dubious social status as "laborers" worked at play (under the pretext of rehearsing for performances at court), often drawing playgoers who were supposed to be at work but who were instead being idle. Indeed, early on Rutter offers some interesting readings of scenes of plays, including *A Midsummer Night's Dream,* in which playwrights seem to be calling attention to the genuine labor that goes into producing drama, defining the theatrical enterprise as legitimate work.

Rutter proceeds to trace the ways that the larger relationship between labor and social status was represented on the Shakespeaean stage. The book's historical narrative is not revolutionary, nor does it pretend to be: Rutter takes the familiar (albeit occasionally recalibrated) story about the social allegiances of the London theaters from the 1590s to 1610 and reinforces rather than complicates it. The starting point is the now more-or-less conventional sense of the London theatrical marketplace propagated by Andrew Gurr and others, one derived largely from readings of surviving play-texts: that Henslowe's company catered to citizen tastes; the children's companies at Paul's and Blackfriars catered to more elite tastes; Shakespeare's company situated itself somewhere in-between; and that these relationships were increasingly muddied over the period.

While the overall narrative about the companies is not new, what Rutter accomplishes in his monograph is a deft illumination of the companies' agendas by exploring different plays' representations of "labor" and "idleness." Among Rutter's greatest achievements is his reading of Dekker's *Shoemaker's Holiday* as tapping into a contemporary debate about workers' rights, especially their right to have time off, which enables them to be at the theater. Such an apprentice-oriented approach in Dekker's play and others from the Henslowe repertory is juxtaposed with several of Shakespeare's more equivocal and complicated representations of labor and idleness in works such as the Henriad (especially noteworthy are clever readings of some of the lines of Prince Hal/Henry V), *Julius Caesar*, and *Hamlet*. (Rutter does a great deal of interesting work with these plays, and it is difficult to do it justice within the confines of this space.)

Meanwhile, in the early revival years, at least, Rutter argues that playwrights at Paul's and Blackfriars intentionally represented the playhouse as free from workers both in the audience and onstage. While Rutter's claims about the children's companies have merit and fit neatly into his overall argument, his treatment of these institutions (with their remarkable differences from the adult companies/professional actors to which Rutter devotes considerably more time) is a bit underdeveloped and less satisfying than other aspects of the book. For example, for institutions Rutter claims were focused on idleness, I wondered what it meant that many of the operator-manager-investors in the children's theaters were in fact from the "middling sort"; what it meant that the boys, especially in the early years, were impressed (and the troubles the Blackfriars company experienced when Henry Evans attempted to impress the child of an influential gentleman named Henry Clifton, who described the boys as "a company of lewd and dissolute mercenary players");[1] and what sort of significance inheres in the fact that, according to a letter by Roland White to Robert Sidney, William Stanley, the sixth Earl of Derby, "put up the playes of the children in Pawles to his great paines and charge."[2] Many of these details do not enter Rutter's narrative. Furthermore, there are points in which Rutter reads events according to social theory (or marketing derived from social theory) when nostalgia and practical considerations seem far more important (the tone of the early plays at Second Paul's and Second Blackfriars and the 1596 petition that prevented the Lord Chamberlain's men from using the Blackfriars theater are examples). None of these quibbles explode Rutter's fine and engaging arguments (indeed, some of the facts I've mentioned obviously could be turned to his advantage), but they do, I think, represent ways in which the boy companies get short shrift in the book.

In the end, however, my qualms about this aspect of Rutter's work are largely a reflection of the nature of Rutter's ambitious project of reading a large and complex society and marketplace. Indeed, *Work and Play on the Shakespearean Stage* is a formidable piece of scholarship. The narrow focus of the book, and Rutter's deft and nuanced handling of it, makes it a worthwhile contribution to our understanding of the London theatrical marketplace and the elements of society that supported it.

Notes

1. Qtd. in Irwin Smith, *Shakespeare's Blackfriars Playhouse: Its History and Its Design* (New York: New York University Press, 1964), 183.
2. Qtd. in W. Reavley Gair, *The Children of Paul's: The Story of a Theatre Company, 1553–1608* (Cambridge: Cambridge University Press, 1982), 118.

The Cartographic Imagination in Early Modern England: Re-writing the World in Marlowe, Spenser, Raleigh and Marvell, by D. K. Smith. Aldershot, Hampshire: Ashgate, 2008. Pp. 254. Hardback, $99.95.

Reviewer: ELIZABETH JANE BELLAMY

Over the last decade or so, a number of influential histories of early modern cartography have forged compelling links between early modern English space and place, such as, to name just two, Andrew McRae's 1996 *The Map of Agrarian England, 1500–1660,* and Lesley Cormack's 1997 *Charting an Empire: Geography at the English Universities, 1580–1620.* These and other studies have rendered virtually impossible any effort to talk about early modern England's status as a "nation" or an emergent "empire" without also taking into account developments in early modern English cartography—its growing preoccupation with increased precision in scope, scale, perspective, and the accurate measuring of space. Fueling this spatial preoccupation were the sophisticated advances in theoretical mathematics (and their subsequent pragmatic applications to the growing science of navigation), and more accurate techniques for surveying the land. Because these technological advances were becoming available to an increasingly literate public, they also created ever greater desires for cartographic precision and accuracy. Cartography, in short, became a national imperative.

Perhaps the first study of the matrix of the new cartography, the new sense of ideological nationalism this cartography engendered, and the imaginative "space" of literature was Richard Helgerson's landmark 1992 *Forms of Na-*

tionhood, and, more recently, Andrew Gordon/Bernhard Klein's 2001 collection *Literature, Mapping, and the Politics of Space in Early Modern England and Ireland.* More particularly, John Gillies's 1994 *Shakespeare and the Geography of Difference* and Garrett Sullivan's 1998 *The Drama of Landscape* have, among others, been instrumental in positioning early modern English drama within the ways in which the new cartography enabled the imagining of space. Picking up where these studies have left off, D. K. Smith's book delves further into the following overarching questions: how did early modern English literature reflect this new spatial organization, what Smith terms early modern England's "cartographical imagination"? And how did this emergent spatial consciousness work its way into, or become assimilated by, the early modern English prose, poetic, and dramatic imagination?

The third and fifth chapters of Smith's book are, respectively, studies of Spenser's *The Faerie Queene* and studies of Marvell's poems *Bermudas* and *Upon Appleton House.* Because readers of this journal will, in all likelihood, be more interested in Smith's discussion of drama, I will offer only brief summaries of these chapters. Smith's third chapter offers valuable insights into the relationship between geography and allegory, i.e., how Spenser converts the vague geographical space of medieval romance into a less fictive, "mappable" allegory of Fairy Land. The fifth chapter investigates how the intriguing collisions between old and new world maps made their way into Marvell's geographic poetry. Smith exposes the tensions between the demands of cartographical precision and the growing anxieties and uncertainties spawned by mid-seventeenth-century political upheavals (the English Revolution, regicide, etc.) that haunted Marvell's poems.

Turning now to Smith's chapters on drama, I believe one of the author's more ambitious arguments is his first chapter, where he backdates the origins of the "new" cartography from roughly midway through the sixteenth century to the later fifteenth century. Smith reassesses common scholarly assumptions that medieval England, more concerned with spiritual than physical geography, had virtually no preoccupation with spatial accuracy. In some ways, Smith picks up where Mary Campbell's key 1988 study of medieval and early modern European travel narratives left off. Campbell argues that for early medieval pilgrims, the land itself scarcely mattered. But Smith turns to the late fifteenth-century popular saint's play, the Digby *Mary Magdalene,* and its representation of pilgrim experience as evidence that there was indeed an emergent language of map-making in medieval England. Smith contends that the Digby *Mary Magdalene* is intriguingly self-conscious about the spatial dimension of travel, where geographical spaces shape the heroine's redemptive quest.

Smith's fifth chapter focuses much of its attention on how Marlowe's *Dr. Faustus* and *Tamburlaine* catered to their audiences' increasing familiarity with such influential world maps as Ortelius's and Mercator's. Smith argues that Faustus, in effect, seeks control of the world. Craving a physical world even more than profit or sensual desire, Faustus seeks possession of the world via the exoticism of travel, only to come full circle back to his tiny study in Wittenberg. The Scythian shepherd Tamburlaine succeeds where the German scholar failed. In this play, Tamburlaine rejects the outdated "triple world" of medieval geography, and then forces the new geography to bend to his conquering will. Readers can judge for themselves how much new ground (beyond Emily Bartels's, Crystal Bartolovich's, Gillies's, and, most recently, Mary Floyd-Wilson's treatments of mapping in *Tamburlaine*) is plowed in Smith's chapter. Perhaps of greater value and originality is his reading of Raleigh's "Discoverie of Guiana" with and against the grain of Marlowe's dramatic cartography. Having barely penetrated beyond Guiana's coastline and feeling the pressure of having to draw a map of empire for a Guiana he does not really know, Raleigh is cogently portrayed by Smith as merely a would-be Tamburlaine. Raleigh does not so much "map" Guiana as fall back on familiar rhetorical and geographic tropes, in the final analysis, composing, in Smith's words, only "a perceived rhetoric of conquest" (139).

This book should have a broad appeal not only to scholars of medieval and early modern drama, but also to anyone interested in histories of mapping and cartographical discourse, especially as they intersect with literary representations of mapped space.

The Figure of the Crowd in Early Modern London: The City and Its Double, by Ian Munro. New York: Palgrave Macmillan, 2005. Pp. x + 256. Hardcover $69.95.

Reviewer: MEG F. PEARSON

Ian Munro reminds us of the extraordinary denseness of early modern London while illuminating the city's vexed responses to that crush. The men and women who occupied this simultaneously claustrophobic and dynamic urban expanse, argues Munro, used the figure of the crowd in their proclamations, poems, and plays as "the visible manifestation of an increasingly incomprehensible city, the tangible referent onto which the desires and fears provoked by London's swelling mass were projected" (1). Appearances of the crowd as event and as discourse help convey early modern London's troubled understanding of itself.

Grounded in the growing body of criticism about London, including the work of critics such as Ian Archer and Lawrence Manley, Munro's well-researched book distinguishes itself by addressing the expansion of the city in terms of people as well as space. The book suggests that to understand the "experiential space" of early modern London, we must take into account the "visible and tangible presence of more and more *bodies*" (4). Munro correspondingly employs the spatial theories of Henri Lefebvre and Michel de Certeau, but he relies most heavily upon the binaries of arboreal and rhizomatic spatial systems articulated by Gilles Deleuze and Félix Guattari. Distinguishing between arboreal, structured systems and rhizomatic, or heterogeneously connective systems enables Munro to illustrate the dangerous unpredictability of crowds in the early modern imagination. The Derridean concept of the supplement further clarifies Munro's figure, for not only are the crowds of London unmanageable and seemingly uncontainable by social hierarchies in the urban literature, their excess threatens to overwhelm and even replace the city's organization. While recent critical work on London has tended to focus upon stabilizing civic institutions and local community, rationalizing London into a legible space, Munro argues for the illegibility of the crowd, its "resistance to being read" (10).

Chapter 1, "Imaginary Numbers: City, Crowd, Theater," defines crowds and crowdedness through a series of royal and civic proclamations against the breaking up of London estates and houses. An explicit tension becomes apparent between the understanding of London as the *camera regis,* the idealized and intact chamber of the monarch, and the proclamations' language of instability and disease. The competing discourses of royal chambers and chamber pots pervade the period's writings, Munro discovers, often driving authors and "urban theorists" like John Stow into a longing for a simpler age (27). Works such as Stow's *Annals* attempt to remember and perhaps construct anew a knowable, legible London by visualizing the city from above. Civic ritual similarly attempted to stabilize the urban world, Munro suggests, but not in the way we might expect.

Munro's readings of urban literatures such as the Lord Mayor's Day processions and shows in chapter 2, "London's Mirror: Civic Ritual and the Crowd," offer important understandings of how the figure of the crowd functions in the context of actual bodies. He does well to trouble what he terms critics' "urban desire," which suggests that the Lord Mayor's Day shows existed to stabilize the relationship between city, crown, and crowd, in keeping with Victor Turner's model of theater as a communion (58). The chapter juggles the civic allegories in shows by Thomas Dekker and Thomas Middleton with the real world of the unruly holiday procession "as part of the process of understanding the interaction of the ideal and real Londons juxtaposed by performance" (53). Shows such as Dekker's *Troia-Nova Triumphans* (1612) locate their pageants' villains and antagonists in areas like Cheapside to emphasize the rowdy mess of the crowd faced by the new Lord Mayor. The city must be vanquished, Munro argues, not reaffirmed.

Leaving the city streets for the playhouse, chapter 3, "Shakespeare's London: The Scene of London in the Second Tetralogy and *Henry VIII,*" zooms through the first and second tetralogies before arriving at *Henry VIII.* Munro shows persuasively that the figure of the crowd is more interesting in history plays than in city comedies (48–49). The first tetralogy, particularly *Richard III*, presents crowds as threats, Munro argues, and stages the urban environment as unsafe. The second tetralogy, on the other hand, does not laud the crowded city so much as shrink it to a theater. The onstage crowds who watch Richard II or Prince Hal are all like theater audiences, powerfully able to disapprove, but familiar and necessary parts of the historical narrative. In his focused reading of *Henry VIII,* Munro draws our attention to the excessiveness of crowds. "The problem with the crowds in the coronation and christening scenes," he argues, "is not that they are subversive but that they are *too much:* they offer *more* joy, *more* loyalty than is needed or desired" (102). Here Munro's interest in Derrida is fulfilled in a compelling reading that avoids what hinders certain parts of the book: an unnecessary reliance upon either/or binaries.

Munro declares a shift from the event of the crowd—actual crowds on stage and in the street—to the discourse of the crowd in chapter 4, "Distracted Multitude: The Theater and the Many-Headed Monster." Here the book turns to the "many headed multitude," an early modern commonplace inherited from Plato's *Republic.* Munro reads nondramatic texts to great effect, particularly George Chapman's *Andromeda Liberata* (1614), an epithalamion to Frances Howard and Robert Carr which employs the multiheaded image to disparage the swirling rumors surrounding their courtship and marriage. Additionally, Munro incorporates several anti-theatricalist pamphlets as compelling examples of how attacks against the multitude are framed in the urban discourses of filth and contagion. Even without a physical crowd, the threat of a multi-vocal, fleshly crowd remains.

In the final chapters' readings—Shakespeare's *Julius Caesar* and Ben Jonson's *Sejanus his Fall* in chapter 5, and Shakespeare's *Coriolanus* in chapter 6—Munro demonstrates how plays sought to negotiate their own relationship to the urban audience using two of the major discourses of the period: Rome and the plague (143). The chapter illustrates how the Rome of *Julius Caesar* resembles early modern London—a place where the crowds demonstrated remarkable power, to the unease of the patricians and rulers—while Jonson creates a "populous absence," suggesting that *Sejanus* represents the unnerving impossibility of representing a crowded city (160). In both plays, eternal Rome is undermined by "the supplement of the prodigy," mysterious and incomprehensible omens and supernatural occurrences that undermine easy conclusions to either play (146).

Meaning seems unavoidable in *Coriolanus,* Munro's final play. After a fascinating discussion of plague literature, particularly pamphlets by Thomas Dekker, chapter 6 "'A Kind of Nothing': Plague Time in Early Modern London," considers how Shakespeare's play manages to excise the plague story contained within Plutarch's history of Coriolanus while sustaining the metaphor of plague. The "idea of contagion in the city leads to a consideration of the complexity of the circulation of urban bodies," a phenomenon of great interest to London during its explosive population growth (183). The juxtaposition of *Coriolanus* with Dekker's pamphlets persuades the reader that *Coriolanus* should be read as an example of the urban literature that flooded London in the early seventeenth century (193).

Munro quotes *Coriolanus* to wonder, "What is the city but the people?" (3.1.198). "If the city is only the people," Munro worries later, "then what is the city but 'a kind of nothing,' identifiable only by its ceaseless change and monstrous, uncontrollable growth?" (199). As this book demonstrates, the figure of the crowd has too much meaning, not too little. The book, like the city Munro imagines, circulates dynamically between genres and texts in service to a central point. Scholars of early modern literature, urban literature, spatial theory, and civic history will all find pieces to their liking in this compact and compelling book.

Male Friendship in Shakespeare and His Contemporaries, by Tom MacFaul. Cambridge: Cambridge University Press, 2007. Pp. x + 222.

Reviewer: BEN LaBRECHE

In the chapters that begin and end his book, Tom MacFaul argues that Shakespeare and other early modern dramatists turned the ideals of friendship to startling new ends. Classical and Renaissance writers such as Aristotle, Cicero, and Sir Thomas Elyot claimed—and more recent scholars have often concurred—that virtuous friendship provided a basis for attributing equality and permanence to social relationships. MacFaul, though, argues that the flip-side of this humanist ethics—*false* friendship—may have been even more important to the work of early modern playwrights. By "coming out on the other side" of ideal friendship, he suggests, their plays established "a new way of looking at individuality" and argued for valorizing personal difference and autonomy (1–2).

This thesis seems to present *Male Friendship in Shakespeare and His Contemporaries* as a historicist project, and MacFaul does set his argument in the same cultural shift from feudal loyalties to rhetorical bonds that Lorna Hutson described in *The Usurer's Daughter*.[1] Generally, though, he pays much less attention to historical contexts than he does to literary characters. His reading presents early modern plays as crowded, hierarchical landscapes where characters—particularly secondary figures like Parolles or Iago—constantly pursue "dramatic self-assertion" and "recognition" by others (e.g., 2, 27). As MacFaul writes, "Shakespeare's characters want to have a proper place in the story, and friendship is the best way apparently minor or subordinate characters can obtain this" (13). Minor characters garner this attention by setting themselves *against* the ideal of friendship and thus generating conflict and a role for themselves in the play's overall plot, and on the whole *Male Friendship* admires these departures from the conventional ethics of friendship. Even while acknowledging the monstrousness of Iago's manipulation of male intimacy, for example, MacFaul also connects his and other characters' betrayals of friendship to "non-heroic modes of selfhood" and to "recognizing and respecting human difference" (195).

MacFaul's decision to associate Iago with "respecting human difference" will certainly raise some eyebrows, but on the whole his thesis offers a very interesting complement to Laurie Shannon's work on friendship in *Sovereign Amity*.[2] Her work presents Renaissance friendship as a factor in the long-term development of political equality and social autonomy. MacFaul, however, shows how in the nearer term false friendship could valorize individuals within *existing* structures of subordination. Taken together, then, Shannon's and MacFaul's books show just how complex and flexible the early modern friendship tradition could be.

Two possible problems do, however, arise as MacFaul develops his argument. First, readers may not be entirely satisfied by how he depicts the canonical texts of classical and humanist friendship. Anyone familiar with these writings will likely object that they are complex, conflicted works in their own right and that dramatists further elaborate their ethical dilemmas rather than inventing them wholesale. Second, MacFaul fails to take up the extratextual implications of his often illuminating work on character. He writes of literary characters who "want to have a proper place in the story," but presumably it is actually early modern playwrights who *want* to work out characters' (and their own) places in dramatic and social hierarchies. Readers will thus find it helpful to read *Male Friendship* in tandem with David Woloch's *The One vs. the Many*, which much more explicitly relates the jostling of characters within literary texts to the social and economic circumstances of their creation.[3]

In contrast to the unified argument of his opening and closing chapters, MacFaul's middle chapters often work almost as independent essays. In keeping with his claim that early modern dramatists steered away from ideal friendship, each of these chapters focuses on a relationship other than friendship: literary patronage, brotherhood, erotic love, servanthood, politics, and common fellowship. As a result, they at times feel rather tangential to the book's main thesis, particularly when they take up relationships that do not "com[e] out on the other side" of ideal friendship so much as simply have nothing to do with it. (This is true, for example, of much of the chapter on servants and of the discussion of Enobarbus and Antony that ends the book.) At other times, however, these chapters provide valuable insights into important literary questions, such as the patronage relationships encoded in sonnet sequences or the pervasive conflict between same-sex friendship and heterosexual love in early modern plays. MacFaul's extended discussions of specific plays could have been enriched, though, by more thorough engagement with current critical debates. This is not to ask for encyclopedic annotations, but simply to say that *Male Friendship* has significant points to make and that these deserve to be put in more explicit dialogue with the ideas of other scholars.

The insightful local readings offered by MacFaul—particularly when he juxtaposes different Shakespearean texts—will, however, prove quite useful to readers. So will his examinations of how friendship and literary genre relate to one another. At the end of his first chapter, MacFaul suggestively connects the recognition of friends and enemies to both Aristotelian *anagnorisis* and a "melancholic recognition [in Shakespeare's plays] that one is fundamentally alone" (20, 27). And his chapter on Shakespeare's sonnets convincingly shows a tension between the momentarily perfect friendship that can exist in individual lyrics and the compromised, more instrumental relationship that emerges over the sequence as a whole (39, 46). It is perhaps in these passages where MacFaul relates social bonds directly to literary form that his book offers its most striking insights into early modern friendship.

Notes

1. Lorna Hutson, *The Usurer's Daughter: Male Friendship and Fictions of Women in Sixteenth-Century England* (London: Routledge, 1994). MacFaul cites her historical framework at page 15.

2. Laurie Shannon, *Sovereign Amity: Figures of Friendship in Shakespearean Contexts* (Chicago: University of Chicago Press, 2002). MacFaul relates his work to her "fiction of equal friendship" at pages 7, 12, 20.

3. Alex Woloch, *The One vs. the Many: Minor Characters and the Space of the Protagonist in the Novel* (Princeton: Princeton University Press, 2003).

Flaunting: Style and the Subversive Male Body in Renaissance England, by Amanda Bailey. Toronto: University of Toronto Press, 2007. Pp. 190. Cloth $65.00

Reviewer: MARGARET ROSE JASTER

For Amanda Bailey, the devil is in the definitions. In *Flaunting,* Bailey offers some intriguing insights into English Renaissance society by tweaking definitions for terms frequently encountered in Renaissance studies. Her central thesis rests on such a tweaking. After echoing the long-established New Historicist tenet that "power . . . resides in the ability to transform the materials of dominant culture into the symbols of subversion . . . ," Bailey attempts a new twist by asserting that "certain young men of the English Renaissance

... did not *assume* the elite signs of privilege, but rather *appropriated* them for their own ends" (4) (italics mine)—a rather fine distinction. Bailey then returns to a comfortable New Historicist insistence that the theater not only produced an awareness that clothes make the man, but also that the theater "encouraged sartorial irreverence among those with little discretionary income and no social authority, and in doing so created the conditions for a subculture of style" (5). The remainder of her introductory chapter addresses other relevant definitions ("fashion," "art," "publish," and "flaunt," among others) as she differentiates her study from earlier scholarly works, and argues for a defiant aesthetics, practiced by the above-mentioned youthful subculture.

In her second chapter, Bailey demonstrates the "monstrous manners" (another useful definition for her discussion) of her subversive young men by linking the clothing laws to early modern theatrical practices. In keeping with a plethora of scholars of the English Renaissance, Bailey extends her definition of "clothing laws" to include a variety of texts that sought to influence sartorial behavior. Including sermons, anti-theatrical tracts, and satires, these texts echo the concerns of the official clothing laws (proclamations and statutes) with the behavior of the "meaner sort" which she defines as "an amorphous group of male apprentices, servants and students" (25). When Bailey cites her primary sources, she is on solid ground: it is gratifying (and not surprising) to learn that Philip Stubbes ranted against young men who rioted and flaunted daily. While Bailey then admits that the "specific behaviors associated with flaunting remain unclear," she assumes that the definition in early modern culture includes the notion that "practitioners openly wrested luxurious items of apparel from their proper place." Further, she suggests that these flaunters *may have* "modified the associations of items traditionally used in certain ways by a particular social group, producing unorthodox combinations" and "exaggerated a particular aspect of a given item"— assumptions not necessarily borne out by the evidence in the primary texts (46). In this chapter, Bailey also identifies the theater as a particularly vital site for the young men's subversive behavior.

Bailey concludes her theoretical chapters by proposing that the young men that she has identified were seen as an "especially subversive minority," a claim that she substantiates by close readings of three plays in the next three chapters. According to Bailey, past interpretations of these plays have been negatively affected because they ignore the presence and particularized behavior of this subversive minority in the plays. To prove this point, Bailey returns to her incisive use of definitions by reminding us that shrewishness was, in this period, a non-gendered form of class conflict: a shrew was a social outcast or newcomer of either gender, and, more importantly for Bailey, someone who challenged authority (76). This broadened definition, along with her careful uses of "brave" and "face," offers Bailey's readers a more nuanced reading of (what we might have considered) a very familiar play.

In her interpretation of Marlowe's *Edward II,* Bailey faults earlier readings of the play which "ignore the play's awareness of the potency of aesthetic defiance and thus fail to illuminate how sexual and stylistic excess are linked in this play and what is at stake in their overlay" (78). Bailey reminds us that while Marlowe is generally loyal to his source for this play (Holinshed), the emphasis on Gaveston's apparel is Marlowe's addition. What is essential about Gaveston's presentation of himself is the Italianate nature of his clothing and comportment (79), a concern that existed more potently in Elizabeth Tudor's court than in Edward Plantagenet's. Because of their low birth, Gaveston and Edward's other favorites infect the English court with another version of flaunting, the Italian vice of *artifiziozo* (a distortion of the venerated *sprezzatura*). While her reading of Marlowe's *Edward* certainly opens up this text to fascinating analysis, the effect is somewhat blunted by Bailey's discussion of Oscar Wilde's style at the conclusion of this chapter. Both Marlowe's play and Bailey's reading stand on their own.

Her chapter on Jonson's *Every Man Out of His Humour* may be Bailey's most convincing. She opens with a headnote from Guilpin's *Skialethia* which reminds us of the importance of St. Paul's Walk as a site of presentation and representation in London, circa 1600. For Bailey, Jonson's play introduces the notion of London as the capital of England—soon to be capital of Western Europe (103). Bailey contends that with the staging of characters who "flouted prescriptions of proper urban comportment" and "used the objects and spaces made newly available to them in an urban context as the material of histrionic self-expression," Jonson moves the London stage experience from the traditional *theatrum mundi* to *theatrum civitatus* (105). In this chapter, Bailey examines the concepts of "behavioral urbanization," "loitering," "shifting," "flamboyance" and "gesticulation" as she argues that Jonson's play is "in conversation with" Thomas Dekker (126) whose *Guls Hornebooke* (1609) is the undoubted handbook for her pompous young men.

The conclusion to this penultimate chapter—that Jonson proves that the theater inevitably "could not contain the very modes of impertinent display that it inspired" (128)—moves the reader comfortably into her final chapter in which she describes how the sumptuousness of her flaunting young gentlemen evolves into the sartorial exhibitionism of style.

While I have quibbled throughout this review with some of Bailey's assumptions and I have found her ultimate comparison of early modern flaunters to zooties, hippies, and punks to be rather facile, I believe scholars of early modern English studies have much to learn from this carefully researched and executed book.

Shakespeare and the Practice of Physic: Medical Narratives on the Early Modern English Stage, by Todd H. J. Pettigrew. Newark: University of Delaware Press, 2005. Pp. 198. Hardcover $43.50.

Reviewer: SAMANTHA MURPHY

Todd H. J. Pettigrew's *Shakespeare and the Practice of Physic,* winner of the 2004 Jay L. Halio Prize in Early Modern Studies, takes, as its title suggests, medical practice very seriously. By focusing on early modern medical practitioners, rather than medical theory, Pettigrew provides a valuable contribution to both Shakespeare studies and the scholarly discourse about early modern medicine. Much recent research into early modern medicine has taken the social construction of medical knowledge as its point of inquiry. What has been overlooked are the representations of actual practitioners. Pettigrew acknowledges his debt to the criticism focusing on early modern medicine's social effects, but his study is primarily concerned with "the political controversy surrounding medical practice, a controversy that touched all levels of society and into which even the grandest men and women of state entered" (28).[1] This close examination of the discourse surrounding medical men and women is the greatest strength of Pettigrew's monograph.

Pettigrew centers his argument around the College of Physicians and their strategies to professionalize and hierarchize medicine. Created in 1518 with authority to regulate medicine in and around London, by Shakespeare's time the College was at "the center of the fight to establish the power of what we now call the profession" (14). They sought to privilege university-educated, licensed physicians at the expense of other types of healers. It is not to the College's legal interventions that Pettigrew attends; instead, he makes a strong case that the use of narrative was their most effective strategy. Supporters of the College produced various texts which aimed to alter the ways in which the English understood the idea of medical practice. These rhetorical productions attempted to make "informal medicine . . . unthinkable for the patient" (14). This rhetoric, however, did not go uncontested. There was still much support for non-licensed practitioners, especially outside of London where trained physicians were unlikely to practice. Shakespeare's plays, Pettigrew argues, contributed to a counter-narrative by displaying skepticism of the claims of the medical establishment while "working to expand the imaginative possibilities of its audience" (60).

Shakespeare and the Practice of Physic is organized in a straightforward manner. Each chapter focuses on a type of medical practitioner, using a representative Shakespearean play to anchor the discussion. *All's Well That Ends Well*'s Helena is given as a prime example of an empiric, while *Macbeth* provides ample fodder on physicians. *Romeo and Juliet* allows for the examination of both apothecaries and beneficed practitioners. Pettigrew concludes his roster of practitioners with two short chapters focusing on surgeons (who do not appear in any of Shakespeare's plays) and magical healers, as represented by Cerimon in *Pericles*.

The main work of the monograph comes in the first four chapters: a detailed introduction followed by readings of *All's Well That Ends Well, Macbeth,* and *Romeo and Juliet*. Together, these plays get at the crux of a generalized medical anxiety in the early modern period—non-trained lay healers, physicians, apothecaries, and medical priests are all censured. While this general medical angst is not highlighted by Pettigrew, it serves as an unacknowledged undercurrent throughout his book. All of his dramatic examples, save one, point to a Shakespearean critique of the narratives of dominance and hierarchy set forth by the College. The *Macbeth* chapter, in particular, does an excellent job of illustrating the pervasive counter-discourse leveled against physicians. Doctors, despite the rhetoric put forth by the College and its supporters, were "still an object of fear, a fear that constantly threatened to undermine the physician's legal and rhetorical strength" (87). In *Macbeth*, Shakespeare invokes the tricky element of reputation in relation to his hapless doctor. Reputation was a physician's greatest commodity, but their intimacy with patients' bodies also made them open to accusations of inflicting intentional harm. The doctor as poisoner was a particularly strong image directed against the profession and was bolstered by various poisoning plots involving royal physicians. *Macbeth*'s impotent doctor, caught between his ethical duty to treat Lady Macbeth and deadly court politics, foregrounds the counter-narrative of "distrust and anxiety" (87) surrounding the physician, thus questioning the College's claim to absolute authority in medical matters.

Pettigrew follows his examination of *Macbeth*'s physician with a compelling reading of *Romeo and Juliet*'s apothecary and medical friar. Importantly, Pettigrew notes that this play serves as the sole exception to Shakespeare's critique of the College's narrative. That is because, in Pettigrew's eyes, *Romeo and Juliet* is primarily concerned with the consequences of privileging personal will over adherence to society's laws. Quoting Francis Bacon, Pettigrew argues that self-interest "putteth the law out of office" (107). Consequently, Shakespeare embraces the College's rhetoric in order to "build the play's commentary on social order" (93). Apothecary and priest act as "dramatic emblem[s] of the importance of law, the requisite rules that give order to society" (105) and, by their actions, "suggest the profound danger of selfish disregard for the law" (108).

In light of Pettigrew's contention that Shakespeare adopts the College's narrative, even if only on one occasion, it is a shame that his monograph does not explicitly acknowledge the underlying anxiousness present in the multiple narratives by and about medical practitioners. As he details in his meticulous use of early modern writings, no medical position went uncontested.

Pettigrew does, persuasively, note this lack of consensus about medical practice: "What is most productive [to examine] . . . is not how medical practice was viewed in general (for there was no general view), but rather the variety of possibilities of representation that medical practitioners provided, and how authors choose the conception that fits their thematic, and consequently ideological, purposes" (109). Confusingly, however, he also argues that there was a "social consensus" (133) which bolstered the College's narrative as the "status quo" (35). At moments like these, Pettigrew seems to undercut his own argument.

Shakespeare and the Practice of Physic, despite a few inconsistencies, is well worth the read. Pettigrew presents a fresh take on Shakespeare's medical practitioners and offers a new direction for the study of early modern medicine. The politics of medical practice and its link to the wider production of social discourse is an avenue well worth pursuing. Drawing on New Historicism, Pettigrew's book takes on a previously overlooked "spiral of discourse" (160)—early modern narratives about medical practitioners. Hopefully his monograph will inspire others to follow this path of study. "The cycle of culture," as Pettigrew concludes, "continues" (160).

Notes

1. Pettigrew particularly singles out the work of Gail Kern Paster and Jonathan Gil Harris. He notes that their work inquires into how "health, illness, and related experiences were conceived" (29). In other words, they ask about how early modern bodies were socially constructed, while Pettigrew's book is more concerned with the social constructions put forth by and about the people practicing medicine.

Food in Shakespeare: Early Modern Dietaries and the Plays, by Joan Fitzpatrick. Ashgate: Aldershot, Hants, England and Burlington, VT, 2007, Pp. ix + 166. Hardcover $99.95.

Reviewer: AMY L. TIGNER

In the last few decades, food and its constituent concerns of cooking, eating, and diet have all captured the imagination of the post, postmodern psyche. In the average bookstore (assuming one still occasionally frequents such a physical space), the sheer number of cookbooks and the expanding categories of cooking styles (from raw to barbeque; French to Balinese; Julia Child to the Barefoot Contessa) are staggering; meanwhile, just down the aisle, a surfeit of dietary guides (from the dramatically titled *Alkalize or Die* to *Dr. Atkins' New Diet Revolution; Eat Right 4 Your Type* to *The South Beach Diet; The Juice Fasting Bible* to *The Bible Diet*), all of which promise to trim our expanding girths and cure the ailments of our overstuffed, junked-up, techno-toxic bodies. Our twin cultural obsessions of consuming a wider and wider variety of tastes (both naturally and artificially produced from a petroleum-fueled, global market), and of maintaining an idealized slenderness associated with youthfulness (even as our youth are becoming increasingly obese) illustrate the paradoxical state of an economically driven population that values gratification over limitation. In such an environment, it is not surprising that scholars have formulated food and dietary studies, investigating the theoretically underpinnings of how societies view food and the body, eating and health. One such exploration is Joan Fitzpatrick's *Food in Shakespeare: Early Modern Dietaries and the Plays,* which focuses on the study of dietaries in the English context, exemplified in Shakespeare's dramatic works.

Proffering the caveat that her book is not an exhaustive study of all Shakespeare's plays nor of Elizabethan culinary practice more generally, Fitzpatrick declares, "This book is the first detailed study of food and feeding in Shakespeare's plays" (1). Indeed, Fitzpatrick's text participates in the burgeoning field of food and early modern English literature and provides a treasure trove that unlocks various nuances of food-related moments in many of the plays. Curiously, her use of the passive, and albeit alliterative, term "feeding" coupled with "food," rather than the more active and succinct word "eating" emphasizes the almost animalistic act of consumption in the plays, as if the characters lack control of their own attitudes toward food. Certainly, such a bestial or perhaps even swinish approach to diet aptly applies to Fitzpatrick's first case study: Sir John Oldcastle, otherwise known as Falstaff. Fitzpatrick explains that Sir John's original moniker, Oldcastle, links him to the historical Protestant martyr who was accused of heresy and then executed under Henry V. As Oldcastle's descendants complained of Shakespeare's depiction of their ancestor as a buffoon and a glutton, his name was summarily modified to Falstaff. Though scholars argue whether Shakespeare was lambasting Catholics or Puritans with his depiction of Sir John, Fitzpatrick's argues that what is more significant is Shakespeare's "development of a gluttonous figure and his perspective on the moral consequences of excessive culinary indulgence" (20). What follows is Fitzpatrick's explication of how Elizabethans would have read the gluttonous Sir John as a vice figure and how diet, in Galenic terms, directly affects personal behavior, thereby illuminating food as a signifier of morality in the play and the culture more generally.

In Fitzpatrick's next chapter, concerned with *Henry V* and *Macbeth,* we learn interesting facts about specific foods and what they represent in the plays. Figs and leeks in *Henry V* provide subtle clues as to how national identity politics function in the play. Most fascinating, however, is Fitzpatrick's reading of the witches' brew in *Macbeth,* as she unearths the association between the famous line, "Double, double, toil and trouble" (4.1.10) and early modern brewing practices, specifically the allusion to double, double beer, a concoction of tremendous alcoholic strength. This double, double beer was so powerful that Queen Elizabeth ordered brewers to stop producing it, as indeed it caused too much "toil and trouble" in the populace. Fitzpatrick also explains the connection between the witches in *Macbeth* and successful female beer and ale brewers, who were often themselves accused of witchcraft. Turning to the vegetable world in the third chapter, Fitzpatrick makes a case for the Pythagorean philosophy of vegetarianism in *As You Like It* and *The Winter's Tale*. Though Fitzpatrick's argument about Jacques's vegetarian ethics are convincing, I find the author's assertion that Perdita serves a meatless meal at the sheep festival dubious. Certainly, Perdita sends her adopted brother out with a shopping list that includes only vegetarian ingredients (sugar, rice, currants, mace, dates, nutmegs, ginger, prunes, and raisins), but why should a shepherdess send out for a leg of lamb? Given the popularity of mutton and lamb in the early modern English diet, as the work of both Ken Albala and Joan Thirsk attest, it is highly unlikely that the festival lacks a springtime lamb on the table.[1]

Fitzpatrick's fourth chapter considers how gluttony and insatiable sexual desire are associated in three of Shakespeare's plays, *Sir Thomas More, Coriolanus,* and *Pericles*. Her readings of these less popular and seldom performed plays through the lens of gustatory and erotic appetite are interesting. However, even considering the author's beginning caveat, I am surprised that Fitzpatrick did not include in this chapter *Antony and Cleopatra,* as it is in this play that Shakespeare is most explicit in representing early modern anxieties of gluttony and sexuality and their inherent affiliation with female power and foreign culture and rule. In her final chapter, Fitzpatrick presents readings of the strange and repulsive, spanning from Hamlet's reference to eating a crocodile to the Timon's comparison of friendship with rotten food and finally to the cannibalistic feast that Shakespeare dramatizes in one of his earliest plays, *Titus Andronicus*. Overall, Fitzpatrick's book is full of wonderful details about food and its meaning in Shakespeare's plays, and it lays the groundwork of what is promising to be a truly fruitful field. Any general reader who lusts after the newest glossy cookbook or finds Michael Pollan's call for sustainable eating irresistible or any scholar who follows the development of food studies will find Fitzpatrick's *Food and Shakespeare* a must-read.

Note

1. Ken Albala, *Eating Right in the Renaissance* (Berkeley: University of California Press, 2002), 272; Joan Thirsk, *Food in Early Modern England: Phases, Fads,*

Fashions 1500–1760 (London: Hambledon Continuum, 2007), 46, 53, 80, 237, 240–41.

A Power to Do Justice: Jurisdiction, English Literature, and the Rise of Common Law, by Bradin Cormack. Chicago: University of Chicago Press, 2007. Pp xiii + 406. Hardcover $55.

Reviewer: ANDREW MAJESKE

Bradin Cormack's *A Power to Do Justice* is an important study of an all too neglected area of jurisprudence, jurisdiction, in the context of its relation to culture—in this case Renaissance English literature. Cormack's book constitutes a substantial reworking of his dissertation of substantially the same name, with the subsequent addition of new material in chapters 2 and 6. Extant reviews of this book have labeled it as "brilliant" (Carla Spevack) and "big and bold" (Carolyn Sale). Fran Dolan, who wrote a more extended and penetrating review essay addressing this and another book, fashions it "boldly conceived."

What these reviews fail to emphasize, however, is the extremely ambitious and admittedly controversial nature of Cormack's work. Cormack denies categorically the very "idea of a discursive position beyond the law" (2); he asserts that a life "beyond law" is merely a "phantasm" (2). In essence he is claiming that when studying the era, at least from the perspective of the productive study of law and literature—and probably more broadly than this—there is no use in looking beyond "free national or civic identity," because "subjection to one or another jurisdiction was in fact the source of historical rights and privileges" (2). Expanding upon the admittedly provocative position that aesthetics is essentially a "political mode," Cormack further radicalizes this stance by subordinating the political to the legal via the mechanism of jurisdiction (5). Thus, Cormack establishes that all literature is political, and, by his expansion on Rancière, subsumed within the legal sphere.

Cormack distinguishes his work by elevating process over substance and procedure over doctrine. This realignment allows him to engage the "shifting jurisdictional realities" and the "complex but nonopositional relation" of literature and law in early modern England, and to avoid what he considers to be the "tenacious binaries" of much law and literature scholarship (2). Cormack's language frequently defies paraphrase, so I will use his own words to describe his overall purpose as well as his chapter arguments. Cormack asserts that a "governing thought in this book is that jurisdiction and literature both evade easy analysis because they open the culture in which they function onto more complex orders than those through which they seem to do their work" (12). Cormack "ventures to show how deeply engaged early modern literature was with the *technical production* of legal order, and to define the ways in which jurisdictional topics provoked a metacritical perspective on the management of legal meaning and literary meaning both" (12). More elusively, Cormack remarks that the "various and provisional literary subjectivities indexed in this book, obliquely rather than directly reactive to the state, are not so much subversive of their juridical-political counterparts as continuous with it: at once by-products, vivid supports, and dialectical partners of the political in formation" (42). Cormack, perhaps realizing how difficult at times his book can seem, rhetorically poses the question why someone would "write a book on the legal and literary negotiations of jurisdiction," a question to which he "punningly" replies:

> In cultural history and political theory alike, jurisdiction has been overlooked as merely a technical matter. But exactly as a principle of *mere* distribution—undilutedly [OED a^2, Lat. *merus*, "undiluted"], the administration and management of juridical boundaries [OED sb^2, OE *gemaere*, "boundary"] themselves—jurisdiction holds out for critique all the odd promise of a dynamic that orients us in the world through the disorienting force of its potentiality. (44)

In chapter one, Cormack addresses Skelton's play *Magnyfycence* about Henry VIII's "household economy," and argues that the play "analyzes the impact on the Tudor Crown of the fiscal exploitation of *Prerogativa Regis* and the jurisdictional compressions aimed at through the *quo warranto* proceedings" (84). Chapter 2 speaks to equity and jurisdiction in Thomas More's *Utopia,* by proposing "an important and underappreciated continuity between [More's] early and late thought, as a way of demonstrating, somewhat against the standard view, the central role of More's legal training in his textual production" (85). Chapter 3 then examines books 5 and 6 of Spenser's *Faerie Queene,* and is "concerned with Spenser's reaction to the reconfiguration of English law in response to its contact with Ireland and to the congruent deformation of the native Irish or Brehon law" (133). In chapter 4, Cormack surveys Shakespeare's history plays as he looks "to the problem French posed for English legal nationalism as a way to unfold at the microlevel the odd pressures involved in representing the crisis of Conquest so as both to embrace and disavow its meaning" (181). Chapter 5 explores Shakespeare's *Cymbeline* and *Pericles* as "engagements with the idea of jurisdiction at a moment when the category came under pressure as a consequence of the political union of 1603 and in response to a still evolving construction of *imperium* as a specifically supranational authority" (228). The book closes with chapter 6, a reading of Webster, Rowley, and Heywood's play *Cure for a Cuckold,* and purports "to show how the charged legality produced as an effect of jurisdictional plurality could sustain . . . a comic freedom constituted jurisdictionally as one formal norm's response to another" (291).

I continue to wonder whether the "shifting jurisdictional realities" Cormack views as controlling might in the end provide an unstable foundation upon which to build a stable and fully comprehensible argument. It is possible that Cormack seeks in this book to satisfy too many masters—the list of readers in the acknowledgments is as impressive and diverse as it is extensive. I eagerly look forward to his forthcoming book on Shakespeare and the law in which I hope he will begin to move somewhat away from the perspective of the technical and procedural and in the direction of the substantive and even doctrinal, a movement which I believe will provide a more stable foundation for his work, and make it less theoretically elusive.

"Hamlet" without Hamlet, by Margreta de Grazia. Cambridge: Cambridge University Press, 2007. Pp. xii + 267. Cloth $101.00; paper $41.99.

Reviewer: SAYRE GREENFIELD

Margreta de Grazia's *"Hamlet" without Hamlet* rejects two hundred years of psychological readings of the play's hero to ground her interpretation of *Hamlet* in ground itself, in "the close relationship between human and humus, man and manor," and even Hamlet and hamlet (6). This attention to the land resurrects both the political nature of the play as a dynastic struggle and resurrects the plot, too often ignored since Coleridge in favor of character. Overall, de Grazia's book provides a refreshing view of the tragedy, though this view makes the play less exceptional among its Renaissance fellows and more connected, in the end, to the late medieval tradition of drama.

De Grazia begins by summarizing the psychological approaches to the play from Coleridge and Hegel through Lacan and Nicolas Abraham, for all of whom *Hamlet* is a play of "futurity" (19), ahead of its time in its attention to the mental states of the hero: "Since 1800, he has proven capable of accommodating each new modification of inwardness, including the unconscious and the unconscious that is structured like language" (22). One might note that this connection of *Hamlet* to "futurity" actually goes back a hundred years earlier, to 1702, when Edward Bysshe applies that label to the "To be or not to be" soliloquy in *The Art of English Poetry.* Bysshe's sense of "futurity," however, was supernal, while the numerous romantic and postromantic appropriations of Hamlet that de Grazia coherently surveys make Hamlet of the future by his always conforming to successive modern theories of psychology.

To undo these modernizations by showing what the play "could not possibly be after 1800 and as long as Hamlet's interiority was taken as the vortical subject" (5), de Grazia then examines the deracination of modern Western man. Hegel's narrative of how the Reformation turned within (not to sacred sites) to find holiness and Marx's narrative of how early modern capitalism converted people into rootless vendors of their own labor make it hard for us to see *Hamlet*'s connections to land. In the play itself, Hamlet is not so disconnected: a series of puns and other pointers that de Grazia unearths keeps the dirt, stage space, and empire over which Hamlet conflicts with the gravedigger, Laertes, and Claudius in our faces: for example, *mole* and *mold* (29), *moor* as an insult for Claudius and as a place (33), *hide* as a unit of land (35), *plot* (36–37), *groundlings* (44), the false etymology of *clown* as *colonus* "a tiller of the soil" (44, 132), and even such phrases as Hamlet's "my wit's diseased," the last word sharing "both spelling and pronunciation with *dis-eized:* to be illegitimately dispossessed of lands" (157). I could, perhaps pedantically, add to de Grazia's store of wordplay connecting Hamlet to the land his line on "the skull of a lawyer": "where be his quiddits now, his quillets . . . ?" There is a statute from 1597–98, concerning Beynershe (Benhurst) in Berkshire noting that "the sayde Hundred doth consiste onely of five small Villages and thre small Quylletts or Hamletts" (*The Statutes of the Realm,* 1819, vol. 4, part 2, chap. 25, p. 929). This area is, interestingly, close to the route from London to Stratford.

Besides noting the continual puns on land in *Hamlet,* de Grazia details, in close readings of various passages, "the play's own preoccupation with the process of history, the alternations of state that punctuate world history, as one kingdom gives way to another in what might be called a premodern imperial schema that assumes the eventual fall of all kingdoms and their final subsumption by the apocalyptic kingdom-to-come" (65). That large-scale view of the shape of history in chapter 3 gives way in chapter 4 to *Hamlet*'s concerns with generational turnover and thwarted inheritance. Thus Hamlet's disgust with his mother becomes in part a matter of how her new marriage to Claudius has changed the succession (with the connivance of the council). Also, in this view, the fixation of Hamlet, Laertes, and Polonius on female sexuality, represented in terms of gardens and flowers, is very much concerned with political control over land. The only problem such a reading creates is that it tends to give the dull-witted Rosencrantz and Guildenstern, in their insistence on Hamlet's ambition, more insight into his melancholy than other characters.

The competition for land is not only among the court members, and chapter 5 completes de Grazia's picture of a worldly *Hamlet* by studying the class struggle for control of real estate, particularly in the grave-scene rivalry between dispossessed Hamlet and the gravedigger, with the latter's language of "arms" and land ownership. By invoking doomsday and the Garden of Eden, and the presumed equality at both ends of human history, the peasant challenges the upper class's entitlement to property. The Hamlet-Laertes fight in Ophelia's grave also becomes a territorial battle between two men as "Both men are pushed over the edge by the blasted image of their patrilineal dream" (145). The hole in the ground is not a Freudian sexual symbol or a "generalized or intransitive" signifier as in Lacan (156), but more literally about earth and the death of future prospects for family and dynasty.

Chapter 6 relates only tangentially to the book's earlier concerns about land control and inheritance, instead revisiting the book's initial attack on the modern psychological readings of Hamlet. De Grazia concentrates on Claudius's prayer scene and Hamlet's delay in his vengeance here, as well as the discomfort critics have felt since the mid-eighteenth century with the hero's desire to damn Claudius, and she records how the nineteenth- and twentieth-century critics psychoanalyzed this desire away. Instead, de Grazia links Hamlet's diabolic desire with the Vice figure and the play's structure of delay with medieval mystery cycles and morality plays, trying to recuperate again an unmodern Hamlet.

De Grazia's reading of Hamlet against modernity has coherence and great appeal. A few minor modernizations could be made to her own references, however. She notes (15) the *OED*'s first citation of "psychological" as 1812, but the 2008 draft *OED Online* has already postdated the first use to 1688, and the *ECCO* database turns up a number of uses from the 1760s and 1770s. She relies on Paul Conklin's *A History of Hamlet Criticism* (1947) for enumerating allusions to the play in the seventeenth century (40), though that compilation has trouble telling common idioms from specifically Shakespearean quotations. And she credits *Daiphantus* to Anthony Scoloker (8), an attribution common in scholarly writing but shown without foundation by Josephine Roberts in *Library Chronicle* 42 (1978). Nonetheless, de Grazia's more terrestrial and less psychological view of *Hamlet* seems well based, on the whole, and her work will make it easier to think of the play and teach it as belonging to the drama of its own era.

Shakespeare and the Idea of the Book, by Charlotte Scott. Oxford: Oxford University Press, 2007. Pp. 256. Hardback, $110.00.

Reviewer: JAMES J. MARINO

During a period of enormously productive scholarship on the history of the book, Charlotte Scott has written a very different, but scarcely less important, work about the iconography of the book on Shakespeare's stage. Scott persuasively identifies the book as a central and fraught symbol for early moderns, with an enormous range of cultural associations and "a powerful place within religious, political, legal and pedagogic discourse" (4). Even more important, the appearance of a book on stage conjoins two of the era's master metaphors, casting each in the other's terms. If both the theater and the book are fundamentally ideas about the world, and fundamental tools for imagining and representing that world, then a book in the theater becomes a nexus of enormous semiotic complexity. Scott views the book, fundamentally, as a limit case for the theater's representational powers, with the book's own semiotic potential alternately amplifying and short-circuiting that of theatrical performance.

With so much at stake, this book raises issues larger than any single volume can exhaust, and presents its author with tantalizing and painful choices. The book figures in virtually every one of Shakespeare's works, in great ways and small, and the very symbolic multiplicity that Scott takes as her subject makes it very hard to limit any discussion to a single set of concerns. The "religious, political, legal and pedagogic," to say nothing of the erotic, somatic, performative, and patriarchal discourses are endlessly implicated in one another through the locus of the book, and no matter what issue Scott examines, another set of discursive meanings is always temptingly at hand. Scott, to her credit, does not attempt to fit the rich tangle of her subject matter into the limits of an artificial or simplified argument, nor does she pretend to do so. "There is no uniform pattern to Shakespeare's idea of the book," Scott writes in her conclusion, "nor does he use it to make any claim about the nature of authorship, sectarianism, or personal ambition" (187). Scott resists any imperative "to provide a categorical answer to questions of interpretation, to offer an opinion of William Shakespeare's personal value judgment of the book, or to suggest a clear trajectory of intellectual or dramatic development." Instead she marks the number of "conversations" that the figure of the book engages: "the dynamic between the body and mind, the scream of silence, faith, justice, and the thought in motion, . . . the Reformation, iconoclasm, skepticism, humanism, and the developing distance between the word and its essence" (187). Scott clearly has a large and complicated territory to cover. She works through a number of key issues in largely independent chapters, exploring one or two plays per chapter in nuanced and erudite meditations. The first and final studies operate as bookends of a kind, exploring fairly fundamental questions of theatrical semiotics posed firstly by the presence and lastly by the pointed absence of books on Shakespeare's stage. During the interim Scott investigates feminine erotic education and its discontents, post-Reformation religious identification and the integrity of self-identity, and questions of memory and amnesia. Throughout she engages carefully with, and contributes to, the critical debates surrounding each of the plays she examines.

Scott's first case deals with Ovid's *Metamorphoses,* the only "specific material book" to appear in Shakespeare (26), as a stage property in *Titus Andronicus* and *Cymbeline.* Scott argues that Ovid's book is a disruptive presence, "appear[ing] at the moment when theatre comes into contact with its own limitations" (26), and creating openings for polyphony in the text. The semiotic effects are multiple: "voices of dissent emerge, bodies are dismantled, and memories are compromised" (56). Even so, Scott points out that the book functions differently in *Titus* than in *Cymbeline.* She likewise finds very different erotic dynamics at work in *Love's Labor's Lost* and *The Taming of the Shrew,* and indeed in the Katherina and Bianca plots. Lucentio's seduction of Bianca superficially validates an early modern script of humanist seduction, simultaneously eroticizing a woman and educating her into silence and docility, but Petruchio's coercive "education" of Katherina produces the end of humanist instruction by other means, and more securely. However equivocally *The Taming of the Shrew* endorses the humanist (and Ovidian) model of pedagogical seduction, however, *Love's Labor's Lost* implicitly refutes it, depicting the "relationship between women and the book [as] . . . mutually exclusive" (81), and the literary language of the male wooers as self-defeating.

Scott's chapters on *Richard II, Hamlet,* and *The Tempest* are equally learned and nuanced, and as they deal with single plays their underlying coherence translates more easily to their surfaces. The chapter on *Richard II* locates Richard on the fault lines of Catholic and Protestant iconography, of the visual and the verbal, of the manifest and the occulted, of the divine book and the divine body. Scott situates Hamlet, as Shakespeare's "icon of the scholar self" (131), within a complicated set of dialogues between writing and remembering, the novel technology of print and the old technology of memory training, the imperative of remembering and the necessity of forgetting, humanist scholarship and modern experience. The chapter on *The Tempest* deals not with the visible but the invisible book: with Prospero's unseen, incessantly cited library. Scott considers the library not merely as a collection of books but as a network of intertextual reference, providing a structure not only for Prospero's power but his imagination of power. (Although Scott does not make the connection so baldly, Prospero's library functions like the script or "book" of an early modern play, both imposing a controlled structure on the performance and licensing its moments of seeming chaos or anarchy but itself remaining invisible to the spectators.) The library is imagined both as a refuge from the public sphere and as a public sphere of its own, a polity of letters.

Scott has a keen eye for paradox, for cultural anxiety, and for internal contradiction; they enrich her readings, and this book is full of thoughtful, penetrating details. *Shakespeare and the Idea of the Book* opens a treasure house of questions about this important topic, and I expect that future scholars will be citing Scott's work for many years to come.

Index

Aliens, 161–63
Anne of Denmark, 143, 146, 149
Arden editors, 58, 59
Arden of Faversham, 17–33
Ariosto, 68
Armada, 65, 77
Attribution studies, 17–33
Authorship, 17–33

Bacon, Francis, 130
Bacon, Roger, 67
Bailey, Amanda, 180–82
Bellamy, Elizabeth Jane, 173–75
Berry, Herbert, 142–43, 149, 150, 155
Betterton, Thomas, 54
Blaeu, Willem Janszoon, 143–44
Boas, Frederick, 18
Book, 192–94
Braun, George, 154
Burden, Clive and Philip, 142, 154–55

Carnival, 119–20
Cardenio, 46
Cecil, William, Lord Burghley, 130
Chapman, George, 47–49, 56, 57
Character, 86–113
Church festivals, 117–18
Cibber, Colley, 53, 54
Clark, Peter, 117
Coleridge, Samuel Taylor, 30, 55, 56
Common Law, 188–90
Cormack, Bradin, 188–90
Crowd, 175–78
Curran, John E., 86–113
Curtain Playhouse, 142, 155

Davenant, William, 53–54
De Grazia, Margreta, 190–92
Dekker, Thomas, 129

Dietaries, 185–88
Doran, Madeline, 86
Dramatic verse, 17–33

Eavesdropping episodes, 39
Economics, 164–70
Editing, 34–62
Elizabeth I, 79–82, 128, 143, 150, 152
Englishness, 161–63
Erasmus, 88

Field, Nathan, 88
Fisher, Sidney, 155
Fitter, Chris, 114–41
Fitzpatrick, Joan, 185–88
Fletcher, John, 45–46, 57, 80–81, 86–113
Food, 185–88
Ford, John, 48, 49, 57
Forker, Charles R., 161–63
Forman, Valerie, 164–66

Garnier, Robert, 17
Geoffrey of Monmouth, 66–67
Gheeraerts, Marcus, 143
Globe Playhouse, 119–21, 127, 131, 136
Grav, Peter F., 167–70
Greene, Robert, 26, 27, 63–85, 129
Greenfield, Sayre, 190–92

Harman, Thomas, 129
Helgerson, Richard, 154
Hill, Christopher, 135
Hirsch, James, 34–62
Hogenberg, Franz, 154
Hondius, Jodocus, 145
Hondius II, Jodocus, 149
Howard, Jean E., 119

Jackson, MacDonald P., 17–33
James VI and I, 143, 149, 152, 153

195

Jaster, Margaret Rose, 180–82
John of Bordeaux, 73–74

Kermode, Lloyd Edward, 161–63
King Leir, 18
Kipnis, Jeffrey, 52–53
Klein, Bernhard, 153, 154
Koselleck, Reinhart, 77–78
Kyd, Thomas, 17–33

LaBreche, Ben, 178–80
Levin, Richard, 87, 91
Liberties, 119, 121, 125, 136
Lodge, Thomas, 26, 129
Love, C. Bryan, 170–73
Lyly, John, 26

MacFaul, Tom, 178–80
Mahood, M. M., 20, 30
Majeske, Andrew, 188–90
Male body, 180–83
Male friendship, 178–80
Manning, Roger, 125
Maps (of London), 142–57
Maps (in early modern England), 173–75
Marino, James J., 192–94
Marlowe, Christopher, 20, 74, 124
Massinger, Philip, 86–113
Medicine and theater, 183–85
Merlin, 66–67, 69
Moisan, Thomas, 60
More, Thomas, 121, 126
Munro, Ian, 175–78
Murakami, Ineke, 164–66
Murphy, Samantha, 183–85

Norden, John, 142–157

Ornstein, Robert, 86

Parish administration, 118–19
Pearson, Meg F., 175–78
Peele, George, 70
Pepys, Samuel, 54
Pettigrew, Todd H. J., 183–85
"Play," 170–73
Poetry, 17–24
Potter, Jonathan, 145
Prophecy, 63–85

Raffel, Burton, 59
Rutter, Tom, 170–73

Saxton, Christopher, 145
Schlueter, June, 142–157
Scott, Charlotte, 192–94
Seneca, 87, 88, 89, 99
Shakespeare, William: *A Midsummer Night's Dream,* 25; *All's Well that Ends Well,* 24, 44–45; *Antony and Cleopatra,* 22; *As You Like It,* 114–41; *Coriolanus,* 127; *Hamlet,* 34–62, 190–92; *Henry V,* 133; *1 Henry VI,* 20, 25; *2 Henry VI,* 18–20, 24, 27, 28, 31, 122, 133; *3 Henry VI,* 24, 28; *Henry VIII,* 46, 80–81; *Julius Caesar,* 21, 40; *King John,* 18–19; *King Lear,* 41, 42, 122, 127, 133; *Love's Labour's Lost,* 26, 120; *Macbeth,* 22, 24, 29; *Much Ado About Nothing,* 39; *Othello,* 42–44, 124; *Richard II,* 35, 65; *Richard III,* 22; *Romeo and Juliet,* 20, 30; *Taming of the Shrew,* 18, 28, 31, 45–46; *The Merchant of Venice,* 29, 41, 89; *The Merry Wives of Windsor,* 25; *The Rape of Lucrece,* 21, 23, 24; *The Two Noble Kinsmen,* 46; *Two Gentlemen of Verona,* 24, 29; *Venus and Adonis,* 23, 28
Sharp, Buchanan, 135; Sharpe, J. A., 129
Sinfield, Alan, 86
Smith, D. K., 173–75
Soliloquy, 34–62
Soliman and Perseda (Anon.), 17, 21, 23, 25, 27, 28, 31
Speed, John, 144–46, 149–50, 150, 152–54
Spencer, Eric V., 167–70
Spenser, Edmund, 63–85
Succession, 63–85
Swinburne, A. C., 31

Taylor, Neil, 56, 57
Theater (playhouse), 155
Thomas, Keith, 121
Thompson, Ann, 56, 57
Tigner, Amy L. 185–88
True Tragedy of Richard III, The, 79, 82
Tudor government, 115–16, 128–29

Vagrancy, 114–141
Van Den Ende, Jasua, 144

Van Langren, Arnold and Hendrick Florenzoon, 149
Vestry, 114–141
Vickers, Brian, 18, 21, 30
Virgil, 67–68, 69

Visscher, Claes Janszoon, 145, 149

Walsh, Brian, 63–85
Woodbridge, Linda, 129
Work, 170–73